K'UNG-TS'UNG-TZU

Princeton Library of Asian Translations

K'UNG-TS'UNG-TZU

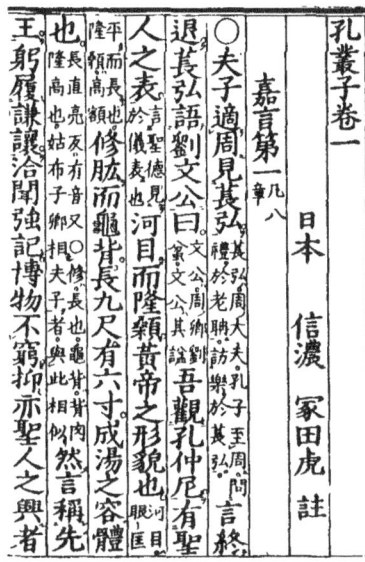

THE
K'UNG FAMILY
MASTERS'
ANTHOLOGY

*A Study
and Translation of
Chapters 1–10, 12–14*

YOAV ARIEL

PRINCETON UNIVERSITY PRESS

Princeton, New Jersey

Copyright © 1989 by Princeton University Press
Published by Princeton University Press, 41 William Street,
Princeton, New Jersey 08540
In the United Kingdom: Princeton University Press, Guildford, Surrey

All Rights Reserved

Library of Congress Cataloging-in-Publication Data

Ariel, Yoav, 1946–
  K'ung-Ts'ung-Tzu.

  (Princeton library of Asian translations)
  Bibliography: p.
  Includes index.
  1. K'ung, Fu, ca. 264–208 B.C. K'ung Ts'ung-tzu. 2. Philosophy, Confucian.
I. Title. II. Series.
B128.K853K8533 1989   181'.09512   88-22521
ISBN 0-691-06770-8 (alk. paper)

Publication of this book has been aided by a grant from the Paul Mellon Fund of
Princeton University Press
This book has been composed in Linotron Times Roman

*Clothbound editions of Princeton University Press books are printed on acid-free
paper, and binding materials are chosen for strength and durability. Paperbacks,
although satisfactory for personal collections, are not usually suitable for library
rebinding*

Printed in the United States of America by Princeton University Press,
Princeton, New Jersey

להורי, ונדה ואברהם אריאל, שאינם

In memory of Hsiao Yee-hung

CONTENTS

ACKNOWLEDGMENTS		ix
NOTE ON SOURCES AND NOTATION		xi

Introduction

SECTION 1	The Nature, Structure, and Contents of the *KTT*	3
SECTION 2	The *KTT* in History	12
SECTION 3	The Authenticity, Date, and Authorship of the *KTT*	56

K'ung-ts'ung-tzu—PART A, CHAPTERS 1–10, 12–14

CHAPTER 1	Words of Praise (Chia-yen)	75
CHAPTER 2	Discussion of the *Book of Documents* (Lun-shu)	79
CHAPTER 3	Record of Righteousness (Chi-i)	87
CHAPTER 4	On Punishment (Hsing-lun)	93
CHAPTER 5	Recorded Questions (Chi-wen)	98
CHAPTER 6	The Various Doctrines and the Teachings of the Sage (Tsa-hsün)	102
CHAPTER 7	Living in Wei (Chü Wei)	107
CHAPTER 8	Imperial Tours of Inspection (Hsün-shou)	113
CHAPTER 9	The Minister Kung-i (Kung-i)	116
CHAPTER 10	Holding Firm to Personal Ideals (K'ang-chih)	120
CHAPTER 12	The Philosopher Kung-sun Lung (Kung-sun Lung)	130
CHAPTER 13	Confucian Clothes (Ju-fu)	135
CHAPTER 14	A Dialogue with the King of Wei (Tui Wei-wang)	140

NOTES	147
GLOSSARY	185
BIBLIOGRAPHY	203
Editions and Commentaries of the *KTT* Consulted	203
Classical Chinese Works and Traditional Sinology	203
Recent Works in Chinese and Japanese	207
Works in Other Languages	209
INDEX TO THE INTRODUCTION	217

ACKNOWLEDGMENTS

Many individuals have contributed their time, patience, learning, and material assistance as the kernel of an idea was transformed first into a doctoral dissertation at Tel Aviv University and then into the present book. At each stage in this transformation, colleagues and friends provided valuable criticism as well as support and encouragement.

Guiding me throughout my graduate-school career was Professor Ben-Ami Scharfstein—philosopher, teacher, and mentor—who read every draft of the book and helped me to refine my research.

Professor Andrew Plaks carefully scrutinized the entire text of the translation. Very many of his insightful suggestions are incorporated into the present translation. His guidance and support were invaluable.

For their indispensable contributions to different parts of the present book, I am especially grateful to Professors Ch'i-yün Ch'en, Richard B. Mather, Wang-yi T'ung, Irene Eber, and Ronald Kiener.

During the years of my work on this text, I have benefited immensely from the aid, advice, criticism, and encouragement provided by Professors Willard Peterson, Nathan Sivin, Wei-ming Tu, Benjamin Schwartz, Wm. Theodore de Bary, Allyn Rickett, Fung Hu-hsiang, Kim Young-oak, Michael Nylan, Howard Goodman, and the late Dora Shikman and Vitaly Rubin.

A number of former and present colleagues in the philosophy department of Tel-Aviv University deserve a special note of gratitude for their suggestions and support: Joseph Agassi, Shlomo Biderman, Dan Daor, Asa Kasher, Donald Leslie, Avraham Meidan, and Jacob Raz.

My library research in Taiwan, England, and the United States was supported by grants from the Fulbright Foundation and the Pacific Cultural Foundation, and by sabbatical grants from Tel Aviv University.

For bringing this work to press, and for their editorial guidance, I thank the former and present Asian editors of Princeton University Press, Miriam Brokaw and Margaret Case.

My friend Avner Levi provided me with the freedom to devote much of my time to this project.

I dedicate my book to the memory of Hsiao Yee-hung, a distinguished writer who was both my friend and my Chinese teacher, and to the memory of my father and mother, whom I continue to see everywhere.

Finally, to Raya, I want to express my deepest love.

Tel Aviv
January 1988

NOTE ON SOURCES AND NOTATION

The *K'ung-ts'ung-tzu* is abbreviated throughout as *KTT*. Unless otherwise specified, references to the *KTT* are to the *Ssu-pu ts'ung-k'an* edition. The letters "A" and "B" represent either the first (*ch'ien*) or later (*hou*) part in that edition. References to the translation of the *KTT* are to the chapter and section number respectively.

Unless otherwise indicated, citations of Chinese works are in accordance with the pagination of the *Ssu-pu ts'ung-k'an* (*SPTK*) edition.

References to the standard histories are according to the pagination of the recent *Chung-hua shu-chü* edition (Peking, 1959–1974).

Unless otherwise noted, references to the Chinese texts of the Chinese classics are according to James Legge's *The Chinese Classics* (Hong Kong, 1961 [reprint]), 5 vols.

Throughout the book, Charles O. Hucker's *A Dictionary of Official Titles in Imperial China* (Stanford, 1985) is abbreviated as "Hucker, *Titles*" and is followed by the number of the title in that dictionary.

All the Chinese characters transliterated in the Introduction appear in the glossary. It is assumed that the reader of the translation has the Chinese text of the *SPTK* edition at hand; therefore, transliterations that appear in the body and the notes of the translation may not appear in the glossary.

Introduction

SECTION

1

THE NATURE, STRUCTURE, AND CONTENTS OF THE *KTT*

The *KTT* or *The K'ung Family Masters' Anthology*, which purports to record episodes, dialogues, and statements connected with various members of the K'ung family from the time of Confucius (551–479 B.C.) to the middle of the Later Han (A.D. 25–220), is a philosophically oriented work distinguished by its polemical Confucian nature. Throughout the centuries, scholarly assessments of the *KTT* have wavered between that of bona fide authority and that of peripheral pious forgery.[1]

During the seventh and up to the eleventh century, the *KTT* was widely acclaimed: the major bibliographies of this period usually ascribed the text to K'ung Fu (264–208 B.C.), an eighth-generation descendant of Confucius. The important encyclopedias of the T'ang (618–907) and the Northern Sung (960–1126) dynasties regularly cited it, and by 1058 the publication of the Sung Hsien commentary to the text under imperial auspices heralded a new prominence for the work.

In the Southern Sung dynasty (1127–1279), however, with the rise of a more critical approach to the authenticity of ancient texts, it was argued that the *KTT* was a late fabrication and was therefore to be regarded as a work of little worth. This disparaging attitude was expressed in even stronger terms by Chu Hsi (1130–1200), who labeled the *KTT* a worthless forgery.

As a result of Chu Hsi's deprecation, the *KTT* until the beginning of the seventeenth century had an enormous stigma attached to it. Any attempt at a reappraisal of its contents—outside of this now conventionally accepted conclusion—would have meant a rebellion against the scholarly and authoritative pronouncement of Chu Hsi.

From the seventeenth century on, however, attitudes toward the text underwent a major change. First a reaction against Chu Hsi's derogatory opinion of the text emerged both in China and Japan with the issuing of new commentaries to the text. Second, textual scholars of the seventeenth and eighteenth centuries stated that the striking similarities they uncovered between the *KTT* and various works of Wang Su (A.D. 195–256) indicated that the author of the *KTT* was none other than this famous exegete of the third century A.D.

In the last two hundred years no significant advance has taken place in the study of the *KTT*. Chinese scholars have been unable to move the study of the *KTT* beyond the parameters set by their predecessors. As for Western sinology, it dutifully cited the *KTT* in the appropriate scholarly indexes or notes as the need arose, but generally an attitude of almost fastidious neglect prevailed.

There should be little doubt that contemporary scholarship can utilize the *KTT* toward new and exciting ends. If, as it pretends to be, the text is an authentic product of the K'ung family, then its study might shed light on some long-lost currents of early Confucianism. Alternatively, if, as in all likelihood, the text is a third-century A.D. fabrication of Wang Su, then it inevitably becomes a critical witness to the mind of a third-century Confucian in particular, and third-century A.D. Confucianism in general.

The issues surrounding the *KTT* are particularly compelling. First, one should be reminded that the practice of writing under the cover of a distinguished name is universal. The fact that the "forger" in many cultural traditions attempts to leave his marks on the course of events by consciously concealing all signs of personal identity might provide an interesting comparative framework for the reexamination of such values as individuality, creativity, and uniqueness.[2]

Moreover, study of a forgery can provide a window of kaleidoscopic complexity concerning the sociological, political, cultural, and psychological setting of its formation. The dissemination of "forgeries" in a particular time or place usually denotes a situation of great political and cultural pressure. It is not surprising, therefore, to find that large numbers of spurious works flooded China from the Later Han to the Wei-Chin (A.D. 220–420) era. The study of the *KTT* as a single item in this corpus is especially interesting because in contrast to many other works that are spuriously attributed to famous individuals and cover a limited period of time, the *KTT* deals with many personages, and its feigned historical scope spans about 650 years. Surely the third-century author's attempt at recapitulating, transmitting, and interpreting the development of Confucian thought in a pseudepigraphic form is of major significance to our understanding of both the fragmentation of the mind of a third-century Confucian scholar and the intellectual setting of post-Han China.

Second, the most interesting point in regard to the *KTT* is that the text introduces a unique kind of Confucian response to the third-century philosophical milieu. According to some Western scholars, Confucianism appears to have been in decline during the end of the Late Han and the Wei-Chin era.[3] They argue that orthodox Confucianism, which had dominated Chinese intellectual life for centuries, had lost its prestige. The fall of the Han imperium and the failure of Confucianism to deal with the resultant social and political upheavals were accompanied by the revival of a number of the older schools of thought. The Legalists, Taoists, Dialecticians, and even the Mohists gradually made a comeback. These schools, some of which had been absorbed into the Confucian synthesis during the Former Han (206 B.C.–A.D. 8), now tended to go their own way, aiming, it seems, to replace the Confucian orthodoxy, which appeared to have failed.

What was the Confucian response to the course that Chinese intellectuals now took, a course that reached its culmination point at the beginning of the Wei-Chin era? As a school of thought, so runs the present consensus, Confucianism made a fundamental shift from classical learning to a "Neo-Taoistic" metaphysics known under the name of *hsüan-hsüeh* (Dark Learning). From a psychological standpoint, intellectuals seemed to rediscover their individuality and to lose interest in political problems. Many even became devotees of the *ch'ing-t'an* (Pure Conversation) movement, the apotheosis of the age.[4] To risk a generalization, the image of third-century Confucianism that emerges from most studies of the period is Taoistically metaphysical and, from a personal standpoint, individualistic and escapist.[5]

The study of a third-century work such as the *KTT* will help to bring about a modification of this conventional portrayal of the preceding characterization of Confucianism. The Confucianism of the *KTT* is decidedly aggressive. The author of the text regards the Way advocated by Confucius and his followers as an inexhaustible mine of ever-lasting truths, and the learning of the classics as the exploration of the written manifestations of these truths. At the same time he bitterly attacks almost every non-Confucian school as well as any position that expresses a negative attitude toward classical learning in general and the "Old Text" school in particular. He attacks the Legalist methods and Han Fei Tzu; he denigrates immorality and jokes about its aspirations; he denounces the *chu-tzu* ("The various philosophers"); he labels Kung-sun Lung "a petty sophist" and claims that Mo Tzu's work is worthless. In short, the *KTT* appears to perpetuate a type of polemical third-century Confucianism that has been long-neglected until now.[6]

The Arrangement of the *KTT*

The *KTT* contains approximately thirty-eight thousand characters, about the same number as the *Mencius*. In printed editions and in bibliographical references, the typical table of contents of the *KTT* generally lists either seven or three *chüan* (books) containing the following twenty-three titled *p'ien* (chapters):

1. "Chia-yen" (Words of Praise), in eight sections
2. "Lun-shu" (Discussion of the *Book of Documents*), in sixteen sections
3. "Chi-i" (Record of Righteousness), in ten sections
4. "Hsing-lun" (On Punishment), in eight sections
5. "Chi-wen" (Recorded Questions), in eight sections
6. "Tsa-hsün" (The Various Doctrines and the Teachings of the Sage), in nine sections
7. "Chü Wei" (Living in Wei), in nine sections
8. "Hsün-shou" (Imperial Tours of Inspection), in one section
9. "Kung-i" (The Minister Kung-i), in nine sections
10. "K'ang-chih" (Holding Firm to Personal Ideals), in seventeen sections
11. "Hsiao *Erh-ya*" (Concise *Erh-ya*), in thirteen sections
12. "Kung-sun Lung" (The Philosopher Kung-sun Lung), in three sections
13. "Ju-fu" (The Confucian Clothes), in seven sections
14. "Tui Wei-wang" (A Dialogue with the King of Wei), in five sections
15. "Ch'en shih-i" (Recounting Scholars' Righteousness), in ten sections
16. "Lun shih" (Discussion of Crucial Conditions), in nine sections
17. "Chih-chieh" (Holding Fast to Moral Integrity), in fourteen sections
18. "Ch'i Mo" (Criticizing Mo Tzu), in nine sections
19. "Tu chih" (Superlative Mastery), in six sections
20. "Wen chün-li" (Questions about Military Rites), in one section
21. "Ta wen" (Answering Questions), in five sections
22. "Lien-ts'ung-tzu, shang" (Appendix to the Masters' Anthology: Part "A"), in eleven sections
23. "Lien-ts'ung-tzu, hsia" (Appendix to the Masters' Anthology: Part "B"), in ten sections

Chapter headings in the *KTT* usually mark a shift in focus from the preceding chapter.[7] These chapter headings always refer to a distinctive feature of the opening section of each chapter. The distinctive feature might be the general content of the opening section, such as in chapters 1 and 17; its literary structure, as in chapters 5 and 21; a name of a book under discussion, as in chapter 2; a concept under focus, as in chapters 3 and 4; or a name of a personality, as in chapters 9 and 12. When the consecutive sections of a chapter are logically tied to the opening section, the chapter heading, obviously, refers to the whole chapter, such as in chapter 4.

The twenty-three chapters form a mosaic of some two hundred sections written mainly in the form of episodes containing the dialogues of members of the K'ung family. These sections are mostly introduced by a short contex-

Nature, Structure, and Contents

tual remark delivered by an anonymous narrator who then seemingly steps aside as the episode itself transpires. The two hundred sections form an anthology that purports to recount the philosophical debates, the scholarly pursuits, the political activities, and the personal exploits of various members of one particular genealogical chain of the K'ung family from the end of the Ch'un Ch'iu period (722–481 B.C.) to the middle of the Later Han (A.D. 25–220). Unlike other philosophical compositions, the *KTT* does not bear the name of a single author, no doubt because of its anthological form. Instead, it imparts the impression of a cumulative effort of the K'ung family, covering a period of nearly 650 years. Thus, because it is an anthology, the work is entitled *K'ung-ts'ung-tzu*, that is, *The K'ung Family Masters' Anthology*,[8] or, as it was called in the third century A.D. and very often during other periods up to the T'ang (A.D. 618–907), *K'ung-ts'ung*, or *The K'ung Family Anthology*.[9]

The *KTT* starts with Confucius (551–479 B.C.) and ends with the death of Chi-yen (A.D. 124), a twenty-first-generation descendant of Confucius. The table of the twenty-one generations of the K'ung family, which appears on the next page, is derived from genealogical data that I have culled from the *KTT*. Family members of whom the *KTT* says very little are marked with one asterisk (*), while those who play major roles in the text are marked with two asterisks (**). Members of the family of whose existence we learn from other sources, such as the *K'ung-tzu chia-yü*'s Postscript, the *Shih-chi*, and the *Han-shu*, but who are not mentioned in the *KTT*, appear in parentheses. The genealogical table also contains references to the corresponding chapter number in the *KTT* in which the respective members of the K'ung family play a role, as well as biographical dates whenever such dates are available.

Protagonists of the *KTT*

The genealogical table demonstrates that among the *KTT*'s twenty-one generations of the K'ung family, the following nine play a major role and can therefore be considered the protagonists of the *KTT*:

Confucius (551–479 B.C.), chapters 1–5
Tzu-ssu (479–402 B.C.), chapters 5–10
Tzu-kao (312–262 B.C.), chapters 12–14
Tzu-shun (293–237 B.C.), chapters 15–17
Tzu-yü (K'ung Fu) (264–208 B.C.), chapters 18–21
K'ung Tsang (fl. 150 B.C.), chapter 22
Tzu-feng (fl. A.D. 50), chapter 22
Tzu-ho (fl. A.D. 86), chapter 23
Chi-yen (d. A.D. 124), chapter 23

The *KTT*'s Genealogical Table of the K'ung Family

Name/Adult Name		Dates	*KTT*'s	Chapter Number
Confucius		551–479 B.C.	**	1–5
(Li)	(Po Yü)	d. 483 B.C.		
Chi[a]	Tzu-ssu	479–402 B.C.	**	5–10
Po	Tzu-shang	429–383 B.C.	*	6, 7
(Ch'iu)	(Tzu-chia)	390–346 B.C.		
(K'o[a])	(Tzu-chih)	351–306 B.C.		
Ch'uan	Tzu-kao	312–262 B.C.	**	12–14
Wu	Tzu-shun	293–237 B.C.	**	15–17
Fu	Tzu-yü	264–208 B.C.	**	18–21
Tzu-hsiang			*	22
Tzu-wen			*	22
Yen[a]			*	22
(Chung)				
An-kuo		fl. 150 B.C.	*	22
Tsang		fl. 150 B.C.	**	22
Lin[a]			*	22
Huang			*	22
Mou			*	22
Tzu-kuo			*	22
Tzu-ang			*	22
Chung-huang			*	22
Tzu-li			*	22
Tzu-yüan			*	22
Tzu-chien			*	22
Jen			*	22
Tzu-feng		fl. A.D. 50	**	22
Tzu-ho		fl. A.D. 86	**	23
Chang-yen			*	23
Chi-yen		d. A.D. 124	**	23

SOURCE: "The K'ung-Family-Masters' Anthology and Third-Century Confucianism" by Yoav Ariel. In *Confucianism: The Dynamics of Tradition*, ed. Irene Eber. Copyright © 1986 by Macmillan Publishing Company, a Division of Macmillan, Inc.

Framework of the *KTT*

As the genealogical table shows, the *KTT* exhibits a coherent framework throughout its twenty-three chapters. It chronicles the K'ung family from the neighborhood of 500 B.C. to A.D. 124. Nevertheless, it focuses on four different periods which form the following four distinctive parts of the *KTT*:

The first part consists of chapters 1–10. It deals with the activities of Confucius and his grandson Tzu-ssu and covers the approximate years 500–400 B.C.

Nature, Structure, and Contents

The second part, which consists of chapters 12–21, covers the years 300–200, approximately. It starts in the middle of the Warring States period with Tzu-kao, a sixth-generation descendant of Confucius, and ends shortly after the "burning of the books," with the death of K'ung Fu (eighth generation). Tzu-shun (seventh generation) also plays a central role in this part.

The third part consists of the first half of chapter 22. It concentrates on the writings of K'ung Tsang (150 B.C.), a tenth-generation descendant of Confucius.

The concluding fourth part consists of the last sections of the second half of chapter 22 and the whole of chapter 23. It recounts the events connected with the K'ung family between the years A.D. 50 and 124. Tzu-feng (nineteenth generation), Tzu-ho (twentieth generation), and Chi-yen (twenty-first generation) are the celebrated figures of this part.

Contents of the *KTT*

The *KTT* contains a great variety of subjects, some of which appear repeatedly. The following ten themes recur:

1. Politics, that is, the value of political criticism, the duties of rulers, officials, and subjects; the appointment of administrators, the function of the administration; the methods of governing the people; the way to assess crucial situations, the essential steps in diplomacy, warfare, and economics.
2. The rites, that is, the mourning rites, the rites of warfare, the sacrificial rites, the rites of the family, the rites among colleagues and friends, and the rites as performed in everyday relations between people of various ranks and classes.
3. Morality, that is, numerous cases within differing contexts that illustrate paradigms of morality.
4. History, that is, descriptions of past legendary institutions and discussions of various historical anecdotes.
5. Education, that is, the preferable methods in pedagogy, punishment versus the rites, and the value of learning.
6. Psychology, that is, analyses of the interrelationship between various states of mind and their corresponding external actualities.
7. Confucian classics, that is, analysis of various sections of Confucian classics such as the *Shu-ching* and *Shih-ching*.
8. Lexical expositions of various items.
9. The individual philosopher, that is, the self-image of the lone Confucian, an exposition of his psychological training, and his equal value to that of past sages.

10. Philosophical debates. This seems to be the backbone of the *KTT* and is premised on the conviction of the supremacy of the world view, the ideals, and the values that the K'ung family members represent, as against the ideals and values represented by their opponents.

The *KTT* has numerous targets of philosophical criticism, including the method of ruling the people by means of punishment; the method of approaching philosophical problems with sophisticated arguments; heterodox teachings; Taoist priests who teach the Way to become immortal; the method that propagates the supremacy of administrative techniques; vulgar Confucians—the Modern Text scholars; students of interior applications; the various pre-Ch'in philosophers; Kung-sun Lung Tzu; Han Fei Tzu; and Mo Tzu.

The Integral Nature of the *KTT*: Some Possible Reservations

In contrast to the general nature of the *KTT*, the eleventh chapter, "Hsiao Erh-ya," contains neither discourse, dialogue, nor personages. It is a dictionary that is structurally modeled after one of the Confucian classics, namely, the early Han period dictionary *Erh-ya*. Despite its atypical literary form, there is no doubt that this chapter constitutes an integral part of the whole *KTT*. First, other sections of the *KTT* are not exclusively constructed of anecdotes and dialogues. For example, writings by K'ung family members, such as the letters of K'ung Tsang, appear in other parts of the *KTT*. Second, subsequent references to the *KTT* by the early T'ang encyclopedias cite the eleventh chapter as an integral part of the whole *KTT*. Finally, and most conclusively, many of the lexical expositions of the eleventh chapter can be shown to be in explicit reference to terminological problems that arise in the remainder of the *KTT*.[10]

The headings of the last two chapters, "Appendix to the Masters' Anthology: Parts A and B," are not of the same nature as the chapter headings of the *KTT* proper. These headings do not refer to any internal topical feature of the chapters but only to the fact that the contents function as supplements to the *KTT* proper. This unique feature becomes even more pronounced when the anonymous narrator who introduced most of the previous sections of the *KTT* proper is temporarily replaced by an anonymous editor who justifies the inclusion of some letters and rhyme prose written by K'ung Tsang.[11]

As is the case with the *KTT*'s eleventh chapter, I am convinced that these two concluding chapters also form an integral part of the whole *KTT*. First, the contents of these two chapters are congruent with the whole *KTT*. They recount the activities of the K'ung family members in much the same way as the preceding chapters do. Second, these two chapters were referred to by the early T'ang encyclopedias as integral parts of the *KTT*. Finally as I show in section 3, the two chapters contain a self-reference that tries to reinforce the idea that they form an integral part of the cumulative effort of the K'ung family in the making of the *KTT*.

In the light of the above analysis of the *KTT*'s framework and contents, the integral and coherent nature of the work's twenty-three chapters can be now assumed to be fairly well established.

SECTION

2

THE *KTT* IN HISTORY

The *KTT* from the Mid-Third Century A.D. to 656

The first extant bibliographical work that lists the *KTT* is the *Sui-shu ching-chi-chih*.[1] The monograph that forms *chüan* 32–35 of the *Sui-shu* was written by Chang-sun Wu-chi (d. 659) and others and was presented to the emperor in A.D. 656. The compilers incorporated into their monograph features from several now lost pre-T'ang catalogues,[2] including Juan Hsiao-hsü's (A.D. 479–549) *Ch'i-lu*.[3]

The *Lun Yü*'s section of the *Sui-shu ching-chi-chih* reads: "*K'ung-ts'ung* in seven *chüan*, was written by K'ung Fu an Erudite[4] of Ch'en Sheng.[5] In the Liang dynasty,[6] there was a ten-*chüan* book titled *K'ung-chih*. This work was written by a senior military officer named Liu Pei. It is lost."[7]

Elaborating on the *Lun Yü*'s list of books, the editors of the *Sui-shu ching-chi-chih* discuss various works associated with the *Lun Yü* and finally refer once more to the *KTT*, giving a somewhat revised verdict on its authorship: "The *K'ung-ts'ung* and *Chia-yü*[8] both represent the essential ideas of Confucius, transmitted by the K'ung family."[9]

Three points summarize the conclusions of the editorial team of the *Sui-shu ching-chi-chih* concerning the *KTT*: (1) The *KTT* belongs to the group of works related by their nature to the *Lun Yü*; (2) it consists of seven *chüan*; (3) it is an authentic work of the K'ung family. The matter of authorship, however, remains puzzling: which of the two references to the *KTT* represents their final verdict on its authorship? Did they think that K'ung Fu was the sole author, as clearly stated in the first reference, or was the *KTT* the result of a combined effort of various members of the K'ung family, as suggested by the second reference?

Before dealing with this indecisive verdict in the *Sui-shu ching-chi-chih* concerning the authorship of the *KTT*, we should first examine all extant information concerning the *KTT* and K'ung Fu dated prior to A.D 656. Citations and references to the *KTT* will provide a historical sketch of it during the first

The KTT *in History*

four hundred years of its circulation. The biographical accounts of K'ung Fu might help to understand how the composition of the *KTT* came to be ascribed to him.

Biographical Accounts of K'ung Fu

There are four works prior to A.D. 656 with biographical accounts of K'ung Fu: the *Shih-chi*, the *Han-shu*, the *K'ung-tzu chia-yü*'s Postscript, and the *KTT* itself.

Toward the end of the *Shih-chi*'s biography of Confucius, there is a brief biographical account of fifteen of his descendants.[10] According to this account, K'ung Fu, an Erudite in the employ of Ch'en She the King, died at the age of fifty-seven in Ch'en.[11] The *Shih-chi* contains another reference to a certain individual by the name of K'ung Chia, who was an Erudite in the employ of Ch'en She and who died together with his employer.[12] Commenting on the latter, P'ei Yin (fl. A.D. 438)[13] quotes Hsü Kuang (A.D. 352–425) to the effect that K'ung Chia was the eighth-generation descendant of Confucius, that his personal name was Fu, and that his adult name was Chia.[14]

The *Han-shu* repeats the *Shih-chi*'s biographical references to both K'ung Fu and K'ung Chia. It says that K'ung Fu was Shun's[15] son, that he was an Erudite of Ch'en She, and that he died in Ch'en.[16] The bibliographical section of the *Han-shu*, the *Han-shu I-wen-chih*,[17] also lists a work of twenty-six chapters entitled *P'an Yü* (Plates and Vases),[18] whose author is a certain K'ung Chia. In a short comment, Pan Ku (A.D. 32–92) cites two opinions concerning the identity of K'ung Chia, according to which he was an official of the mythical Yellow Emperor,[19] or else one of the Hsia dynasty emperors.[20] Pan Ku then labels both views fallacious.[21]

The *K'ung-tzu chia-yü*'s Postscript is the third biographical account of K'ung Fu. According to this source, K'ung Fu was Tzu-shun's son. His adult name was Tzu-yü, and his later personal name was Chia. The Postscript also states that K'ung Fu was an Erudite and a Grand Preceptor[22] in the employ of Ch'en She the King, and that he died in Ch'en.[23]

Of all the biographical accounts of K'ung Fu, the *KTT* provides the richest data concerning his life and times. In contrast to most of his family predecessors, whose biographical data are randomly interwoven between the lines of their dialogues within the *KTT*, the major events of his biography are explicitly stated and cover a period from his birth and early childhood, to his death. Four chapters record his philosophical dialogues and portray his political activities.[24] The following are the most important biographical references to K'ung Fu in these four chapters:

K'ung Fu was born in the Warring States period, and grew up during military disturbances (B, 31a2).

He dedicated his life to preserving the heritage of his forefathers (B, 31b2).

He was in charge of books of the times of the Ancient Kings (B, 33a4).

He planned the hiding of these books from Ch'in Shih-huang-ti,[25] who wanted them destroyed (B, 32a6).

His names included Tzu-yü, Fu Chia, Tzu-fu, and K'ung Chia (B, 33a6).

Ch'en She the King invited him for counsel and appointed him an Erudite and a Grand Preceptor (B, 33b2).

His advice concerning the crucial battle against the Ch'in army was ignored by Ch'en She the King, who, as a result, was defeated (B, 44a7).

He retired from official service and died in Ch'en surrounded by his disciples, and appointed Shu-sun T'ung[26] his successor as Master (B, 44b1).

The Shih-chi and the Han-shu Accounts

The *Shih-chi* and the *Han-shu* accounts are extremely brief and almost identical. The information derived from them is that K'ung Fu was Tzu-shun's son, that he served Ch'en She the King as an Erudite, and that he died in Ch'en. There is no single reference in either work that K'ung Fu was the author of any book. Both the *Shih-chi* and *Han-shu* refers to him also by the name K'ung Chia. The *Han-shu I-wen-chih* associates a work entitled *P'an Yü* with a certain K'ung Chia. Nevertheless, Pan Ku's commentary makes it clear that the K'ung Chia mentioned is not K'ung Fu. The striking absence of K'ung Fu's name from certain places in these two standard histories must also be noted. The *Shih-chi*'s biographies of both Ch'en She the King, under whom K'ung Fu served as Erudite, and Shu-sun T'ung, who was said by the *KTT* to be K'ung Fu's appointed successor, do not mention K'ung Fu at all. The pre-T'ang commentator of the *Shih-chi*, P'ei Yin, and the commentator of the *Han-shu*, Yen Shih-ku (581–645), who are both aware of K'ung Fu's existence, and who both mention the *KTT* in their commentaries, do not associate the *KTT* with K'ung Fu or with any other figure.

The *K'ung-tzu chia-yü* Postscript and the KTT's Accounts

Both the Postscript and the *KTT* accounts agree with the *Shih-chi* and the *Han-shu* that K'ung Fu was the son of Tzu-shun, that he was an Erudite in the employ of Ch'en She the King, and that he died in Ch'en. They also supply additional information, namely, that he was appointed a Grand Preceptor by Ch'en She. The *KTT* furnishes several names of K'ung Fu that cannot be found in any other source. Neither of these two works attributes to K'ung Fu the writing of a book, though the *KTT* specifies that he was in charge of certain books of the Ancient Kings and that he dedicated his life to the preservation of his forefathers' heritage.

Before the search for the *KTT*'s authorship in the sources of the periods

The KTT in History

under discussion continues, the seeming discrepancy between the *KTT* and the *K'ung-tzu chia-yü* should be noted. This discrepancy concerns the identity of the K'ung family member who, according to tradition, hid the Canonical Books to prevent their being burned by Ch'in Shih-huang-ti. Who in fact can be credited with this act?

The *Shih-chi* says that a copy of the *Shu-ching*, written in archaic characters before the Ch'in dynasty, was in the possession of the K'ung family in the Former Han period.[27]

The *Han-shu* elaborates and specifies the names of the Canonical Books that were recovered from the wall of the K'ung family house during the Former Han.[28]

The *KTT* states that K'ung Fu masterminded the hiding of certain books of the Ancient Kings.

On first reading, the *K'ung-tzu chia-yü*'s Postscript seems to contradict the *KTT*'s view. The Postscript asserts that it was K'ung Fu's brother, Tzu-hsiang, named Teng, who hid the *Hsiao-ching*, the *Shang-shu*, and the *Lun Yü* of his family.[29]

The K'ung An-kuo of the pseudo-K'ung An-kuo's Preface to the *Shang-shu* says that it was one of his forefathers who hid the Canonical books.[30]

The biography of Yin Min in the *Han-chi* credits K'ung Fu with hiding the books.[31]

K'ung Ying-ta's (A.D. 574–648) *Shang-shu cheng-i* quotes the *K'ung-tzu chia-yü*'s Postscript, identifying K'ung Hsiang as the anonymous ancestor mentioned in K'ung An-kuo's opinion.[32]

The *Sui-shu ching-chi-chih* adopts a certain Hui as its choice for the man responsible for concealing the books.[33]

K'ung Yüan-ts'o, a descendant of Confucius of the fifty-first degree, attributes the hiding to K'ung Fu.[34]

The Li Lien Preface to the *KTT*, which appears in the *Tzu-hui* collection (published 1577), as well as Kuei Yu-kuang and Wen Chen-meng, the editors of the anthology *Chu-tzu hui-han* (published in 1626), attributed the hiding to both K'ung Fu and his younger brother (see fig. 13, p. 52).

Finally, Kramers suggests an interesting identification between the above-mentioned K'ung Hui of the *Sui-shu* and K'ung Hsiang of the *K'ung-tzu chia-yü*'s Postscript.[35]

In light of the above discussion one can see that the traditions concerning the hiding of the Canonical Books consist of features that allow conflicting, as well as overlapping, interpretations. Furthermore, there is no substantive discrepancy between the *KTT* and the *K'ung-tzu chia-yü*. The *KTT* refers to a group of unspecified books of the Ancient Kings, while the *K'ung-tzu chia-yü* presents a list of three classical books that were hidden. These books are obviously related to the times of the Ancient Kings. The *KTT* also speaks about the plan to conceal the books, while the *K'ung-tzu chia-yü* speaks about an actual act of hiding. The gap between the *KTT* and the *K'ung-tzu chia-yü* concerning this issue can therefore be easily bridged. To sum up: There is no single biographical account prior to A.D. 656 of either K'ung Fu or any other related figure ascribing the *KTT* or any other book to him.

Citations of the *KTT* Prior to A.D. 656

Citations of the *KTT* in works written prior to A.D. 656 appear both in encyclopedias and in commentaries of other major works. The study of these citations allows one to determine with assurance the *terminus ante quem* of the *KTT*, to gauge its place in intellectual circles during the first four hundred years of its circulation, and to examine its textual material during these early phases of transmission as compared with its present content. Since these citations are all limited to strictly textual considerations and avoid issues of ascription, they do not provide any new information concerning the *KTT*'s authorship.

The Third Century A.D.

Two long-lost works, Wang Su's *Sheng-cheng-lun*[36] and Huang-fu Mi's (A.D. 215–282) *Ti-wang shih-chi*, are works from the third century that were alleged to have referred to the *KTT*. The fact that the *Sheng-cheng-lun* cites the *KTT* has led contemporary scholars such as Lo Ken-tse to claim that the *KTT* could not have been written after the second half of the third century A.D., since this is the approximate date of the composition of the *Sheng-cheng-lun*.[37] Nevertheless, of these two alleged citations, that of the *Ti-wang shih-chi* is verified, while that of the *Sheng-cheng-lun* is not, as shown in the following discussion.

The Sung encyclopedia *T'ai-p'ing yü-lan*, which was completed in 983, quotes the *Sheng-cheng-lun* as follows: "Scholars did not know the adult name of Meng K'o (Mencius). In the *Book of Tzu-ssu* and in the *KTT*, there is a certain Meng Tzu-chü[a] who is K'o[b] (Mencius)."[38]

This passage immediately raises a question: What sort of book was cited by the *Sheng-cheng-lun* as the *Book of Tzu-ssu*, a book that had identical information on Mencius's adult name as the *KTT*? A discussion of this and other problems related to the *Book of Tzu-ssu* will be presented later. For the moment, two critical questions should be posed regarding the alleged reference from the *Sheng-cheng-lun*. First, do the various present editions of the *KTT* duplicate the name Meng Tzu-chü[a]? Second, does the *T'ai-p'ing yü-lan* represent the original text of the *Sheng-cheng-lun* or just a later, reconstructed version?

All extant editions of the *KTT* at my disposal read Meng Tzu-chü[b] and not

The KTT *in History* 17

Meng Tzu-chü^a. Although this discrepancy can be resolved by having recourse to various orthographical explanations, it is sufficient to cast preliminary doubt on the authenticity of the alleged citation of the *KTT* in the *Sheng-cheng-lun*. Still, there is no doubt that the original text of the *Sheng-cheng-lun* did mention Mencius's adult name. This can be seen in Yen Shih-ku's commentary to the *Han-shu I-wen-chih*, in which he states: "The *Sheng-cheng-lun* says that the adult name of Mencius was Tzu-chü[b]. The present record, however, does not have an adult name for Mencius, and the source from which the *Sheng-cheng-lun* obtained Mencius's adult name is not specified."[39]

Yen Shih-ku clearly mentions that the original text of the *Sheng-cheng-lun* did indeed mention Mencius's adult name, since he refers to it at a time when the *Sheng-cheng-lun* was still extant. Yen Shih-ku explicitly states, however, that the *Sheng-cheng-lun* does not specify the source from which it draws its information about Mencius's adult name. Therefore, it can be asserted that the original text of the *Sheng-cheng-lun* did not quote either the *Book of Tzu-ssu* or the *KTT*, and the reference to these two works in the quotation of the *Sheng-cheng-lun* in the *T'ai-p'ing yü-lan* is the result of later interpolation.[40]

This conclusion overturns Lo Ken-tse's argument concerning the *terminus ante quem* of the *KTT*. But there is still Huang-fu Mi's *Ti-wang shih-chi*, which allows one to determine the *terminus ante quem* of the *KTT* in the vicinity of A.D. 250. The *T'ai-p'ing yü-lan* produces a surviving extract from the *Ti-wang shih-chi* that deals with some aspects of the banishment of Emperor T'ai Chia (traditionally reg. 1753 B.C.) to T'ung by his chief minister I-yin.[41] This extract quotes the *KTT*: "The *K'ung-ts'ung*[a] referred to this case as follows: 'For three years he[42] was occupied with remorseful thoughts, regretting his past misconduct. Then he emerged and resumed his position. For this he was called an enlightened Emperor.'"[43]

Now, since the cited paragraph appears in the present text of the *KTT* (A, 16b6–7), one may confidently assume that the author of the *Ti-wang shih-chi*, Huang-fu Mi, consulted the *KTT* when writing his survey of the Ancient Emperors and quoted it as an authoritative historical source. The *terminus ante quem* of the *KTT* can therefore be established as circa A.D. 250.

A.D. 300–600

Extant, as well as reconstructed, works of the fourth century A.D. do not include, to the best of my knowledge, any reference to the *KTT*.[44] The following two centuries, however, provide four citations from the *KTT*, none of which appears in its present form. These include a citation of the *K'ung-ts'ung-tzu* in P'ei Yin's (ca. A.D. 438) *Shih-chi chi-chieh*;[45] a citation of the *K'ung-ts'ung-tzu* in Liu Chün's (A.D. 462–521) commentary to the *Shih-shuo hsin-yü*;[46] and two citations of the *K'ung-ts'ung* in Li Tao-yüan's (d. A.D. 527) *Shui-ching-chu*.[47]

Before proceeding to the seventh century, the omission of the title of the *KTT* from Yü Chung-jung's (A.D. 476–549) *Tzu-ch'ao* should be explained. The table of contents of this no longer extant philosophical anthology is preserved in Kao Ssu-sun's (ca. 1184) *Tzu-lüeh*,[48] and includes no less than 107 book titles. The reason why the *KTT* was not excerpted in that list is that the *Tzu-ch'ao* was a philosophical anthology while the *KTT*, like the *K'ung-tzu chia-yü*, was not considered at the time a philosophical work (*tzu*), but rather a work associated with one of the Classics (*ching*[a]).[49] For that reason neither the *KTT* nor the *K'ung-tzu chia-yü* was included in the *Tzu-ch'ao*.[50]

A.D. 600–656

The beginning of the seventh century marks a significant stage in the history of the *KTT*. The famous encyclopedias of that period quote it widely,[51] and commentators examine it in comparison to other celebrated works.[52] The encyclopedia *Pei-t'ang shu-ch'ao*, written by Yü Shih-nan (A.D. 558–638) and completed before A.D. 618, quotes the *KTT* no less than twenty-eight times. The following is a list of these citations, correlated with the corresponding passages from the *KTT*:

Pei-t'ang shu-ch'ao	*KTT*	*Title Referred To*
16-1b	A, 46b5	*K'ung-ts'ung-tzu*
34-4b	B, 1b2	*K'ung-ts'ung-tzu*
40-3b	A, 21b6	*K'ung-ts'ung-tzu*
43-2a	A, 25a5	*K'ung-ts'ung*[a]
44-2b	B, 62a5	*K'ung-ts'ung*[a] (*chüan* 7)
45-4b	A, 84a8	*K'ung-ts'ung*[a]
49-3a	B, 1a8	*K'ung-ts'ung*
58-1b	B, 51b5	*K'ung-ts'ung-tzu* (*chüan* 7)
79-6b	Not found	*K'ung-ts'ung*
88-4b	B, 58a2	*K'ung-ts'ung-tzu* (*chüan* 7)
93-3b	A, 54a1	*K'ung-ts'ung-tzu*
93-3b	A, 18b1	*K'ung-ts'ung-tzu*
94-3b/4a	B, 19a1	*K'ung-ts'ung-tzu*
97-2a	Not found	*K'ung-ts'ung-tzu*
106-8b	A, 32b2-3	*K'ung-ts'ung-tzu*
123-3b	B, 2b1	*K'ung-ts'ung-tzu*
125-12a	A, 74a1	*K'ung-ts'ung*
134-2b	A, 35b4	*K'ung-tsung*[a]*-tzu*
135-4a	B, 58a2	*K'ung-ts'ung-tzu* (*chüan* 7)
136-17a	A, 78a2	*K'ung-ts'ung-tzu*
137-9b	B, 13b5	*K'ung-ts'ung*[a]
145-5a	A, 51b2	*K'ung-ts'ung*[a]

Pei-t'ang shu-ch'ao	KTT	Title Referred To
145-6a	A, 51a6-7	K'ung-ts'ung[a]
148-10b	A, 79a7	K'ung-ts'ung[a]
152-6b	B, 67a1	K'ung-ts'ung-tzu
155-2b	B, 20a3	K'ung-ts'ung-tzu
160-3a	B, 51b1	K'ung-ts'ung
160-3a	B, 4b3	K'ung-ts'ung

These data indicate, first, that 93 percent of the *Pei-t'ang shu-ch'ao*'s selected citations from the *KTT* also appear in the text of the present *KTT*. Because the *Pei-t'ang shu-ch'ao*'s citations of the *KTT* cover almost all major chapters of the whole text,[53] and because 93 percent of the *Pei-t'ang shu-ch'ao*'s selection of the *KTT* match the present text of the *KTT*, it can be assumed with confidence that the content of the *KTT* at the beginning of the seventh century A.D. was quite similar to its present content.

Second, the above list includes four direct, specific citations from the *KTT*, drawn from its seventh *chüan*, namely, the appendix "Lien-ts'ung-tzu." This shows that the appendix constitutes an integral part of the text of the *KTT*, which Yü Shih-nan used while compiling his *Pei-t'ang shu-ch'ao*.

Yü Shih-nan used four variant titles of the *KTT*: *K'ung-ts'ung-tzu*, *K'ung-ts'ung[a]*, *K'ung-ts'ung*, and *K'ung-tsung[a]-tzu*. The use of the four variants indicates that Huang-fu Mi, P'ei Yin and Liu Chün, and Li Tao-yüan, who referred to the *KTT* by different titles, were referring to the same text, and that the transmission of the *KTT* during the first four hundred years of its circulation was under the above four titles.

Finally, nowhere in the *Pei-t'ang shu-ch'ao* are any of the names of K'ung Fu mentioned. This omission is important because Yü Shih-nan usually indicates the source of his quotation by giving either the title or the author's name, or both. In the case of the *KTT* only the text's titles are mentioned, and nowhere in the entire encyclopedia is there a reference to K'ung Fu as the author of the *KTT*.

Another encyclopedia written prior to 656 that supplies indispensable information about the *KTT* during this period is the *I-wen lei-chü*. The composition of this encyclopedia was directed by Ou-yang Hsün (557–641), who completed it between the years 622 and 624. The following is a list of the *I-wen lei-chü*'s twenty references to the *KTT*, accompanied by the correlated items of the present text of the *KTT*:[54]

I-wen lei-chü	KTT
29/510	A, 78B1
4/58	B, 20A3
17/314	A, 6A3

I-wen lei-chü	*KTT*
21/393	A, 18b3
38/677	B, 58A2
60/1082	B, 2B2
60/1087	A, 73B8
67/1186	A, 34B8
71/1237	A, 20B2
72/1247	A, 19A6
82/1415	A, 69A8 (quoting chap. 11, "Hsiao *Erh-ya*")
83/1427	B, 2B2
85/1451	A, 51A5 (specifying chapter 9's name)
85/1451	A, 18A2
92/1594	B, 20A3
93/1614	A, 72A3
100/1723	VII, 8B1 (in *Sung Hsien* edition only; not found in the *Ssu-pu ts'ung-k'an* edition)
22/404	B, 17B8
24/428	A, 6B4
25/453	A, 79A6

This list allows one to come to several important conclusions about the structure of the *KTT* prior to A.D. 656. First, the *I-wen lei-chü* reaffirms many previous deductions from the *Pei-t'ang shu-ch'ao*: all the citations of the *KTT* in the *I-wen lei-chü* also appear in the present form of the *KTT*. The *I-wen lei-chü*, too, refers to the appendix, the "Lien-ts'ung-tzu," as an integral part of the *KTT*. The *KTT* is variously entitled in the *I-wen lei-chü* as *K'ung-ts'ung-tzu*, *K'ung-ts'ung*, and *K'ung-tsung*ᵃ*-tzu*. Moreover, new facts can be deduced from the *I-wen lei-chü*'s citations. First, the *I-wen lei-chü* refers to the "Hsiao *Erh-ya*'s" chapter as *KTT*. This indicates that prior to A.D. 622 the "Hsiao *Erh-ya*" was considered an integral part of the whole text. Second, the *I-wen lei-chü* specifies *Kung-i*, which is the title of the ninth chapter of the *KTT*, as the sub-source of its citation from the *KTT*. This indicates that the chapter names of the *KTT* were part of the text prior to A.D. 622.

The *Sui-shu ching-chi-chih*'s Two Verdicts on Authorship of the *KTT*

Keeping in mind the transmission of the *KTT* during its first four hundred years, let us return to the *Sui-shu ching-chi-chih* and reexamine its verdicts concerning the authorship of the *KTT*. Several points can be made in view of the initial verdict. First, K'ung Fu could not have possibly written the whole *KTT* because the end of the sixth *chüan* records his own death.[55] The text also

The KTT *in History*

records, throughout the whole seventh *chüan*, the activities of the K'ung family members who lived long after Kung Fu's death. Second, there is no single biographical account of any personality prior to A.D. 656 that ascribes the writing of any book to K'ung Fu. Finally, there is no extant trace of a reference to the *KTT* prior to 656 that ascribes the writing of that text to K'ung Fu.

This leads to the question why Chang-sun Wu-chi's editorial team determined in their first reference to the *KTT* that it was written by K'ung Fu. Was there a source or tradition, of which we have no record today, that associates K'ung Fu with the *KTT*? Usually the shortcomings of such a hypothetical argument are obvious: it is irrefutable and can fill almost any hole of a fragmentary picture that perplexes the historian. In the case of the *KTT*, however, one may find enough clues to suggest the existence of remnants of two such sources, sources which might explain how the two verdicts of the *Sui-shu ching-chi-chih* were reached.

In its first reference to the *KTT*, the *Sui-shu ching-chi-chih* mentions a lost work entitled *K'ung-chih*. This title is obviously one of the 1,064 titles of the already lost works that the *Sui-shu ching-chi-chih*'s editors incorporated from Juan Hsiao-hsü's lost *Ch'i-lu*. It is therefore not improbable that the first *Sui-shu ching-chi-chih*'s reference to the *KTT* is a reproduction of the lost *Ch'i-lu* entry on the *KTT*. In that case, it was the *Ch'i-lu* that first attributed the *KTT* to K'ung Fu, and the editors of the *Sui-shu ching-chi-chih* simply represented the *Ch'i-lu*'s findings in their first reference to the *KTT* together with the *Ch'i-lu* reference to the already lost *K'ung-chih*.

The list of the *Pei-t'ang shu-ch'ao*'s citations of the *KTT* contains two that are no longer extant in the *KTT*'s present form. The citation in the *Pei-t'ang shu-ch'ao*, 97-2a, reads: "The *KTT* says: 'The family possessed collected works of the forefathers. All the brothers made a mutual effort to intone these works without exhaustion.'"

Now, it is quite certain that the edition of the *KTT* presumably listed by Juan Hsiao-hsü in his *Ch'i-lu* contained, like the one examined by Chang-sun Wu-chi's team, the above recovered extract from the *Pei-t'ang shu-ch'ao*. If this is the case, is it far-fetched to assert that K'ung Fu played a decisive role in the final compilation of his forefathers' works?

Thus, it is reasonable to assume that Chang-sun Wu-chi and his assistants accepted a number of points while making their initial verdict as to the authorship of the *KTT*. First, they concurred that the *KTT* must have been an authentic work. This is indicated by both verdicts, which ascribe the *KTT* to one or more members of the K'ung family.

Second, they accepted as true that the appendix, that is, the *KTT*'s seventh *chüan*, which describes the events following the death of K'ung Fu, must have been an authentic part of the *KTT* that was affixed to the *KTT* proper. This second premise justified the ascription of all seven *chüan* of the *KTT* to K'ung Fu.

They further concluded that K'ung Fu dedicated his life to the preservation of his ancestors' heritage, and that the heritage of the forefathers of the K'ung family was transmitted in the form of collected writings within the family. Therefore, they concluded that the end of K'ung Fu's biography marks the end of the *KTT* proper.

As a result, it can be assumed that a previously written catalogue, such as the *Ch'i-lu*, might have suggested a connection between the writing of the *KTT* and K'ung Fu. Its initial verdict was therefore totally supported and hence justified.

Nevertheless, the same editorial team was also aware that internal evidence in the *KTT*, such as the record of K'ung Fu's death, showed that he could not possibly have written the entire text of the *KTT* proper, that is, the bulk of the six *chüan*. There was no external evidence, except that presumably suggested by the *Ch'i-lu*, that would suggest the slightest connection between K'ung Fu and the composition of the *KTT*.

Chang-sun Wu-chi's team therefore retreated from its first verdict to a second, more critical and nonspecific judgment, according to which the *KTT* was the result of a cumulative effort made by K'ung family members, who preserved and transmitted their forefather's lore.

In spite of this, scholars from later periods have focused mainly on the *Sui-shu ching-chi-chih*'s first verdict, which they then reproduced. As I shall demonstrate, from the twelfth century on, other scholars of a more critical nature have found the *Sui-shu ching-chi-chih*'s two verdicts to be both inconsistent and problematic. These later scholars therefore posed two questions: (1) Was K'ung Fu the author of the *KTT*? (2) Was the *KTT* a genuine product of the K'ung family, or a mere forgery?

Before the results of their studies are examined, however, it is necessary to bridge the gap between A.D. 656 and 1058, and to provide a survey of the transmission of the *KTT* during the second four hundred years of its circulation.

A.D. 656–1058

The year 656 marks the first inclusion and evaluation of the *KTT* in a bibliographical section of a dynastic history. In 1058 the first commentary to the *KTT* was completed. The history of the *KTT*'s development between these two important dates does not warrant a detailed discussion. The *KTT* maintained its position in intellectual circles. It was listed in bibliographical works, referred to in various commentaries, and considered a valuable source of cita-

The KTT in History

tions for the important T'ang and Sung encyclopedias. The following chronological list displays notable features in the history of the *KTT* during the period under discussion:

The Li Shan (d. 689) commentary to the *Wen-hsüan*, the *Wen-hsüan-chu*, quoted the *KTT* nearly sixty times, referring to it always as the *K'ung-ts'ung-tzu*.[56]

The T'ang encyclopedia *Ch'u-hsüeh chi* by Hsü Chien (A.D. 659–729) quoted the *KTT* eighteen times, referring sixteen times to the *K'ung-ts'ung-tzu* and two times to the *K'ung-ts'ung*.[57]

The *KTT*, like the *K'ung-tzu chia-yü*, was not included in Ma Tsung's (d. 823) philosophical anthology, the *I-lin*.

The *KTT* was listed under the title *K'ung-ts'ung-tzu* in Liu Hsü's (887–946) *Chiu T'ang-shu* (Old Standard History of the T'ang) and referred to as a seven-*chüan* work by K'ung Fu.[58]

The encyclopedia *T'ai-p'ing yü-lan*, completed in 983, quoted the *K'ung-tsung^a-tzu* 120 times.[59]

The *KTT* was listed in the section of the "Eclectic Philosophers" (*tsa-chia*) under the title *K'ung-ts'ung-tzu* in Wang Yao-ch'en's (1001–1056) catalogue *Ch'ung-wen tsung-mu* as a three-*chüan* work.[60]

The *KTT* was listed under the title *K'ung-ts'ung* in Ou-yang Hsiu's (1007–1072) and Sung Ch'i's (998–1061) *Hsin T'ang-shu* (New Standard History of the T'ang) as a work of seven *chüan*.[61]

The *KTT* was listed in Li Shu's (fl. 1024) *Han-tan shu-mu*[62] as a work of double title: *K'ung-ts'ung-tzu* and *P'an Yü*.[63]

In conclusion, between the years 656 and 1000 the *KTT* was always regarded as a work of the *Lun Yü* category but was very rarely ascribed to K'ung Fu. It was not considered a philosophical work and was therefore not included in the philosophical sections of the dynastic histories or in the philosophical anthology of the corresponding period. It was transmitted under three titles: *K'ung-ts'ung-tzu*, *K'ung-tsung^a-tzu*, and *K'ung-ts'ung*. The general impression conveyed by this survey is that the *KTT* gradually became known under the title *K'ung-ts'ung-tzu*, while the title *K'ung-ts'ung* was gradually discarded. Since A.D. 656, the *KTT* has always been referred to as a work consisting of seven *chüan*. However, after 1000 there was also a reference to an edition of the *KTT* consisting of three *chüan*.[64] The beginning of the eleventh century, furthermore, marked a change in the attitude toward the nature of the text. It was no longer labeled by all bibliographers a classical work. And, for the first time, the *KTT* was identified with the long-lost *P'an Yü*.

A.D. 1058–1647

Between the eleventh and seventeenth centuries, the *KTT* declined in prominence. Although the transmission of the text was positively affected by its reissuing in Sung Hsien's (fl. 1058) revised annotated edition, its value, on the whole, was denigrated. First, many bibliographers removed it from its traditional rubric in the section of the "Classics" to the section of "Confucian Philosophers" and even to the section of the "Eclectics." Second, scholars, utilizing more critical methods, raised strong doubts concerning its authenticity and worth. This critical attitude was expressed in the studies of Hung Mai (1123–1202), Chu Hsi (1130–1200), Ch'ao Kung-wu (fl. 1144), Kao Ssu-sun (fl. 1184), Ch'en Chen-sun (fl. 1234), Sung Lien (1310–1381), Hu Ying-lin (1551–1602), and Li Lien (fl. 1577).

Before a survey of the critical studies of the *KTT* conducted by the abovementioned scholars is undertaken, a full account of both the Sung Hsien's edition with preface and commentary and Wang Lin's (fl. 1188) postscripted edition of the *KTT* must be provided.

The Sung Hsien Edition

Sung Hsien's unprecedented pioneering work on the *KTT* led to the formation of a revised edition, the framework and content of which set the standards for almost all subsequent complete editions of the *KTT*.[65] His commentary, which rendered the *KTT* accessible to readers for the first time, remained unsurpassed until 1795, when the Japanese scholar Tsukada Tora published another commentary on the text.

Sung Hsien, whose adult name was Kuan-chih, was a metropolitan graduate (*chin-shih*) of 1023, and a Gentleman for the Closing Court (*ch'ao-san lang*) who served as a director in the State Farm (*T'un-t'ien*) Division of the Department of State Affairs. His work on the *KTT* was carried out under imperial auspices and was presented to the Secretariat-Chancellery (*Chung-shu*) in 1058.[66]

His preface to the *KTT*, also dated 1058,[67] can be divided into three short discussions. The first is concerned with the authorship and the structure of the *KTT*; the second with the form of the text; and the third with its value.

Sung Hsien's discussion of the authorship of the *KTT* synthesizes the *Sui-shu ching-chi-chih*'s two authoritative views with "new" internal evidence that he found in the text. He opens his discussion by reproducing the *Sui-shu ching-chi-chih*'s first opinion on the authorship of the *KTT*, ascribing the composition of the whole text to K'ung Fu. This is followed by a brief biography of K'ung Fu, mainly adapted from the *KTT*.[68] In an apparent retreat from his opening statement, Sung Hsien then explains that K'ung Fu played a double role in the formation of the *KTT*: he compiled a collective work of the teach-

The KTT *in History*

ings of his family's predecessors, to which he then added his own writings. This corpus consisted of twenty-one chapters in six *chüan*. As for the authorship of the remaining last *chüan*, Sung Hsien concludes that it consisted of rhyme prose (*fu*[a]) and letters (*shu*[a]) that were added to the *KTT* proper by K'ung Tsang, Confucius's descendant of the tenth generation, who was a Chamberlain of Ceremonials during the reign of Emperor Hsiao Wu (140–87 B.C.).[69]

Sung Hsien's discussion of the authorship of the *KTT* attempts to minimize the prominent role traditionally ascribed to K'ung Fu as author of the *KTT*. Sung Hsien wanted to establish the composite character of the *KTT* by denying K'ung Fu the status of sole author, and even exclusive compiler. Nevertheless, the preface indicates his decision to refer the reader only to what he conceives to be the sine qua non in the formation of the *KTT*. He avoids going into a tedious discussion that would fill the lacunae in his preface and reconcile its discrepancies. This vagueness might explain his statement that ascribes the whole seven *chüan* to K'ung Tsang. There is no doubt that Sung Hsien was aware of the fallacy of his statement since he himself wrote a commentary to the final sections of the seven *chüan*, on the activities of K'ung Tsang's family successors who lived long after his death. However, he does not attempt to explain such inconsistencies and prefers to sketch a brief history of the formation of the text. As a result of this approach, many later scholars, who no more than glanced at Sung Hsien's preface, decided that K'ung Fu wrote the *KTT* proper, and that K'ung Tsang wrote the entire seventh *chüan*.[70]

In the second part of his preface Sung Hsien describes the textual material used while issuing his annotated edition of the *KTT*. In the first part of his discussion, he refers to the *KTT* as a seven-*chüan* text consisting of twenty-three chapters (A, 4a5–7). In the second part of his preface he elaborates on the textual nature of the *KTT* and says that to produce a corrected edition he had to examine many copies of the text which he had bought from private collectors. He also states explicitly that he deleted various defective passages from his edition of the *KTT* which he judged to be inauthentic as well as later interpolations. His first remark therefore indicates that by 1058 the text of the *KTT* was circulated in private circles. His explicit statement that he deleted various passages from his edition might explain the absence of certain extracts from the present *KTT*, of whose existence we learn from the various citations of the *KTT* prior to 1058.

The third part of Sung Hsien's preface shows that the *KTT* was losing its prominence in the eleventh century. This is indicated by the somewhat apologetic mood with which he justifies his dedication to the study of the *KTT*. Sung Hsien makes a sardonic reference to the popular status of philosophical texts such as the *Kuei Ku-tzu*, and then he states that the *KTT*, unlike other texts that represent philosophers' thoughts, bears the imprint of the former sages. His rhetorical concluding remark that the *KTT* deserves praise rather than oblivion (A, 4b3–6) suggests that at the time of Sung Hsien the value of the *KTT* was placed in doubt.

The K'ung-ts'ung-tzu shih-wen and Wang Lin's Postscript

The text of the *KTT* in the *Ssu-pu ts'ung-k'an* edition is preceded by two separately written items, Sung Hsien's preface to the *KTT* and his report to the Secretariat-Chancellery. The end of the text of the *KTT* is supplemented by two additional items that form an integral part of the *Ssu-pu ts'ung-k'an* edition, like Sung Hsien's preface and report. The following is a discussion of their nature.

The *KTT*, B, 69a1–79a8, consists of a small appended work entitled *K'ung-ts'ung-tzu shih-wen*, which bears no author's name. This work is arranged according to the chapter order of the *KTT*, containing phonetic spellings of terms and names that occur throughout the whole text. Although the work is anonymous, it is quite certain that it, too, was written by Sung Hsien. His authorship of the *K'ung-ts'ung-tzu shih-wen* can be deduced from the fact that Cheng Ch'iao (1102–1160) listed it, next to the *KTT* itself, and ascribed it to him in his *T'ung-chih*.[71] The importance of the *K'ung-ts'ung-tzu shih-wen* is that it is the first extant work on the *KTT* to be distinguished from the text of the *KTT* and to be circulated under its own title.

The *KTT*, B, 80a1–80b2, which appears on the very last page of the *Ssu-pu ts'ung-k'an* edition, consists of a very short postscript written by Wang Lin and is dated 1188. Wang Lin's postscript describes the formation of his own edition of the *KTT*. The *KTT*, he first says, is a collective work of the former sages, which was rarely circulated in his time. He then states that his edition was initiated by the "Honorable Vice-minister Lin[b] of the Summer Office (*hsia-kuan*)" when the vice-minister filled an office in Chiang-yu. Wang Lin continues that the vice-minister was called back by imperial order and left him with the unfinished editorial project. The abortive edition, however, was flawed. And, on a private visit, he was able to obtain a *Shu*[b] edition of the *KTT*.[72] Wang Lin concludes by saying that he compared his flawed edition with the *Shu*[b] edition and corrected no less than six hundred mistakes, thereby bringing his editorial enterprise to completion.

From Wang Lin's editorial introduction two important points emerge. First, around 1188, the *KTT* was not considered a popular text. And second, there was a complete and intelligible *Shu*[b] edition of the *KTT*, printed prior to 1188 and circulated among private collectors.

Hung Mai's Opinion

Hung Mai's (1123–1202) striking conclusion that the *KTT* is a late fabrication appears in one of his five collections of notes, *Jung-chai sui-pi*.[73] His study of the *KTT* is very short, but its scope and depth remained unsurpassed for a long time. There are eight main points of his discussion:

First, Hung Mai states that there is a passage in the biography of Mei Ch'eng in the *Han-shu*[74] that is duplicated in its entirety in the *KTT* (A, 9a4),[75] and that all early commentaries to the *Han-shu* did not refer to the *KTT* as a source of evidence. This is an implicit but nonetheless extremely significant argument. It implies that soon after the completion of the *Han-shu*, that is, at the time the first commentaries to the *Han-shu* were written, the *KTT* was not in existence as an independent text. It furthermore implies that the author of the *KTT* duplicated the passage under discussion from the *Han-shu*.

Second, Hung Mai refers to Li Shan's *Wen-hsüan chu* as the first source that quotes the *KTT*. This is an important methodological approach in attempting to determine the *ante quem* date of the *KTT*. There are, however, chronologically earlier sources that quote the *KTT*.

Third, Hung Mai points out that the *Han-shu I-wen-chih* does not mention the *KTT*. This indicates that the famous bibliographers of the Former Han, Liu Hsiang and Liu Hsin, did not see the *KTT* at all. Nevertheless, the *Han-shu I-wen-chih* does record in the *Ju-chia* section a book of ten chapters written by the Marquis of Liao, the Minister of Ceremonies K'ung Tsang.[76] The "Lien-ts'ung-tzu," which is the *KTT*'s appendix, also ascribes to K'ung Tsang the composition of a book of ten chapters (B, 45b1–46a1). Therefore, Hung Mai hesitantly points out, the two separately mentioned books could denote the very same book.

This argument refutes the opinion that the *KTT* was compiled in the Former Han because the famous bibliographers of the period did not mention it. Hung Mai then distinguishes between the *KTT* proper and its supplement, the "Lien-ts'ung-tzu," and suggests a bold interpretation according to which K'ung Tsang's ten-chapter book listed in the *Han-shu I-wen-chih* is possibly the same book as the first part of the "Lien-ts'ung-tzu."

Fourth, Hung Mai briefly surveys the tradition that ascribes the authorship of the *KTT* to K'ung Fu. According to this survey K'ung Fu was an Erudite of Ch'en She. He collected the anecdotes dealing with the exploits of his predecessors in twenty-one chapters arranged in six *chüan*, to which he added further anecdotes concerning his own deeds. This survey indicates that the seven-*chüan* edition of the *KTT* continued to be circulated at the time of Hung Mai.

Fifth, Hung Mai states that the *KTT* was not considered a source of reference in periods prior to the T'ang. It was rather Sung Hsien in 1059 whose commentary and explanations first made the text accessible. This brief reference shows that Sung Hsien's commentary was considered a breakthrough in the history of the study of the *KTT* more than a hundred years after its completion.

Sixth, Hung Mai notes that the *KTT* does not reveal the literary characteristics of the period from the end of the Ch'in to the end of the Han. This is a striking stylistic argument that introduces a completely new methodological approach toward the problem of dating and verifying the authenticity of the *KTT*.[77]

Seventh, Hung Mai concludes that the *KTT* was probably produced by an indulgent fabricator who lived in the period between Ch'i (A.D. 420–479) and Liang (A.D. 502–557). This is a convincing conclusion, which undermines the opinions concerning the authenticity and dating of the *KTT* by both the *Sui-shu ching-chi-chih* and Sung Hsien.

Finally, Hung Mai ends his discussion of the *KTT* with what should be considered a totally irrelevant argument. He mentions Yen Shih-ku's argument concerning the authenticity of the *K'ung-tzu chia-yü*, according to which the present text of that work is not the same work as that listed in the *Han-shu I-wen-chih*.[78]

It seems to me that Hung Mai brought up this issue in order to defend his revolutionary argument from any future findings that might jeopardize his whole discussion. Hung Mai was probably aware of the fact that his findings concerning the absence of external references to the *KTT* throughout the Han period might eventually turn out to be flawed. He therefore supplied a response for the future hypothetical counterargument that the inclusion of a certain title in bibliographical lists such as the *Han-shu I-wen-chih* says very little about the authenticity of an extant work with that title.

Chu Hsi's Opinion

Chu Hsi (1130–1200) was certainly the *KTT*'s greatest adversary in history. His various hostile remarks reveal that he unabashedly loathed the text. His *Yü-lei* and *Wen-chi* contain several such derogatory references.[79] Chu Hsi stated that although the *KTT* pretends to be an ancient and authentic book, it is no more than a late forgery. Neither the great scholars of the Former Han, such as Chia I and Tung Chung-shu, nor the standard histories of that period mention the *KTT*. It is common knowledge, concludes Chu Hsi, that the *KTT* is a forgery written in the Later Han period. Furthermore, Chu Hsi observed that the *KTT* shows features that resemble the pseudo-K'ung An-kuo's writings. He also makes much of the *KTT*'s style and character, which he severely faults. On the whole, he concludes that the *KTT* is a worthless work whose content does not merit the slightest attention.

There are two points worth mentioning in connection with Chu Hsi's references to the *KTT*. First, Chu Hsi was the first to draw attention to the stylistic resemblance between the pseudo-K'ung An-kuo's work and the *KTT*. It took Chinese scholars five hundred more years to realize in full the implications of this resemblance. Second, as a result of Chu Hsi's castigations, from the twelfth to the seventeenth century the *KTT* was circulated with an enormous

The KTT *in History*

stigma. Therefore, the possible reappraisal of its contents in a newly written essay or commentary would have meant a rebellion against the scholarly and authoritative status of Chu Hsi.[80]

Ch'ao Kung-wu's Discussion

Ch'ao Kung-wu's opinion of the *KTT* in seven *chüan* appears in his *Chün-chai tu-shu-chih* (preface: 1151). His discussion is divided into two main parts. In the first he summarizes those previous opinions concerning the *KTT* with which he agrees. He therefore refers to K'ung Fu as the author of the *KTT* in twenty-one chapters, and to K'ung Tsang as the author of the "Lien-ts'ung-tzu." He also makes note of Sung Hsien's commentary and duplicates the *Han-tan shu-mu*'s entry on the *KTT*, where it was given an alternative title. In the second part Ch'ao Kung-wu makes an attempt to find a solution to the problem of the *KTT*'s absence from the list of books in the *Han-shu I-wen-chih*.

His argument is constructed along critical lines. Although the *KTT* is not mentioned in the *Han-shu I-wen-chih*, a work of twenty-six chapters is listed there, entitled *P'an Yü*, whose author is K'ung Chia. Now since according to the *KTT* one of the various names of K'ung Fu was K'ung Chia, and since the *Han-tan shu-mu* states that the *KTT*'s alternative title was *P'an Yü*, it is reasonable to assume, first, that the K'ung Chia mentioned in the *Han-shu I-wen-chih* is none other than K'ung Fu, and second, that the *KTT* is the *P'an Yü* less the six chapters[81] that were subsequently lost.[82]

Kao Ssu-sun's Discovery of an Anachronism

Kao Ssu-sun (fl. 1184) reacted negatively to Ch'ao Kung-wu's theory that identifies the *KTT* with the *P'an Yü*. He gave a full presentation of Ch'ao's views in his *Tzu-lüeh*[83] and rejected them on the ground that neither the commentaries to the *P'an Yü*'s entry in the *Han-shu I-wen-chih* nor the total number of the alleged *P'an Yü*'s chapters supported such a theory. Kao Ssu-sun's greatest contribution to the study of the *KTT* was the anachronism he detected in the book. He argued that according to tradition, Confucius died in 479 B.C. His grandson Tzu-ssu lived with Mencius during the reign of Duke Mu (reg. 409–377 B.C) and died at the age of sixty-two. If this is the case, then Tzu-ssu must have been born around 470 B.C., namely, after his grandfather's death. Consequently, he could not possibly have been engaged in philosophical discussion with his grandfather Confucius as recorded in chapter 5 of the *KTT*. This anachronism led Kao Ssu-sun to the inescapable conclusion that the *KTT* was a fabrication of a later period. Now, Kao Ssu-sun's chronology is somewhat deficient. Tzu-ssu, at least according to the *Shih-chi* chronology, must have born before the death of Confucius.[84] Therefore there is no doubt that the *KTT*, as Kao Ssu-sun was the first to indicate, exhibits obvious unreconcilable anachronisms. If Tzu-ssu conversed with his grandfather, it must have been before Confucius's death in 479 B.C., and thus he could not have been alive in the reign of Duke Mu (409–377 B.C.). And if he, together with Mencius, was active during that reign, he could not possibly have talked to his grandfather, because he died at the age of sixty-two.

Ch'en Chen-sun's Discussion

Ch'en Chen-sun (fl. 1234) was the last of the Sung scholars who expressed critical views concerning the *KTT*. In his *Chih-chai shu-lu chieh-t'i* he argued that the *KTT* could not possibly have been written by K'ung Fu, because the evidence in the text, such as the record of the death of K'ung Fu as well as the record of the lives of his successors, indicates the opposite.[85] Ch'en Chen-sun was the first scholar who established the *post quem* date for the *KTT*. In contradiction to Sung Hsien, he held that the twenty-three chapters of the seventh *chüan* of the *KTT* form an integral corpus. He furthermore pointed out that the last line of the twenty-third chapter of the text concludes with the death of Chi-yen, and the text specifies the exact year of his death as A.D. 124. The *post quem* date of the *KTT* was therefore established for the first time as the year A.D. 124.

Sung Lien's and Hu Ying-lin's Views

In the Ming dynasty sharp disagreement occurred between those scholars who argued for the genuineness of the *KTT* and those who thought it was a forgery. Sung Lien (1310–1381) belonged to the latter group. In his *Chu-tzu pien* he recapitulated previous opinions concerning the *KTT* in seven *chüan*, introducing a provocative new hypothesis.[86] According to his idea, the *KTT* was forged by none other than its first commentator, Sung Hsien. Sung Lien presents his hypothesis cautiously, relying on the fact that Wang Shih-yüan not only forged the book of K'ang Sang-tzu, but also added his own commentary to it.[87]

No matter how absurd this may seem to anyone who is versed in the numerous references to the *KTT* in the periods prior to Sung Hsien's time, the fact is that Sung Lien's hypothesis continued to circulate for two hundred more years, until the time of Hu Ying-lin (1551–1602). In his *Shao-shih shan-fang pi-ts'ung*, Hu Ying-lin discussed the *KTT* in seven *chüan* and made a note of Sung Lien's hypothesis.[88] Nevertheless, he discarded it because there was nothing in the literary style of the text to suggest that the *KTT* was a product of a Sung scholar. The insubstantial nature of this counterargument indicates that Hu Ying-lin's study of the *KTT* was not extensive, an assumption which may explain some of his mistaken statements concerning the history of the *KTT*.[89]

It is important to note, however, that even though Hu Ying-lin was aware of the derogatory opinions about the *KTT* previously expressed by Chu Hsi and Sung Lien, he insisted that the *KTT* is, after all, a genuine work. In his estimation, the stylistic character of the *KTT* shows that the text was a product of the Late Han and Wei-Chin periods, but it might have undergone readjustments during the Sung. Accordingly, Hu Ying-lin concluded that the *KTT* was a product of the K'ung family circles during Chi-yen's time and later. These compilers assembled the works of the forefathers of the K'ung family into a corpus including, among the rest, K'ung Fu's own works such as the "Hsiao Erh-ya" and "Ch'i Mo."

The Li Lien Preface

The preface ascribed to Li Lien (1488–1566) concludes the list of critical views expressed by Sung and Ming scholars concerning the *KTT*.

Li Lien's discussion of the text appears in the preface of the *Tzu-hui*'s three-*chüan* edition of the *KTT*.[90] The *Tzu-hui* was an anthology of twenty-four minor philosophers, published in 1577 and attributed to Chou Tzu-i (1529–1587).[91] The first line of the preface starts with a lengthy citation of Mr. Li Lien from Ta-liang,[92] a citation that seems to constitute the whole bulk of the preface. The last line of the preface specifies the date of its composition as 1577.

The above-mentioned dates present an apparent enigma: How could Li Lien, who died in 1566, write the whole preface to the *Tzu-hui* edition of the *KTT*, which is dated 1577? To add to the quandary, the last three lines of the preface, which justify the inclusion of the *KTT* in the *Tzu-hui* collection, could not have been written by Li Lien himself, but by the *Tzu-hui* compiler. We may therefore suggest that the so-called Li Lien preface to the *KTT* was probably the preface to the *KTT* written by Chou Tzu-i, who duplicated the authoritative view of Li Lien[93] concerning the text in the first part of his preface.[94]

The preface itself is divided into two major parts. The first, which quotes Li Lien, consists of nine lines, and the second part, written by Chou Tzu-i himself, consists of ten lines. Li Lien's part of the preface is a repetitious summary of the traditional, noncritical views concerning K'ung Fu and K'ung Tsang with respect to the authorship of the *KTT* and the "Lien-ts'ung-tzu."

Chou Tzu-i's part, however, is important because, contrary to Chu Hsi's derogatory view of the *KTT*, which he quotes in his preface, Chou Tzu-i insists that the text was a product of circles connected with Tzu-feng and Chi-yen, the last protagonists of the *KTT*. His concluding statement that the *KTT* is undoubtedly authentic and should therefore be included in his *Tzu-hui* shows that even in times of severe criticism (i.e., during the Sung and the Ming), the *KTT* was far from being relegated to a doomed status.

The *KTT* in the Ch'ing

During the Ch'ing dynasty, the careful reading and analysis of texts gave rise to a major advance in the study of the *KTT*. It is true that the discussion of the *KTT* by Yao Chi-heng (1647–1715?) in his *Ku-chin wei-shu k'ao* (pp. 173–174) was a mere echo of the discussions conducted earlier by Sung and Ming scholars. However, another Ch'ing scholar of the same period introduced a method of comparative examination of texts that not only put the *KTT* in an entirely different light, but that also established a new framework for the subsequent discussions of its authorship.

Tsang Lin's Discussion

It was Tsang Lin (1650–1713) who pointed out in his *Ching-i tsa-chi* that a careful comparison of the *KTT*, the *K'ung-tzu chia-yü*, and the pseudo-K'ung An-kuo's *Shu-ching* with several of Wang Su's works indicated that all had striking affinities, and that they therefore were written by one person, namely, Wang Su.[95]

Tsang Lin began his argument by quoting an extract from the "Chi-fa" chapter of the *Li-chi* which reads:

> Hsiang-chin yü k'an t'an chi han shu yeh.[96]
> (They approached both the sacrificial pits and altars to offer sacrifices to the Heat and the Cold.)[97]

Tsang Lin next quoted the commentary by Cheng Hsüan to the effect that the characters *hsiang-chin* in the above *Li-chi* extract were erroneous, and that they should be emended to *jang chi*. Cheng Hsüan explained in his commentary that *jang* meant "terminating" and *chi* meant "seeking." In cases of untimely cold or heat, Cheng Hsüan continued, people prayed for the termination of the one while simultaneously seeking the commencement of the other. Prayers addressed to the Cold were performed in sacrificial pits, while prayers addressed to the Heat were performed at sacrificial altars.[98] Tsang Lin then wrote that Wang Su in his commentary to the *Li-chi* advocated, in opposition to Cheng Hsüan, the emendation of the *Li-chi*'s *hsiang-chin* to read *tsu ying*, namely, two separate sacrifices with which greetings are offered to the departure of Cold and the arrival of Heat.[99] Now the only other work that had the same wording as that advocated by Wang Su was the *KTT* (A, 30a6), according to which prayers of greeting were offered, in the pits and at the altars, to the departure and arrival of either the summer heat or the winter cold. Tsang Lin continued that his examination of the *KTT* resulted in finding more affinities among the *KTT*, the *K'ung-tzu chia-yü*, the pseudo-K'ung An-kuo's *Shu-ching*, and the annotated works of Wang Su.[100]

Tsang Lin therefore concluded that it was Wang Su who had forged all three works, attributing them to authoritative figures of the K'ung family, in order to refute Cheng Hsüan's exegesis of the Classics and promote his own.

Chiang Chao-hsi's Redaction

In 1724 Chiang Chao-hsi, a scholar who had conducted several studies of a number of classical books,[101] published a redaction with commentary of the *KTT* entitled *K'ung-ts'ung cheng-i* (fig. 14, p. 53). His redaction consisted of five *chüan* and completely omitted chapters 11, 18, 22, and 23 of the standard editions of the *KTT*. He deleted numerous segments of the text, segments that he thought might blur the correct meaning of the *KTT*. He also added to each section a brief explanatory note that attempted to cast light on the intrinsic meaning and value of the section under scrutiny.

Chiang Chao-hsi's commentary to the *K'ung-tzu chia-yü* has been characterized as very mediocre.[102] In the case of the *KTT*, mediocrity persists as a fitting attribute. Chiang Chao-hsi's work on the *KTT* consisted of his enthusiastic deletion of all the problematic parts. By doing so he ended up with a mutilated text within which were implanted the banal insights he had found in the *KTT*.

Nevertheless, Chiang Chao-hsi's redaction of the *KTT* is notable for it was the first attempt since 1058 to present an alternative textual study to the Sung Hsien commentary on the *KTT*. In particular, in contradiction to Chu Hsi's derogatory opinion of the text, which Chiang Chao-hsi quoted in his introduction,[103] he insisted that the *KTT* was an authentic product of Late Han members of the K'ung family, and that it was close both in dating and in nature to the *K'ung-tzu chia-yü*.[104]

The Opinion of the Ssu-k'u ch'üan-shu tsung-mu's Editors

The authoritative editors of the *Ssu-k'u ch'üan-shu tsung-mu* did not arrive at any new findings in their 1777 synopsis of the *KTT*.[105] They made a careful survey of previous treatments of the *KTT*, omitting very few. They discussed the *Sui-shu ching-chi-chih*'s second verdict on the *KTT* and rejected it because they found the *Sui-shu ching-chi-chih* flawed in the case of the *K'ung-tzu chia-yü*. They explained that contrary to the *Sui-shu ching-chi-chih*, according to which the *K'ung-tzu chia-yü* was a genuine product of the K'ung family,[106] their findings indicated that this work was no more than an historical fiction written by Wang Su.[107] Because the *Sui-shu ching-chi-chih* coupled the title of the *KTT* with that of the *K'ung-tzu chia-yü*, stating that both works were authentic products of the K'ung family,[108] and because their findings indicated that the *K'ung-tzu chia-yü* was inauthentic, the editors decided to reject the *Sui-shu ching-chi-chih*'s opinion of the *KTT* as well. They then proceeded to mention the striking similarities among the *KTT*, the *K'ung-tzu chia-yü*, and the pseudo-K'ung An-kuo's *Shang-shu*, but they hesitated to attribute the *KTT* to any particular individual. They pointed out that chapter 11 of the *KTT*, the "Hsiao *Erh-ya*," featured elements of the third and fourth centuries B.C., but it was only in their synopsis of the *Kung-sun Lung-tzu* that they explicitly determined that the *KTT* was a forgery written in the period between the Han and the Chin.[109]

The Tsukada Tora Commentary

In 1795, the Japanese philosopher Tsukada Tora (Tsukada Tamon) (1745–1832) published his commentary to the *KTT* (fig. 15, p. 54), an example of the most painstaking scholarship and a major stage in the history of *KTT* criticism.

Tsukada Tora, a native of Shinano, was a scholar of immense scholarship who wrote philosophical essays as well as numerous commentaries on classical and philosophical texts. In his study of the *KTT* he struggled with countless textual difficulties and supplied the necessary background for almost all the anecdotes that form the narrative framework of the text. He referred his readers to the various classical and nonclassical works from which the author of the *KTT* had drawn, he clarified the meaning of hundreds of concepts, he traced the identities of various personages, and he pinpointed the sources for many titles as well as the locations of cities, towns, and provinces.

Tsukada Tora's lengthy preface demonstrates that he was familiar with the Sung Hsien commentary, which he explicitly regarded as insufficient (4a1), and with the so-called Li Lien preface, which he fully quoted (4b1–6a1). His preface is concerned with the authenticity, dating, authorship, nature of previous views, and value of the *KTT*. He seems to be irritated by Chu Hsi's low opinion of the *KTT*, an opinion which he sardonically rejects several times throughout his preface (1a2–3; 2a1–3). For him, Chu Hsi's derogatory opinion of the *KTT* was affected by his preoccupation with the "principle of mind and nature" (*hsin-hsing chih li*), which was a metaphysical concept close to Buddhism (2a6). Classical Confucianism, however, argued Tsukada Tora, was devoid of this metaphysical orientation, and since the *KTT* represented classical Confucianism, Chu Hsi was reluctant to deal with it (2a7).

Tsukada Tora thought that the *KTT* was an authentic product of the K'ung family, but he argued that the text was the work of many hands. He regarded the first ten chapters as the genuine words of Confucius and Tzu-ssu, and chapters 12–21 as the assembled works of their successors collected by the disciples of K'ung Fu. The "Lien-ts'ung-tzu" was for Tsukada Tora a reminiscence of the Confucian heritage as reflected in the activities of K'ung Tsang, Tzu-feng, and Chi-yen during the Han.

The Nineteenth Century

In the nineteenth century no major innovations in the history of the *KTT* occurred, and scholars continued to be occupied with previous views concern-

The KTT *in History* 35

ing it. Four scholars should be mentioned in this regard: Chou Chung-fu (ca. 1800); Ting Yen (1794–1875); Shen Chia-pen (1840–1913); and Yao Chentzung (1842–1906).

Chou Chung-fu should be noted for his discussion of the nature of the various editions of the *KTT*.[110] Ting Yen intensified the use of a comparative method for textual analysis. In a long, detailed essay he pointed out the similarities among the pseudo-K'ung An-kuo's *Shang-shu*, the *K'ung-tzu chia-yü*, and the *KTT*, determining that they all were written by Wang Su.[111] Shen Chia-pen made a careful summary of all historically major views of the *KTT*.[112] Yao Chen-tzung shared the view that it was Wang Su who forged the *KTT*. In his *San-kuo-chih i-wen-chih* he included the *KTT* as a book dating from the Wei era, and he quoted various sources that attributed its composition to Wang Su.[113]

Modern Discussions of the *KTT*

During the present century, such scholars as Chin Shou-shen,[114] Huang Yün-mei,[115] and Hu Yü-chin[116] have generally reinforced the line of argument according to which the *KTT* was a work of the Wei-Chin era probably forged by Wang Su.

The *Ku-shih-pien* contains two discussions concerning the *KTT*.[117] The first is by Lo Ken-tse, who prepared bellicose paraphrases of many of the previous discussions of the *KTT* that had focused on the anachronisms in the text as indicating its spuriousness.[118] His argument that Wang Su was connected with the composition of the *KTT* also repeated previous arguments. Nevertheless, Lo Ken-tse developed a new argument, which shifted the *terminus post quem* of the *KTT* from A.D. 124 to A.D. 201. In the past, it was generally argued that the *post quem* date of the *KTT* was A.D. 124, since this was the date specified by the last line of the *KTT* as Chi-yen's year of death. Lo Ken-tse, however, drew attention to the fact that Chao Ch'i (d. A.D. 201) explicitly stated in his preface to his commentary to the *Mencius* that there was no source referring to Mencius's adult name.[119] The *KTT*, continued Lo Ken-tse, did contain *Tzu-chü*[b] which was said by the *KTT* to be Mencius's adult name. If such was the case, it would mean that the tradition attributing an adult name to Mencius commenced only after Chao Ch'i's death, that is, after A.D. 201. Since the *KTT* had an adult name for Mencius, the *KTT* therefore must have been written after A.D. 201.

Lo Ken-tse's argument was reinforced from a different angle by Hsin Shih in another critical essay in the *Ku-shih-pien* on the *KTT*.[120] Shin Shih argued that the reading of Kao Yu's (ca. A.D. 198) commentary to the *Lü-shih ch'un-ch'iu* indicated that at the time of the composition of this commentary, the *KTT* was not extant. For example, there is a debate in the *Lü-shih ch'un-ch'iu* between Kung-sun Lung and a certain K'ung Ch'uan concerning Mr. Tsang's three ears. In his commentary to this debate Kao Yu refers to the two participants as two sophists.[121] In chapter 12 of the *KTT*, however, this debate is recorded once more; this time, K'ung Ch'uan is Tzu-kao, Confucius's descendant of the sixth generation, who is portrayed as a Confucian Master and as the chief opponent of Sophism. It is quite certain, therefore, that Kao Yu, the commentator of the *Lü-shih ch'un-ch'iu*, was not familiar with the tradition that identified K'ung Ch'uan as Tzu-kao of the *KTT*, probably because this tradition began only after his time, namely, after A.D 198.

Ch'ien Mu's discussions of the *KTT* revealed a variety of anachronisms in the text indicating not only that the author of the *KTT* was unfamiliar with the dates of various members of the K'ung family but that his knowledge of the history of the pre-Ch'in period was incomplete.[122]

Hu Tao-ching raised new internal evidence that indicated that the *KTT* was a product of the Han to Chin era. In his elaboration on chapter 12 of the *KTT*, Hu Tao-ching strengthened the argument that the *KTT*'s systematic correction of Kung-sun Lung's thesis, "A white horse is not a horse," to "A white horse is not a white horse" was a typical late error of Han to Chin era.[123] This argument emphasized the fact that the *KTT* contained elements typical exclusively of the Late Han to Wei-Chin era and therefore could have been written only during that period.

Chang Hsin-ch'eng presented a masterful survey of all the historically significant references to the *KTT* and declared the *KTT* a definite forgery.[124]

Three recent studies of the *KTT* conclude the list of important references to the *KTT* in modern times. In 1975 Yen Ch'in-nan published his dissertation, *K'ung-ts'ung-tzu chiao-cheng*.[125] His industrious study consists of numerous textual emendations, textual comparisons, and a description of all major extant and no longer extant editions of the *KTT*. In 1977 Yen Ling-feng included a definitive list of all extant and nonextant editions, redactions, and reproductions of the *KTT* in his *Chou Ch'in Han Wei chu-tzu chih-chien shu-mu*.[126] Finally, in 1982 Huang Chang-chien published his collection of essays concerning the Old Text and the New Text schools of the *Shang-shu*.[127] His scholarly study contained an essay that dealt with the authorship of the pseudo-K'ung An-kuo's *Shang-shu*. In it he lists all the striking similarities among the pseudo-K'ung An-kuo's *Shang-shu*, the *KTT*, and Wang Su's own commentary to the *Shang-shu*.[128]

The *KTT* in Western Literature

The *KTT* has scarcely received attention in Western literature. Wylie and Legge were the first, to the best of my knowledge, to mention the *KTT*.[129]

The KTT in History

Forke mentioned the *KTT* several times,[130] as did Graham, who even translated a few of its lines.[131]

The most fully developed treatment of the *KTT*, however, has been that of Kramers. In his study of the *K'ung-tzu chia-yü* he several times discussed the nature and the relation of the *KTT* to the *K'ung-tzu chia-yü*, and he noted Lo Ken-tse's opinion that Wang Su was its forger.[132] His greatest contribution to the study of the *KTT* was his discussion of the relationship between the genealogy of the K'ung family that appears in the *K'ung-tzu chia-yü*'s Postscript and the genealogy of the family in chapter 22 of the *KTT*.[133] Kramers found that it is possible, but not certain, that the writer of the genealogy of the K'ung family in the *K'ung-tzu chia-yü*'s Postscript borrowed some unique features from the genealogy of the same family that appears in chapter 22 of the *KTT*. He also concluded that Wang Su, or some other person under his influence, overhauled various parts of the *K'ung-tzu chia-yü*.[134]

Transmission of the *KTT* under Other Titles

A study of the *KTT* in history would be incomplete without mentioning the parallel transmission of several of its chapters under titles other than the *KTT*. The following is a list of these chapters and their corresponding titles:

KTT's Chapter Number	Title Transmitted Under
5-10	*Tzu-ssu Tzu*
11	*Hsiao Erh-ya*
12-14	*Lan-yen*; also *Ts'an-yen*
22	*K'ung Tsang*

The KTT *and the Tzu-ssu Tzu*

I have already mentioned the *Book of Tzu-ssu* in connection with the determination of the *terminus ante quem* of the *KTT*. A twenty-three-chapter work titled *Tzu-su* is listed in the *Han-shu I-wen-chih* and is ascribed, by Pan Ku, to Confucius's grandson, Chi[a], that is, to Tzu-ssu.[135] During the Late Han to T'ang periods, works under the titles *Tzu-ssu* or *Tzu-ssu Tzu* were scarcely referred to either by major commentaries or by the various encyclopedias. The *Sui-shu ching-chi-chih* listed a seven-*chüan* work entitled *Tzu-ssu Tzu* in the philosophers' category, ascribing it to K'ung Chi, that is, Tzu-ssu.[136]

The present text of the *Tzu-ssu Tzu*, however, is mainly the work of Wang Chuo, who in 1200 reproduced almost all extant references to Tzu-ssu from various sources.[137] These sources were classical books, encyclopedias, and philosophical anthologies such as the *I-lin*.[138] Wang Chuo incorporated in his *Tzu-ssu Tzu* the major part of chapters 5–10 of the *KTT*, which narrate the activities of Tzu-ssu.[139]

Two facts are intriguing in connection with the transmission of the *Tzu-ssu Tzu*. First, it was already 1151 when Ch'ao Kung-wu included the *Tzu-ssu Tzu* in his *Chün-chai tu-shu-chih* and quoted a long passage from it.¹⁴⁰ This passage, which consisted of a dialogue between Tzu-ssu and Mencius, also appeared at the end of chapter 6 of the *KTT* (A, 38b4–39a1). This means that there was at least one work titled *Tzu-ssu Tzu* before 1200, that is, prior to Wang Chuo's reconstructed work, containing certain parts of the *KTT*.¹⁴¹

Second, the Ming encyclopedia *Yung-lo ta-tien* contains at least two references to the *Tzu-ssu Tzu*, neither of which appears in Wang Chuo's *Tzu-ssu Tzu* but rather in chapters 1 and 3 of the *KTT*.¹⁴² As has been mentioned, Tzu-ssu starts to play his role in the *KTT* in the fifth chapter, while the first four chapters narrate the activities of Confucius alone. This is why these four chapters of the *KTT* were not included in the *Tzu-ssu Tzu* of Wang Chuo. The inclusion of two quotations from the first and third chapters of the *KTT* under the title *Tzu-ssu Tzu* in the *Yung-lo ta-tien*, therefore indicates that possibly all of the first ten chapters of the *KTT* were transmitted under the title *Tzu-ssu Tzu*, not just chapters 5–10.¹⁴³

The KTT and the Hsiao Erh-ya

A work entitled *Hsiao Erh-ya*, which was most probably not related to the *KTT*, was listed in the *Han-shu I-wen-chih*, the *Sui-shu ching-chi-chih*, and the *Chiu T'ang-shu ching-chi-chih*.¹⁴⁴ From the Sung onward, however, the *KTT*'s eleventh chapter began to circulate as a separate work of K'ung Fu, under the title *Hsiao Erh-ya*. This *Hsiao Erh-ya* was a subject of various commentaries and studies, some of which pointed to the lexical affinities between this work and Wang Su's writings.¹⁴⁵

The KTT, K'ung Tsang, and the Ts'an-yen

Two works relating to the *KTT* are listed in the section of philosophers of the *Yü-han shan-fang chi-i-shu*. The first is the *K'ung Tsang shu*, a title that is not followed by any of its alleged text.¹⁴⁶ A ten-chapter work of K'ung Tsang is listed in the *Han-shu I-wen-chih*.¹⁴⁷ Its alleged author, K'ung Tsang, is directly referred to and quoted three times by the *I-wen lei-chü*.¹⁴⁸ All three citations are found in the present twenty-second chapter of the *KTT* (B, 51a6; B, 49a6; B, 48b4).

The second work listed by the *Yü-han shan-fang chi-i-shu* is a three-chapter work entitled *Lan-yen* or *Ts'an-yen*, whose supposed author is K'ung Ch'uan, that is, Tzu-kao.¹⁴⁹ This work consists entirely of chapters 12, 13, and 14 of the *KTT*. Ma Kuo-han explains the reasons for the inclusion of these three chapters of the *KTT* as a reconstructed work in his anthology:¹⁵⁰

First, the *Han-shu I-wen-chih* lists two works entitled *Ju-chia-yen* and

Ts'an-yen.[151] Pan Ku explicitly states that the authors of both works are unknown.

Second, the *K'ung-tzu chia-yü*'s Postscript states that Tzu-kao, namely, K'ung Ch'uan, wrote down the *Ju-chia-yen* and entitled them *Ts'an-yen*.[152] The seeming discrepancy between Pan Ku's opinion of the authorship of the *Ts'an-yen* and the opinion expressed in the Postscript of the *K'ung-tzu chia-yü* might be explained as follows: The anthology containing the *Ts'an-yen*, that is, the *KTT*, began to circulate, together with the *K'ung-tzu chia-yü*, no earlier than the end of the Late Han. Therefore, it is no wonder that the identity of the author of the *Ts'an-yen* was not known earlier to Pan Ku (A.D. 32–92), the compiler of the *Han-shu I-wen-chih*.

Finally, Ma Kuo-han notes that although Yen Shih-ku, in his commentary to the *Han-shu I-wen-chih*, rejects the opinion expressed in the Postscript of the *K'ung-tzu chia-yü*,[153] he does not specify the reasons for his rejection, and therefore the *K'ung-tzu chia-yü*'s opinion is sustained.[154]

In sum, various parts of the *KTT* both circulated and were mentioned in connection with titles other than the *KTT*. Contrary to the *KTT*, all of these titles were listed in the *Han-shu I-wen-chih*, a fact whose relevance to the composition of the *KTT* will be discussed later.

Major Available Editions of the *KTT*

Throughout this historical survey, several notes have referred to various editions of the *KTT* that are no longer extant. Among these are the seven-*chüan* editions listed in the bibliographical monographs of the dynastic histories of the Sui and T'ang, the three-*chüan* edition mentioned by the *Ch'ung-wen tsung-mu*, and the printed *Shu*[b] edition mentioned by Wang Lin in his 1188 postscript to the *KTT*. Several other lost editions of the *KTT* are listed in various bibliographies, such as Shao I-ch'en's (1810–1860) *Ssu-k'u chien-ming mu-lu piao-chu*[155] and Yen Ling-feng's contemporary *Chou Ch'in Han Wei chu-tzu chih-chien shu-mu*, which is an encyclopedic list of traditional editions and modern reprints of the *KTT*.[156]

The following sixteen figures are a record of the history of the *KTT* as a printed text and serve as a list of all major available editions of the work.

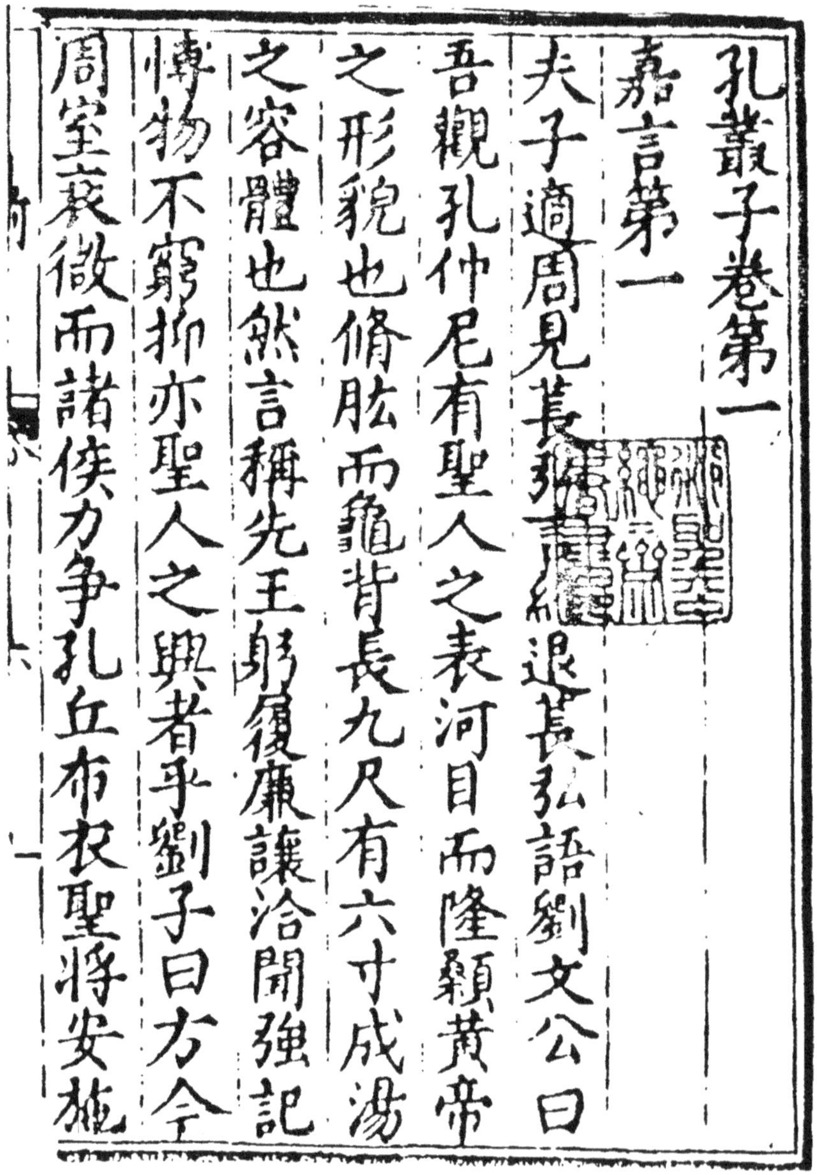

孔叢子卷第一

嘉言第一

夫子適周見萇弘語劉文公曰吾觀孔仲尼有聖人之表河目而隆顙黃帝之形貌也脩肱而龜背長九尺有六寸成湯之容體也然言稱先王躬復廉讓洽聞強記博物不窮抑亦聖人之興者乎劉子曰方今周室衰微而諸侯力爭孔丘布衣聖將安施

FIGURE I The *Ssu-pu ts'ung k'an* edition, published in Shanghai by the Commercial Press in 1920. This is a facsimile reprint of a Ming reproduction of a Sung copy, in a two-part, seven-*chüan*, noncommented edition. It includes the Sung Hsien preface and the letter to the Secretariat-Chancellery as well as his *K'ung-ts'ung-tzu shih-wen*. The edition also includes three fragments of comment by Wang Lin and his postscript to the *KTT*. These features are distinctive imprints by Wang Lin's (1188) and Sung Hsien's (1058) editions, which indicate that the above-mentioned Sung copy, reproduced in the Ming, was based on these two editions.

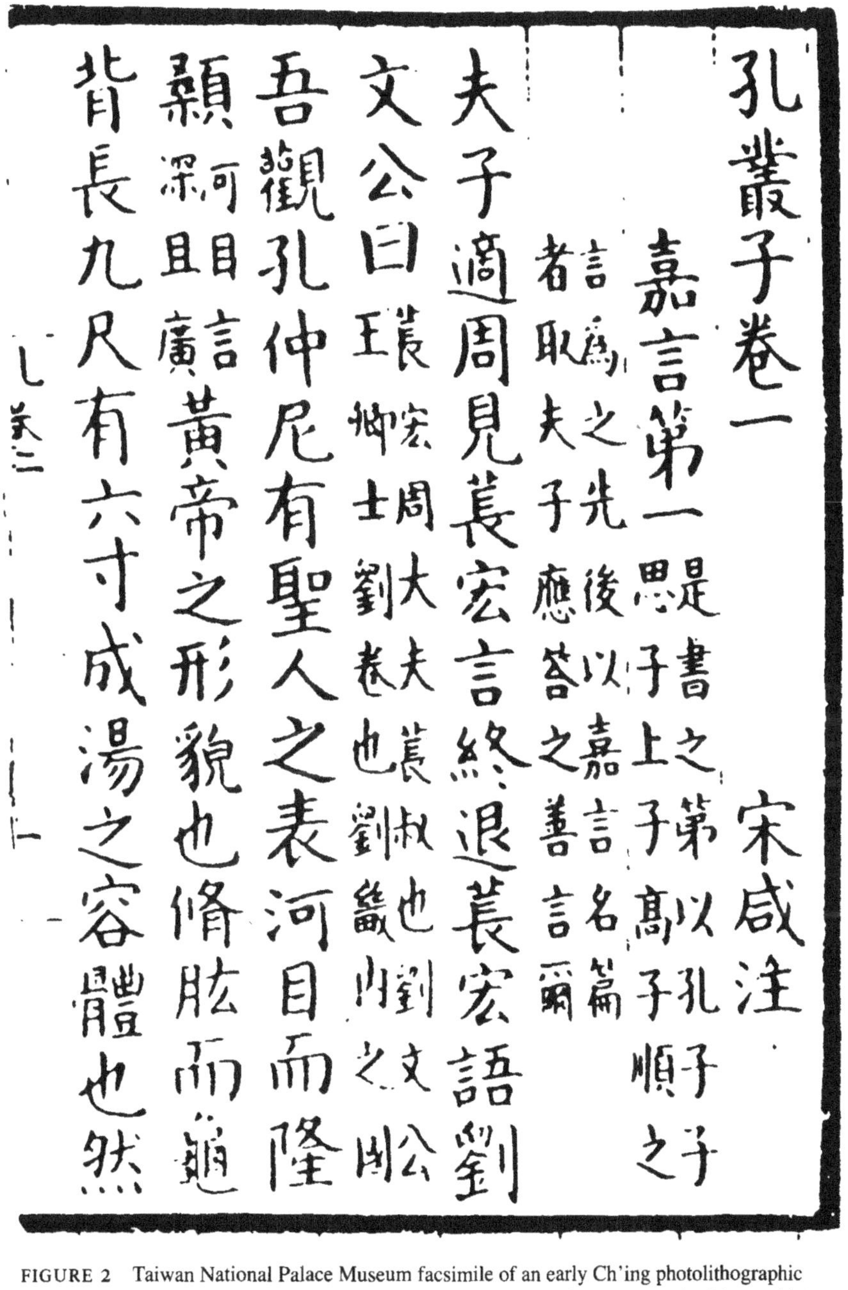

孔叢子卷一　　　宋咸注

嘉言第一　是書之第一思子上子高以孔子順之子以嘉言名篇

夫子應答之嘉言善言爾

者取為之先後之

文公曰環鄉士周大夫劉棼也萇叔也劉文公

夫子適周見萇宏言終退萇宏語劉

吾觀孔仲尼有聖人之表河目而隆

顙河且廣黃帝之形貌也脩肱而趙

背長九尺有六寸成湯之容體也然

FIGURE 2　Taiwan National Palace Museum facsimile of an early Ch'ing photolithographic manuscript of a seven-*chüan* Sung copy. The copy is Sung Hsien's commented edition, which includes the Sung Hsien preface and letter to the Secretariat-Chancellery.

孔叢子卷一

宋 宋咸 注

嘉言第一 是書之第以孔子子思子上子高子順之言為之先後以嘉言名篇者取夫子
應荅之善言爾

夫子適周見萇弘言終而退 覽三百六十六補 而字原脫依御萇弘語
劉文公曰 萇弘周大夫萇叔也劉文公劉卷也劉蟄內之國吾觀孔仲尼有
聖人之表其狀河目而隆頯 字原脫依御覽三百六十 河目言深且廣。其狀二
六十六補 黃帝之形貌也修肱而龜背長九尺有六寸
成湯之容體也然言稱先王躬履謙讓洽聞強記博物不

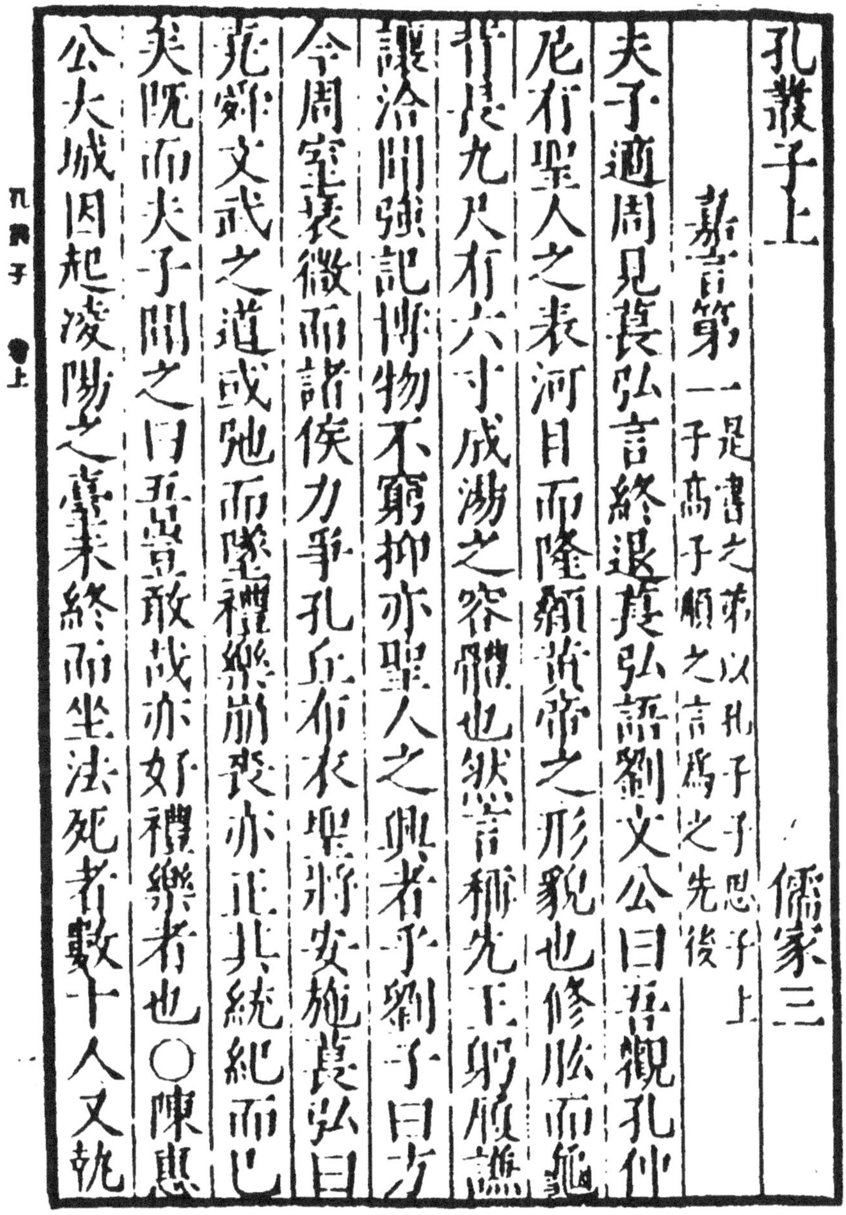

FIGURE 4 The *Tzu-hui* three-*chüan* edition of the *KTT*, 1577, which set the standards for successive three-*chüan* editions. Reprinted by various presses, among which is the above reprint by the Commercial Press (Taipei, 1971), Jen-jen wen-k'u library. The edition contains fragments of Sung Hsien's commentary and the Li Lien preface.

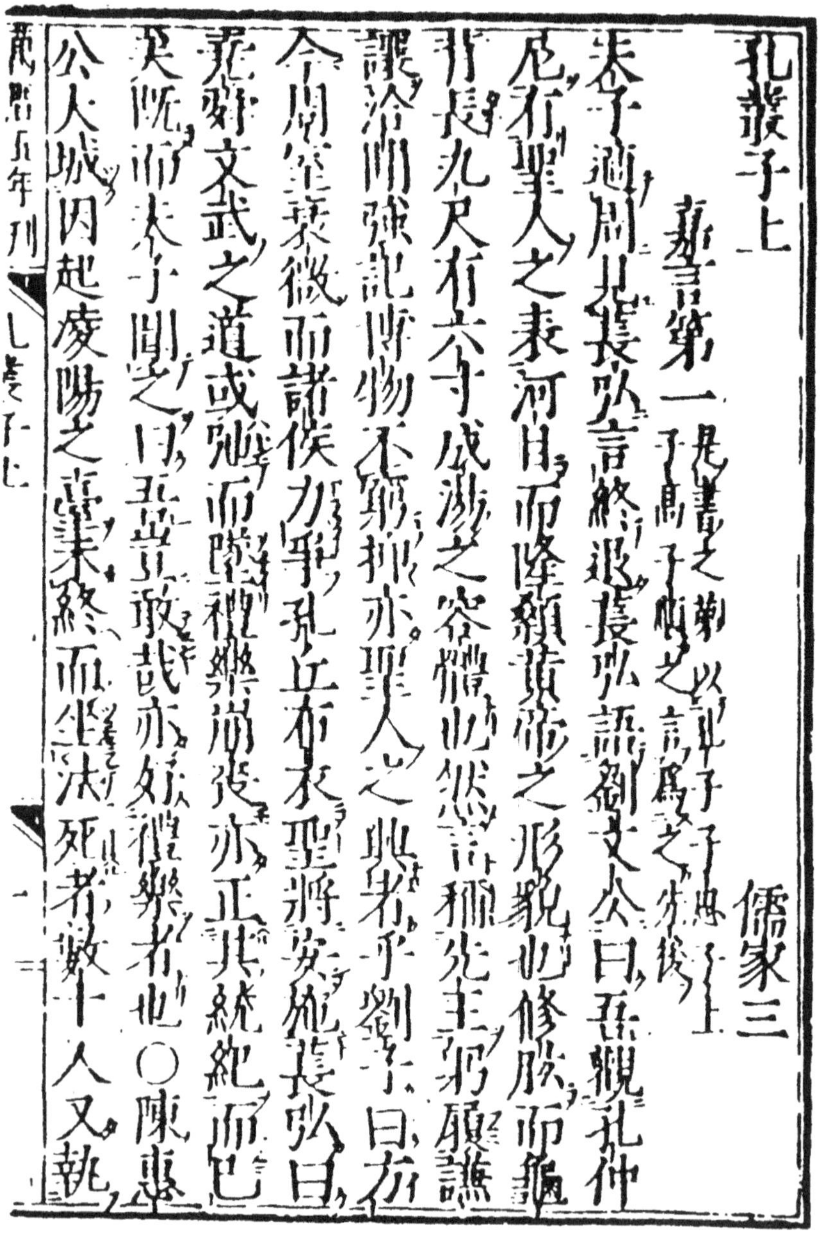

FIGURE 5 A 1789–1800 Japanese reproduction of the *Tzu-hui* edition. See figure 4. Edited by Nagasawa Kikuya, in vol. 1, pp. 481–527, of his *Wa-koku-bon shoshi taisei* (Tokyo, 1975). In addition to the *Tzu-hui* edition it also includes a table of contents and a traditional Japanese reading of the classical Chinese text of the *KTT*.

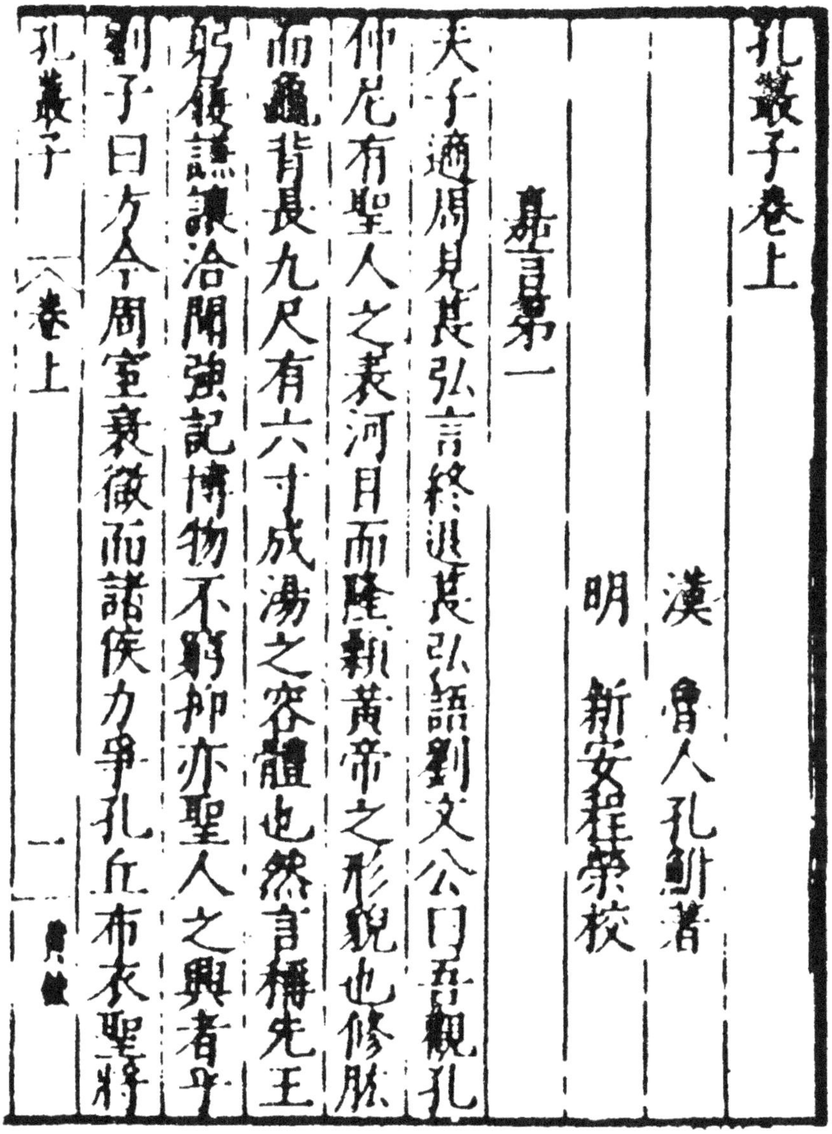

> 孔叢子卷上
>
> 嘉言第一
>
> 漢　魯人孔鮒著
> 明　新安程榮校
>
> 夫子適周見萇弘言終退萇弘語劉文公曰吾觀孔仲尼有聖人之表河目而隆顙黃帝之形貌也修肱而龜背長九尺有六寸成湯之容體也然言稱先王而後諫諍洽聞強記博物不窮抑亦聖人之興者乎劉子曰今周室衰微而諸侯力爭孔丘布衣聖將

FIGURE 6   The *Han-Wei ts'ung shu* (serial A) three-*chüan* edition of the *KTT*. Based on the *Tzu-hui* edition (see fig. 4). Compiled by Ch'eng Jung in 1592. Reprinted in two volumes by Hsin-hsing Press (Taipei, 1967). It includes the Li Lien preface, fragments of the Sung Hsien commentary, and a table of contents.

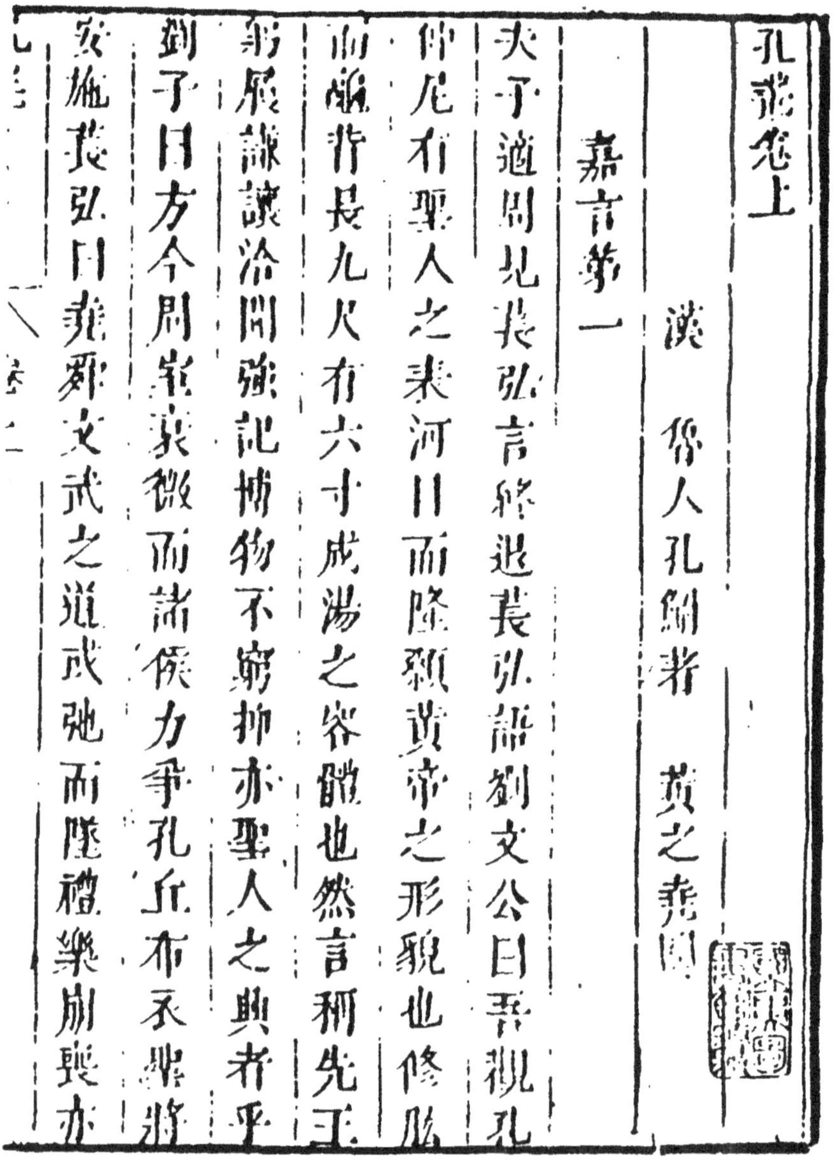

孔叢卷上

　　　　漢　俗人孔鮒著　黃之𡊄[?]

嘉言第一

夫子適周見萇弘言終退萇弘語劉文公曰吾視孔
仲尼有聖人之表河目而隆顙黃帝之形貌也修肱
而龜背長九尺有六寸成湯之容體也然言稱先王
躬履謙讓洽聞強記博物不窮抑亦聖人之興者乎
劉子曰方今周室衰微而諸侯力爭孔丘布衣將
安施焉弘曰堯舜文武之道或弛而隆禮樂崩喪亦

FIGURE 7 Taiwan Central Library exemplar of the *KTT* in the *Kuang Han-wei ts'ung-shu* (serial B), compiled by Ho Yün-chung, 1628. This is an abbreviated, two-*chüan* reproduction of serial A (see fig. 6). Chapters 11, 22, and 23 of the *KTT* are missing. Chapter 18 is appended at the end of the edition. A modified version of the Li Lien preface, which justifies some of the textual omissions of this edition, is included.

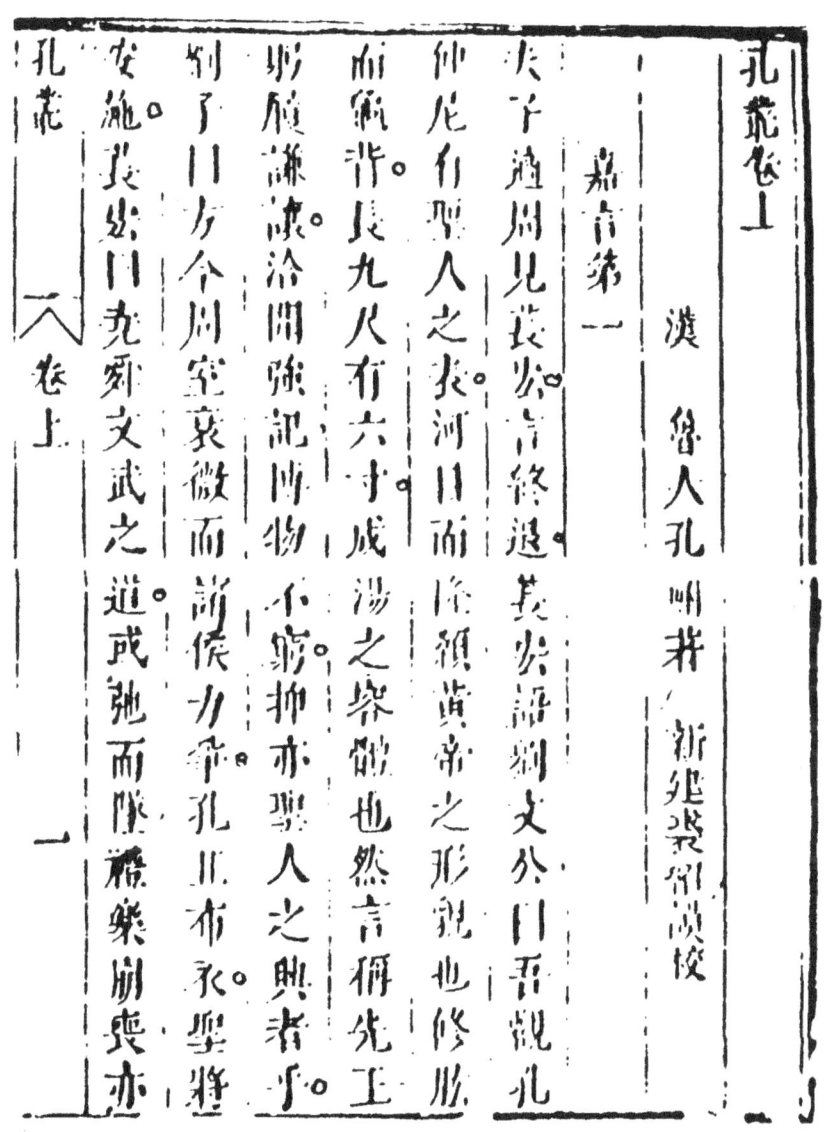

FIGURE 8 The *Tseng t'ing, Han-Wei ts'ung-shu* (serial C) edition of the *KTT*. Printed by Wang Mo in 1791. A punctuated duplication of the serial B edition (see fig. 7). Reprinted in vol. 3, pp. 1577–1621 by the Ta hua Press (Taipei, 1983).

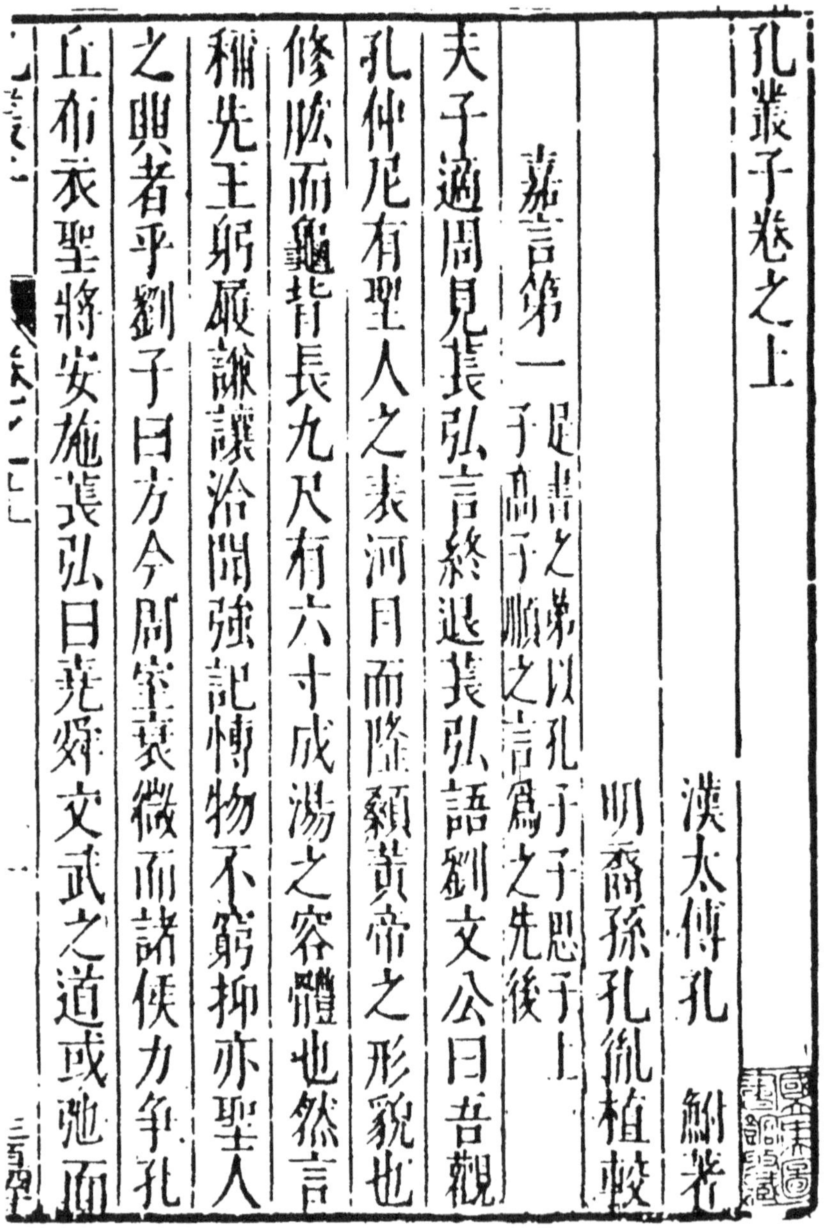

孔叢子卷之上

漢太傅孔　　鮒著
明裔孫孔胤植校

嘉言第一

夫子適周見萇弘言終退萇弘語劉文公曰吾觀孔仲尼有聖人之表河目而隆顙黃帝之形貌也修肱而龜背長九尺有六寸成湯之容體也然言稱先王躬履謙讓洽聞強記博物不窮抑亦聖人之興者乎劉子曰方今周室衰微而諸侯力爭孔丘布衣聖將安施襲弘曰堯舜文武之道或弛而

子思在魯嘗同業次書之弟以孔子之言為之先後子思順之言

FIGURE 9 Taiwan Central Library exemplar of K'ung Yin-chih's edition of the *KTT*, 1633. This is a three-*chüan* edition containing a table of contents, fragments of the Sung Hsien commentary, the Li Lien preface, and a postcript written by K'ung Shang-ta. The division of this edition into three *chüan* and the inclusion of the Li Lien preface indicate that K'ung Yin-chih made use of the *Tzu-hui* edition (see fig. 4).

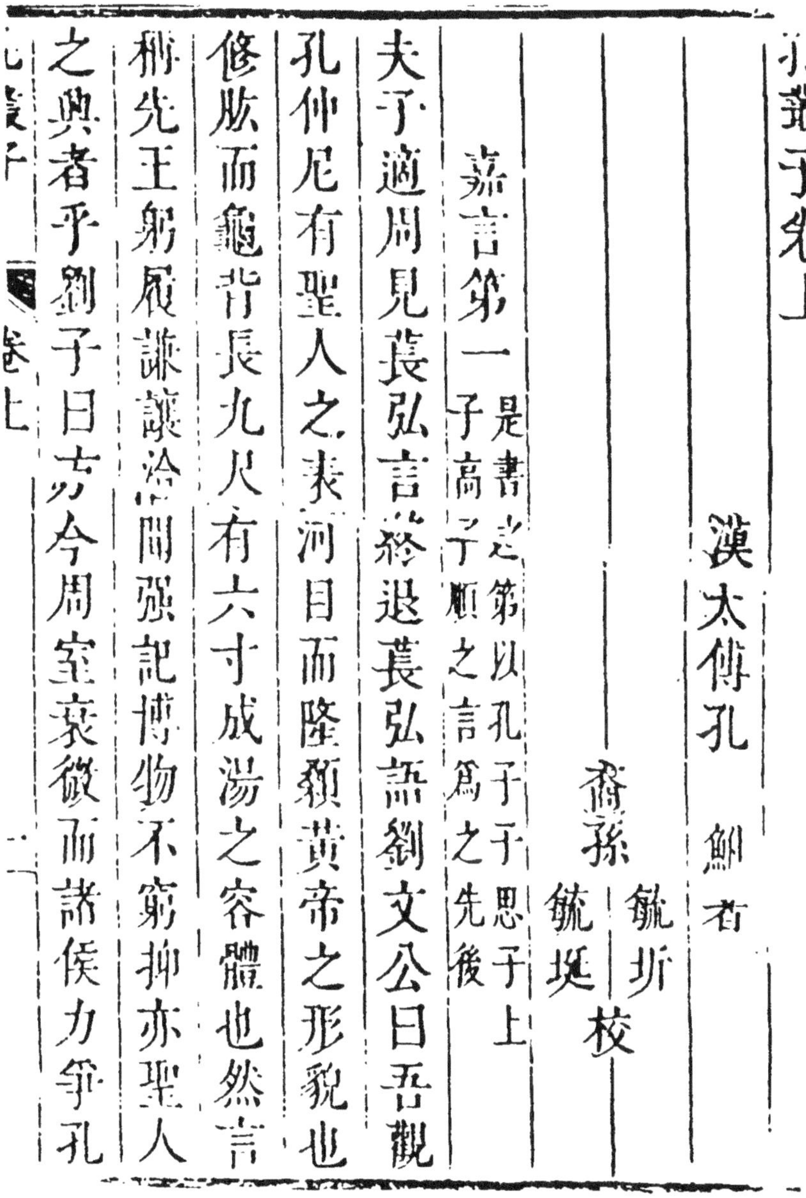

孔叢子卷上

漢太傅孔　鮒　著

裔孫　毓圻

毓埏　校

嘉言第一

是書之第以孔子于思子上子高子順之言為之先後

夫子適周見萇弘言終退萇弘語劉文公曰吾觀

孔仲尼有聖人之表河目而隆顙黃帝之形貌也

修肱而龜背長九尺有六寸成湯之容體也然言

稱先王躬履謙讓洽聞強記博物不窮抑亦聖人

之興者乎劉子曰方今周室衰微而諸侯力爭孔

FIGURE 10 Taiwan National Palace Museum exemplar of K'ung Yü-ch'i and K'ung Yü-yen's edition of the *KTT*, 1697. This is a three-*chüan* edition based on the K'ung Yin-chih edition (see fig. 9).

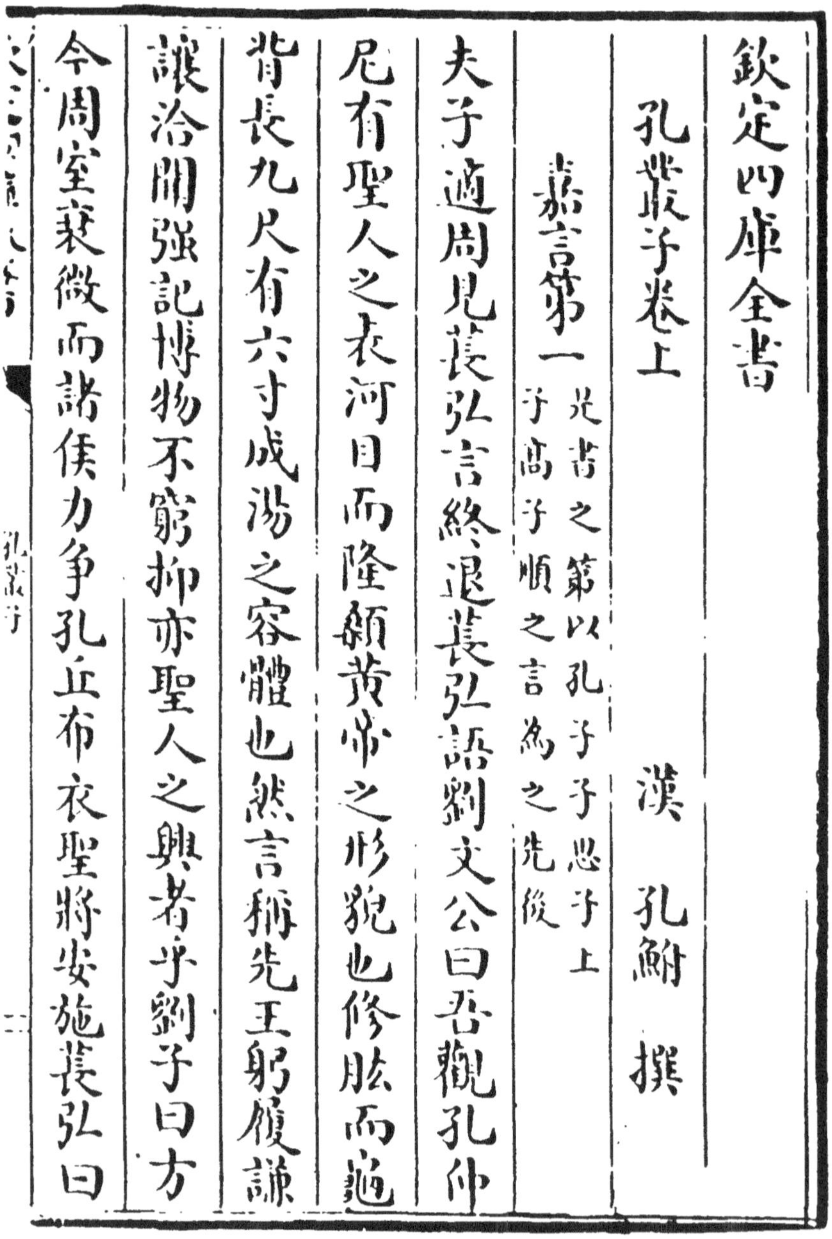

欽定四庫全書

孔叢子卷上

　　　　　　　　　　漢　孔鮒　撰

嘉言第一 足書之第以孔子子思子上
　　　　 子高子順之言為之先後

夫子適周見萇弘言終退萇弘語劉文公曰吾觀孔仲
尼有聖人之表河目而隆顙黄帝之形貌也修肱而龜
背長九尺有六寸成湯之容體也然言稱先王躬履謙
讓洽聞強記博物不窮抑亦聖人之興者乎劉子曰方
今周室衰微而諸侯力爭孔丘布衣聖將安施萇弘曰

FIGURE 11 The *Ssu-k'u ch'üan-shu* edition of 1777. Reproduced in vol. 695, pp. 307–368, in the multiple-volume reproduction of the *Ssu-k'u ch'üan-shu* by the Commercial Press (Taipei, 1985). This is a three-*chüan* edition containing table of contents, fragments of the Sung Hsien commentary, and the synopsis of the *KTT*, which appear in the *Ssu-k'u ch'üan-shu* edition.

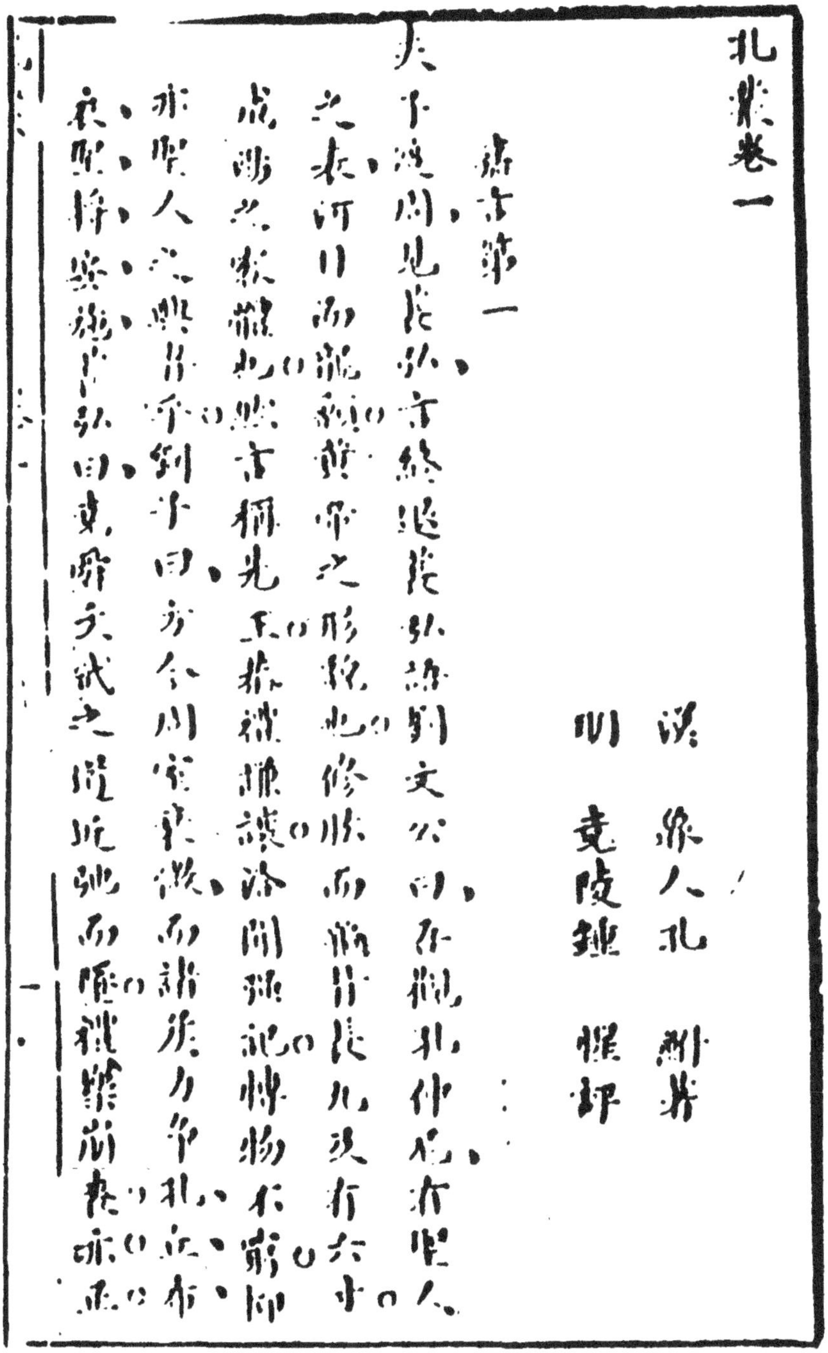

FIGURE 12 Taiwan National Palace Museum exemplar of a four-*chüan* selection of various sections of the *KTT* in the *Mi-shu chiu-chung*, 1612. Edited by Chung Hsing (d. 1625).

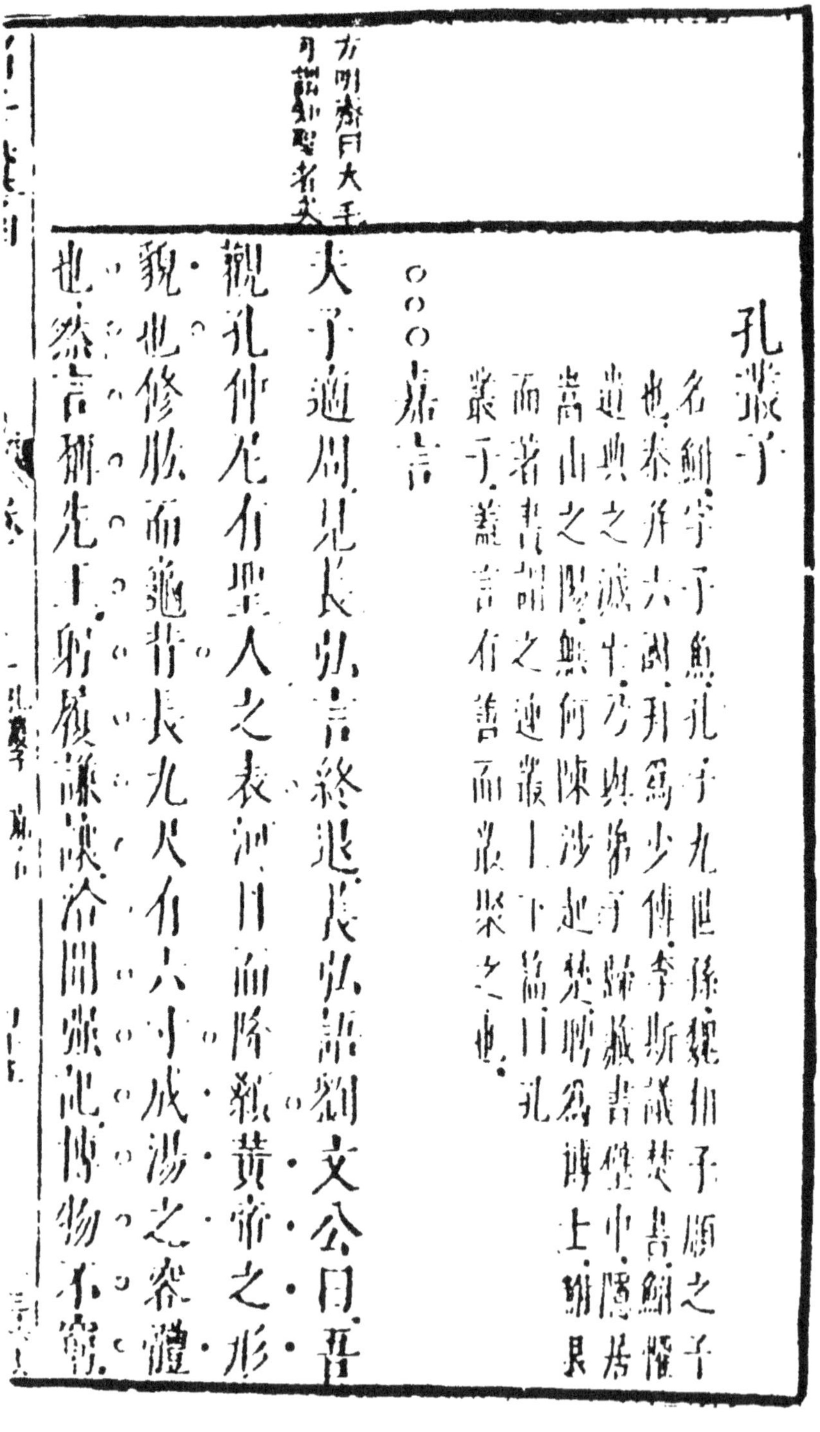

孔叢子

名鮒字子魚孔子九世孫魏相子順之子
也秦并六國幷爲少傳李斯議焚書鮒懷
道典之滅生乎抱負歸藏書壁中隱居
嵩山之陽無何陳涉起楚聘爲博士朝見
而著書謂之連叢上下篇曰孔
叢子叢言有善而叢聚之也

○○○嘉言

子子適周見長弘言終退長弘語劉文公曰吾
觀孔仲尼有聖人之表河目而隆顙黃帝之形
貌也修肱而龜背長九尺有六寸成湯之容體
也然言稱先王躬履謙讓治聞強記博物不窮

FIGURE 13 A National Taiwan University copy of a selection of nine chapters of the *KTT* in Kuei Yu-kuang and Wen Chen-meng's anthology, *Chu-tzu hui-han*, 1626.

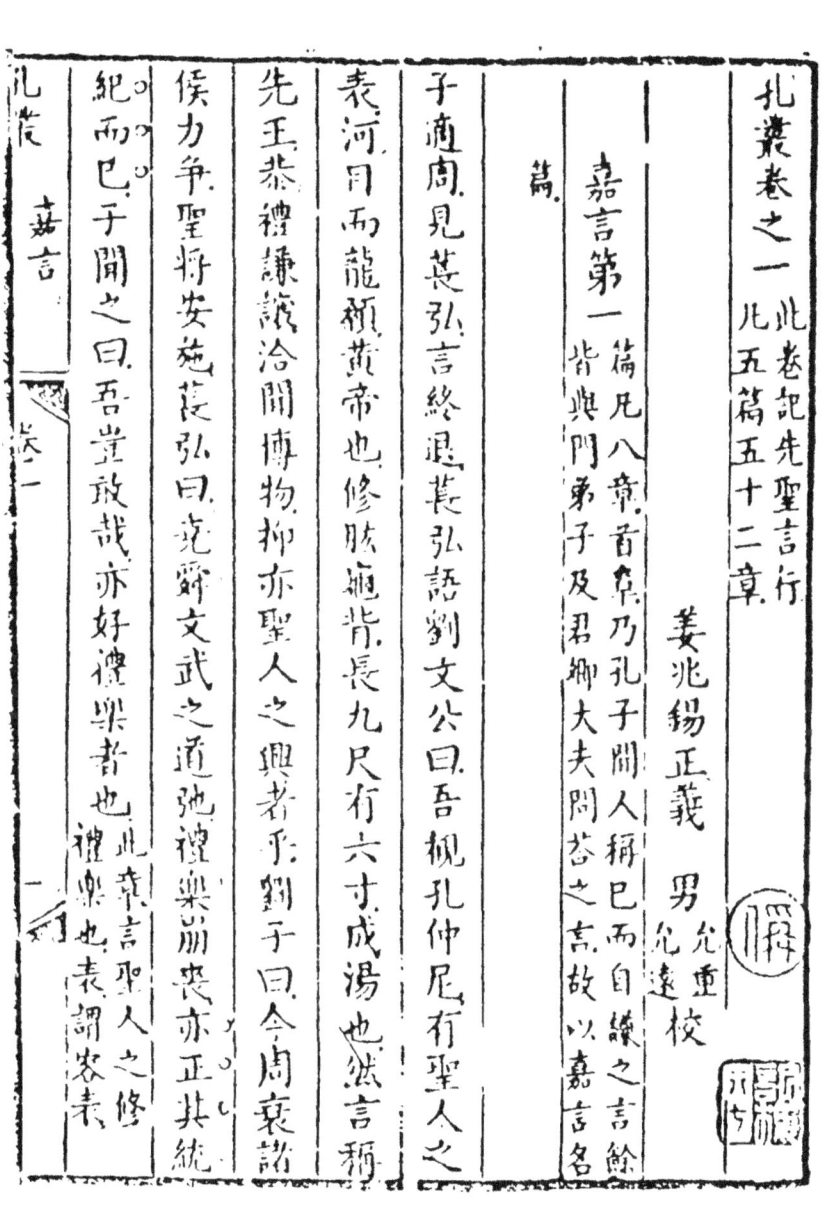

FIGURE 14 Kyoto University library exemplar of the Chiang Chao-hsi five-*chüan* commented redaction of the *KTT*, 1720.

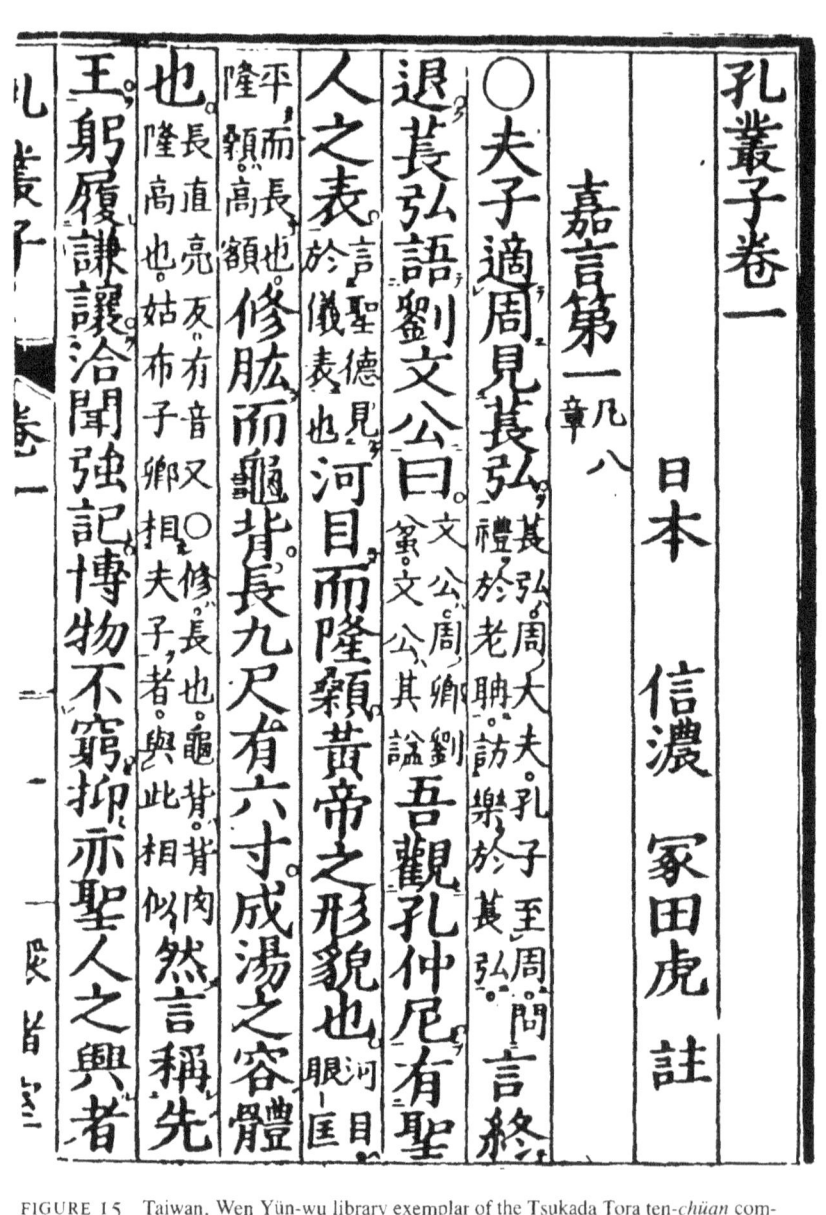

FIGURE 15 Taiwan, Wen Yün-wu library exemplar of the Tsukada Tora ten-*chüan* commented edition of the *KTT*, 1795.

孔叢子卷第一

嘉言第一

夫子適周見萇弘言終萇弘語劉文公曰吾觀孔仲尼有聖人之表河目而隆顙黃帝之形貌也脩肱而龜背長九尺有六寸成湯之容體也然言稱先王躬履謙讓洽聞強記博物不窮抑亦聖人之興者乎劉子曰方今周室衰微而諸侯力爭孔丘布衣聖將安施其弘曰堯舜文武之道或弛而墜禮樂崩喪其亦正其統紀而已矣既而夫子聞之曰吾豈敢哉亦好禮樂者也

陳惠公大城因起凌陽之臺未終而坐法死者數十人又執三監吏將殺之夫子適陳聞之見陳侯與俱登臺而觀焉夫子曰美哉斯臺自古聖王之為城臺未有不戮一人而能致功若此者也陳侯默而退遽赦所執吏既而見夫子問曰昔周作靈臺亦戮人乎答曰文王之興附者六州六州之衆各以子道來故區區之臺未及期日而

成何戮之有夫　[中華書局]

SECTION

3

THE AUTHENTICITY, DATE, AND AUTHORSHIP OF THE *KTT*

The various findings that emerge from this study of the *KTT* make it possible to embark upon a final discussion of the problem of its authenticity, dating, and authorship.

Let me first set the problem: The *KTT* pretends to be the K'ung family's anthology of lore accumulated over 650 years by prominent members of the family. In other words, the text creates the impression that it genuinely records the philosophical activities of various members of the K'ung family, and that a good deal of its content is the authentic writings of some of the K'ung family members. Is the impression created by the *KTT* true? To put the problem more bluntly, is the *KTT* an authentic product of the K'ung family or just a late fabrication?

Before answers to the problem are suggested, the conclusions derived from the survey of the *KTT* critical literature should be considered. This study has disclosed that the *KTT* ought to be regarded as a compilation that could not possibly have been written by either K'ung Fu, K'ung Tsang, or any other protagonist of the text.

This conclusion helps little in the effort to determine the authenticity of the *KTT*. It is useful only for the purpose of refuting the verdicts of those Chinese scholars who attributed the composition of the whole *KTT* to one of its protagonists. The *KTT* does not pretend to be definitively edited by any of its protagonists. As the historical survey shows, the bibliographical tradition that attributes the writing or compilation of the *KTT* to one of its protagonists probably arose as late as the sixth century A.D. and therefore is irrelevant to the present discussion.

To recapitulate, this study has established that there was no external reference to the *KTT* prior to ca. A.D. 250. In theory, this finding can be used as an argument that the *KTT* was not extant before ca. A.D. 250. It must be admitted, however, that this argument has force only if one accepts the late bibliographical tradition that ascribed the writing of the *KTT* to K'ung Fu. For how could the *KTT* be mentioned by philosophers such as Tung Chung-shu (ca. 179–ca. 104 B.C.), or be listed in bibliographies such as Pan Ku's (A.D. 32–92) *Han-shu I-wen-chih*, if its final line specifies the year A.D. 124, the year of the death of its last protagonist? Nevertheless, the implication of two facts must not be overlooked: First, during the period between A.D. 124 and ca. A.D. 250 the *KTT* was not referred to by any of the Confucian philosophers of the period. Second, commentators such as Kao Yu (ca. A.D. 198) and Chao Ch'i (d. A.D. 201) were not aware of the supposed existence of the *KTT*. As the study of the *KTT* in history showed, Kao Yu's commentary to the *Lü-shih ch'un-ch'iu* referred to Tzu-kao as a sophist rather than a K'ung family member, while Chao Ch'i's commentary to the *Mencius*, in contradiction to the *KTT*, stated with assurance that there was no tradition ascribing an adult name to Mencius.

These two facts add weight to the argument that the *KTT* was probably not extant prior to ca. A.D. 250, while the possible counterargument that the *KTT* was not circulated outside the K'ung family until ca. 250 appears groundless.

The survey mentioned the opinion of scholars such as Chu Hsi and Hung Mai, according to whom the style of the *KTT* indicated that it was written in the period between the Late Han and the Wei-Chin. Karlgren, however, labeled such an argument "arbitrary."[1] At any rate, in the case of the *KTT* anyone who argues for its authenticity can claim that since the work was formed over a period of 650 years, it could not escape later editorial, redactional, and stylistic readjustments. This counterargument can also be used for the occurrences of late grammatical features in the *KTT*, which imply a later dating for its composition.[2] In the case of the *KTT*, however, such grammatical features say very little about the authenticity of the text. The only certain deduction is that some of the *KTT*'s early material was linguistically altered by the final editor of the work in the Late Han, in all likelihood for the sake of his contemporary readers. Nevertheless, in spite of this counterargument, the fact remains that the *KTT* contains late grammatical and stylistic features.

The discussion indicated that the *KTT* contains features that belong exclusively to the third century A.D. This argument is particularly persuasive. It maintains that several parts of the *KTT*, namely, those that contain such late features, are spurious. Among these features are the *KTT*'s reference to Mencius's adult name. It is improbable that Mencius had an adult name known only to the K'ung family members, who concealed it during many hundreds of years. The *KTT*'s systematic correction of Kung-sun Lung's thesis, "A white horse is not a horse," to "A white horse is not a white horse" was a misunderstanding of the sophist's case. This misunderstanding was unprecedented in the time of the historical Tzu-kao (312–352 B.C.) but very common in the third century A.D. Finally, the *KTT*'s reference (A, 11a4) to the *Shu-*

ching's "forged" and late-incorporated chapters, "The Counsels of the Great Yü" and "I and Chi,"³ is also an instance of an exclusive feature of the third century A.D. anachronistically recited by the Confucius of the *KTT*.

The study made note of the many anachronisms embedded in the *KTT*. It can therefore be stated with certainty that all parts of the *KTT* in which anachronisms appear are spurious. For how can it be explained that the Tzu-ssu of the *KTT* participated in philosophical debates with both Confucius and Mencius when we know that Mencius was born a hundred years after Confucius's death? If one nevertheless persists in arguing that all these parts are authentic, it will be necessary to discard all other historical and biographical sources of the K'ung family and to use the *KTT* as the only source.

To recapitulate the problem of the authenticity of the *KTT*, is it true that, in accordance with the impression it creates, the *KTT* is the genuine anthology of lore accumulated during 650 years by prominent members of the K'ung family?

In view of the previous discussion, the answer is decisive: the *KTT* cannot possibly be regarded as authentic in the sense just described. It is a late product of the first half of the third century A.D., most probably compiled by someone who was not a member of the K'ung family.

Is it therefore to be concluded that the *KTT* was compiled with the explicit intention to deceive? Two questions will help to clarify the ultimate answer to this crucial problem: First, is "truth" a value in the *KTT*? And second, does the *KTT* contain any view of itself?

Li^a and $shih^a$ are the representative terms for "truth" in the *KTT*. In the text they usually denote either "truth in principle" or "the actual state of things." In the most general sense of the word, truth is a central value that provides the framework for the evaluation of the various theories, accounts, and practices that appear throughout the *KTT*. The *KTT*, as a rule, rejects a priori all arguments that bear the sophists' imprint, because the profusion of their persuasive words are untrue "in principle." Take the case of A, 76a5–76b6 (12.2 in the translation), where it is clearly stated that Kung-sun Lung presented the thesis of "Mr. Tsang having three ears" in a perfected eloquent style. This "perfected eloquent argument" is not given any consideration but is immediately discarded on the grounds that it might be true in theory, but definitely not in reality.

It can also be stated with assurance that the author of the *KTT* was aware of the power of aphorisms plausible though falsely attributed to authoritative sources. In A, 79a6–80a6 (translation, 13.3 and 13.4), there are two cases in which one of the *KTT*'s protagonists, Tzu-kao, has to deal with such fabricated words turned against his forefather Confucius. In the first case, Prince P'ing-yüan is trying to force Tzu-kao to drink wine by quoting old proverbs according to which Confucius, as well as other famous sages, was a drinker. In the second case, Prince P'ing-yüan refers to two traditions that imply that Confu-

Authenticity, Date, and Authorship 59

cius was licentious. Tzu-kao's response in both cases is belligerently negative. He states that both the quoted proverbs and the two referred traditions were "fakes" created by fabricators who wanted to justify their own perversions. This line of argument reaches its culmination in chapter 18, "Ch'i Mo" (B, 24a–30b), where K'ung Fu shows that the *Mo Tzu* contains numerous anachronisms, which makes its criticism of Confucius sheer nonsense.

In light of this uncompromising adherence to "truth," two passages can certainly be considered striking modifications of the author's idea of "truth." In A, 50a1 (translation, 9.4), Tzu-ssu confronts the following allegation: Duke Mu quotes someone to the effect that Confucius's words recorded in Tzu-ssu's book are not authentic, and that they are actually Tzu-ssu's own words. Tzu-ssu's response to the allegation is that he would justify the attribution of words to Confucius even though Confucius might have never said them, providing that the book is on the whole flawless and genuinely conveys his grandfather's line of thought.

In the second passage, B, 19b4–20, a somewhat similar problem is presented to Tzu-shun: Someone wrote a book of discussions and gave it the canonical title *Ch'un-ch'iu*. Tzu-shun's response to this seemingly plagiaristic attitude toward the canon's title is striking. According to him, the sages do not have a monopoly on their books' titles, nor can they be considered the only ones able to produce everlasting masterpieces.

The idea in both cases is obvious: truth or authenticity are matters of intrinsic, not extrinsic evaluation. It is the philosophical core of a book that should be subjected to the various categories connected with "truth," not the book's framework or setting. The implication of this attitude is that an author is free to draw from various sources while setting the framework of his book. It further implies that a certain book may contain some nonfactual details as long as the ideas embodied in it are truthful in principle.

In sum, "truth" is a high value in the *KTT*. It must be noted, however, that "truth" was interpreted in the *KTT* as "truth in principle" or the "actual state of things." This approach to "truth" paved the way for the introduction of an argument by which certain admittedly spurious texts could be reevaluated as "truthful."

By the same token, the attitude of the *KTT* toward manipulative fabrications was decisively negative. The *KTT* held that it was morally right to borrow from other sources, as long as it was for the sake of manifesting "truthful" ideas. And finally, the *KTT* stated that it was in the power of contemporary scholars to produce a masterpiece of canonical value.

The *KTT*'s References to Itself

Let us now turn to the passage in A, 50a1, where Duke Mu refers to a book written by Tzu-ssu as a flawless book containing words spuriously attributed to Confucius. It is true that the book referred to might have been the *Chung-yung*; but then why did Duke Mu not specify this very title, as had been done previously in the *KTT* at the end of the seventh chapter (A, 45b5–6; translation, 7.10), where the text reports that Tzu-ssu wrote a book entitled *Chung-yung* in forty-nine chapters? It seems to me that there is another plausible explanation, according to which the book referred to by Duke Mu was none other than chapters 1–4 of the *KTT* itself.

This hypothesis can be supported as follows: Throughout the whole text there are several cases in which the *KTT* refers to itself. In the eighteenth chapter, B, 29b1, a positive assessment is made by a certain Ts'ao Ming of the whole of K'ung Fu's critique of Mo Tzu expressed in the foregoing pages of the chapter. In B, 45b6–46a–1, the anonymous compiler of the "Lien-ts'ung-tzu" refers to the successive pages of the text and justifies the inclusion of the "righteous" rhyme prose and letters of K'ung Tsang in them. In B, 62b5, there is an explicit reference to the "Lien-ts'ung" as an authoritative source that truthfully records the transmission of the heritage of the K'ung family. Finally there is the *Pei-t'ang shu-ch'ao*'s citation (97–2a) of a no longer extant paragraph of the *KTT*, which refers to a corpus of the forefathers' writings for centuries in the possession of the family.

In view of these self-references in the *KTT*, and in view of the fact that the *Chung-yung* was not specified by the *KTT* as the book referred to by Duke Mu, it is plausible that the unidentified book of Tzu-ssu was none other than that part of the *KTT* in which Confucius's words were recorded, namely, chapters 1–4.

I stress this point because it seems to me that, throughout the whole text, the author of the *KTT* was unconsciously trying to convey to his future readers that, even though his *KTT* might not be authentic in the strict sense of the word, the whole fabric of his anthology of the K'ung family holds true because it conforms to the above-mentioned values of creativity and standards of truth. In other words, the *KTT*'s author's view of his own work was that it was authentic in the sense that its degree of verisimilitude derived from its truthful representation of the philosophical heritage of the K'ung family. Under these circumstances, although the *KTT* remains inauthentic, it cannot be bluntly labeled a forgery because this derogatory term denotes an explicit intention to deceive. Can John DeFrancis's recently published "Singlish Affair" be considered a forgery or, as he himself calls it, "a figment of the imagination," a literary vehicle for exposing the "truth" about the myth of the universality of the Chinese written language?[4] The author of the *KTT* definitely wants to expose the "truth" about a myth such as the apocryphal image of Confucius. In this sense he can no longer be considered a fabricator attempting to manipulate or deceive, and his book cannot be neatly rubricated into one of Chang Hsin-ch'eng's nine categories of forgeries.[5] On the contrary, by compiling the anthology he became equal in his own eyes to the sage, a K'ung family member who truthfully recreated and transmitted the heritage of his adopted family. As for the heritage itself, it had to be selected, revised, and reedited into the framework of the anthology from the great variety of sources of relevant material that existed in the first half of the third century A.D. Among many other works the following can be regarded as the treasury of Confucian lore from which the *KTT*'s author took various passages in his anthology: the *Shih-chi*, *Han-shu*, *Lun-yü*, *Mencius*, *Hsün Tzu*, *Li-chi*, *Ta-tai li-chi*, *Tso-chuan*, *Lü-shih ch'un-ch'iu*, *Kuo yü*, *Chan-kuo ts'e*, *Yen-tzu ch'un-ch'iu*, *Shuo-yüan*, *Hsin-hsü*, *Han-shih wai-chuan*, and *Shang-shu ta-chuan*.

This conclusion can be illustrated with the case of the parallelism between the *Shang-shu ta-chuan* and the *KTT*. As I specify in my translation of chapter 4 of the *KTT* ("On Punishment"), many passages of the two works use the very same wording concerning Confucius's negative view of punishment in education. Now, since the *Shang-shu ta-chuan* existed before the *KTT*,[6] and since no earlier extant text uses the very same wording as the *KTT* on Confucius's view on the subject, it is very plausible that the author of the *KTT* simply duplicated whatever he found relevant in the *Shang-shu ta-chuan* for the Confucius of his anthology. However, he did so within the following constraints: Convinced that the idea of the supremacy of the rites over punishment was as an authentic idea of Confucius, he located in the *Shang-shu ta-chuan* what he regarded as authentically elaborated statements of Confucius on the subject that matched his conviction. He then reproduced all these statements in the fourth chapter of his anthology "On Punishment," shaping them to fit the general framework of the anthology. Thus, the *KTT*'s author could in self-defense vary Confucius's aphorism, "I transmit faithfully and do not innovate,"[7] with "I transmit faithfully and innovate only the context."

The Authorship of the *KTT*

Having concluded that the *KTT* is a late product of the first half of the third century A.D., one finally comes to the question of its authorship. In studying the *KTT* in history, I have already made note of the most significant opinions expressed by Chinese scholars from the beginning of the Ch'ing until the present. These discussions have covered a considerable range of comparative and textual studies that explored striking similarities between the *KTT* and various works and commentaries associated with Wang Su. As a result of these studies, the name of Wang Su became the sinologist's first choice whenever the problem of the authorship of the *KTT* as a fabrication was discussed.

Wang Su deserves to be considered the primary candidate for authorship of the *KTT*. First, the date of the composition of the *KTT*, the first half of the third century, is congruent with Wang Su's dates (A.D. 195–256). Second, the philosophical and exegetical character of the *KTT* are congruent with Wang Su's intellectual biography. And third, there are numerous and striking textual similarities between the works of Wang Su and the *KTT*.

Discussions of the authorship of the *KTT*, including the present one, have not uncovered new data that might lead to another figure, outside the circle of Wang Su, to whom the composition of the *KTT* might be attributed. The name of Wang Su has long been associated with the composition of several other works, such as the *K'ung-tzu chia-yü*,[8] the forged chapters of the *Ku-wen Shang-shu*,[9] and the pseudo-K'ung An-kuo's *Commentary and Preface* to the *Shang-shu*.[10]

It must nevertheless be stated that the authorship of the *KTT* will not be categorically settled as long as all the evidence continues to be merely suggestive. No matter how many more textual similarities between Wang Su's works and the *KTT* can be pointed out, even if we use the kind of software now being produced to determine authorship by means of features of style,[11] we will never be able to deduce definitive authorship from them. Suggestive evidence can merely expose the Wang Su-ian nature of the *KTT* and can therefore only solidify the hypothesis that he was most likely the author of the *KTT*.

The above assumptions hold true for other cases of problematical authorship. Take, for instance, the case of the symphony discovered in early 1982 at Odense in Denmark. The symphony was ascribed to the young Mozart and was labeled K 16a. Although the symphony has typical early Mozartian characteristics, the question remains whether the symphony was a genuine product of the eight-year-old Mozart or whether it was written by another individual of the Mozart circle, such as his father Leopold.[12]

The *KTT*, too, is the product of a definite characteristic, namely, Wang Su-ian. Nevertheless, it could have been also written by another individual of Wang Su's circle, such as his daughter. She was a gifted textual scholar who had mastered the *Analects* and was considered exceptional by Wang Su's father, Wang Lang.[13] Can one categorically exclude the possibility that she could have been the one who wrote the *KTT* as a tribute to her father's scholarship?

I would therefore suggest that unless some external, direct evidence turns up, the ascription of the authorship of the *KTT* to Wang Su will remain a matter of conjecture, and one must always be prepared to be proved wrong when suggesting such a probability.

I shall therefore attempt in the following discussion only to show that the *KTT* is certainly, like the *K'ung-tzu chia-yü*, a work of Wang Su-ian nature, thus strengthening the assumption that the *KTT* was composed by Wang Su.

Wang Su's scholarly activity has been the subject of several important studies conducted by Western and Chinese scholars such as Kramers, Goodman, Li Chen-hsing, Chin Po-hsien, and Hsü Ch'un-hsiung.[14] These studies have resulted in authoritative accounts of Wang Su's life, exegetical works, intellectual pursuits, and political activities. A summary of all these studies should be undertaken; in this instance, I will confine my discussion to the distinctively Wang Su-ian features and show how they are echoed, in my opinion, in the *KTT*.

Wang Su was an "Old Text" scholar.[15] The *KTT* is, no doubt, a paradigm of an Old Text work. K'ung An-kuo, a celebrated figure in the Old Text tradition, is reverently mentioned in the twenty-second chapter of the *KTT*. The chapter also refers to such typical Old Text works as the *Ku-wen shang-shu* and *Tso-chuan* as prominent classical texts. The references to Old Text scholars and works incorporate explicit statements degrading the "Vulgar New Text" scholars (e.g., B, 45b2–5; B, 49b7–51a5). Finally, the overall philosophical tone of the *KTT* is purely rational, unlike the supernatural orientation of the "New Text."[16] This rational tone is also apparent in the image of Confucius portrayed throughout the first five chapters of the *KTT*. He is, like the Confucius of the *K'ung-tzu chia-yü*,[17] a typically Old Text Confucius, that is, a human being, a sage, but certainly not the divine personage or semigod as is the Confucius of the Apocrypha.

Wang Su revolted against the *chang-chü* (explanations by paragraphs and sentences) method of explaining the classics.[18] The *chang-chü* was a widespread method of textual criticism in the Former Han. This was a lengthy and tedious method of classical learning, focusing on each individual character or phrase, with no reference to the general meaning of the text. Gradually it became the symbol of anachronistic traditionalism.[19] It should be noted that the *KTT* (B, 64a8–65b6) specifically refers to the *chang-chü* as a useless method of studying the classics, a method that is totally opposed to that advocated by the members of the K'ung family.

Wang Su was influenced by such scholars as Ma Jung (A.D. 79–166) and by some Ching-chou Taoist trends.[20] Therefore, the *KTT*'s favorable attitude toward Lao Tzu,[21] in contrast to its generally hostile attitude toward non-Confucian philosophers, is no longer surprising. The *K'ung-tzu chia-yü* has a similar attitude, which is shared by Old Text scholars such as Ma Jung, who was Wang Su's model for classical learning.[22]

According to Wang Su's biography, he presented memorials to the throne denouncing the administrative expenditures and the extensive use of capital punishment,[23] and at least one-third of the *KTT* is concerned with the subject of government and politics. The *KTT* denounces expenditures and corrupt officials.[24] Its enthusiastic arguments against the use of penalties constitute the bulk of its fourth chapter, and its objection to capital punishment (A, 28a8–28b1) can be considered a paraphrase of Wang Su's own words which appear in one of his memorials to the throne.[25]

Wang Su criticized and belittled the school of Cheng Hsüan (A.D. 127–

200), the preeminent Han exegete.[26] The main arguments of this famous controversy were recorded in the *Sheng-cheng-lun*.[27]

It can be stated with assurance that whenever an exegetical problem is presented in the *KTT* it is followed, as in the *K'ung-tzu chia-yü*, by a distinctive Wang Su-ian interpretation, which is always contrary to Cheng Hsüan's view. The following are two unique examples of affinities between the *KTT* and quotations ascribed to Wang Su by the *Sheng-cheng-lun*, in connection with that debate.

1. Cheng Hsüan held that the "Six Honored Ones" to whom the "Pure Sacrifice" was offered[28] were six Celestial Spirits.[29] Wang Su, in contrast, advocated that the "Six Honored Ones" were the four seasons, cold and heat, sun and moon, stars, floods and droughts.[30] The *KTT*, A, 13a6 (translation, 2.8), is identical to Wang Su's theory.

2. Cheng Hsüan considered both *tsu* and *tsung* as one sacrifice.[31] Wang Su, however, argued that *tsu* and *tsung* designated two kinds of sacrifice or halls for storing the tablets of those meritorious and virtuous ancestors who no longer had temples of their own.[32] The *KTT*, A, 14a2–7, shares Wang Su's opinion, using almost the very same wording that is recorded in the *Sheng-cheng-lun*.

Wang Su was preoccupied with the subject of rites, especially the "light" and the "heavy" in mourning rites.[33] On this specific subject he wrote a book entitled *The Essential Points Concerning Mourning Rites*.[34]

The *KTT* abounds with discussions concerning various aspects of the rites, including the "light" and the "heavy" in mourning rites. The rites advocated by the *KTT* are identical with those expressed by Wang Su in his various commentaries. For example, the T'ang encyclopedia *T'ung-tien* has a section entitled "On the Mourning Dress of the Reburying Ceremony." The section consists of a collection of authoritative references on this subject. One of these references is an excerpt by Wang Su recounting Tzu-ssu's answer to the question of Minister of Education Wen Tzu concerning the reburial of the minister's uncle in another grave.[35] The *KTT* is the only other text, to the best of my knowledge, in which the dialogue between the minister and Tzu-ssu occurs (A, 55b2–4; translation, 10.7), using the identical wording as quoted in the *T'ung-tien*.

The above-mentioned affinities are only a few examples among many others. In studying the *KTT* in history I have noted scholars like Tsang Lin (1650–1713) and Ting Yen (1794–1875) who, arguing for Wang Su's authorship of the *KTT*, pointed out the similarities between his comments to the *Shang-shu*[36] and the second chapter of the *KTT*, "Discussing the *Book of Documents*," which focuses on various sections of the *Shang-shu*. Recently Huang Chang-ch'ien has published his study on the authenticity and authorship of the *Ku-wen Shang-shu* and the pseudo-K'ung An-kuo's *Shu-ching*.[37]

Huang's study also contains a definitive list of affinities between the *KTT*'s and Wang Su's discussions of the *Shu-ching*. Since the translation of the *KTT* below also contains references to many such affinities,[38] there is no need at this time to discuss the issue in further detail.

In sum, in light of the above considerations, the *KTT* can be categorically said to be a work that reflects various dimensions of Wang Su's mind as they are manifested in his intellectual biography. The *KTT* can therefore be labeled a purely Wang Su-ian work.

Regarding the *KTT*'s specific authorship, I suggest that Wang Su's authorship is highly probable. The possibility must also be entertained, however, that the composition of the *KTT* could be attributed to another personality from Wang Su's circle, that is, someone who wrote the *KTT* under the direct influence or inspiration of Wang Su.

The *KTT* and the *K'ung-tzu chia-yü*

Under ordinary circumstances this study could be concluded at the present point for the contents, framework, and philosophical context of the text have been reviewed and analyzed, and the necessary sinological setting for the study of the *KTT* as a philosophical text has been established. However, certain problems concerning Wang Su's intellectual biography remain.

Why did Wang Su compile, in addition to the *KTT*, a work like the *K'ung-tzu chia-yü*, which possesses a similar character and shares many parallels with the *KTT*? And why did Wang Su, furthermore, explicitly identify himself with the ideas expressed in the *K'ung-tzu chia-yü*, for which he even wrote a commentary, while he never referred to the *KTT*?

The supposition is, of course, that Wang Su himself composed both works. This conclusion is not illogical for the following reasons: First, the attribution of the *KTT* to Wang Su is now highly probable. Second, the attribution of the *K'ung-tzu chia-yü* to Wang Su has also been shown to be highly probable.[39] Third, the many affinities between the *KTT* and the *K'ung-tzu chia-yü* that have been pointed out already are sufficiently convincing to allow one to say that both works were written by the same author.[40]

Kramers avoided the problem in his masterful study of the *K'ung-tzu chia-yü*, although he provided a note on the connection between Wang Su and the authorship of the *KTT*.[41] In light of his conclusion regarding the authenticity and authorship of the *K'ung-tzu chia-yü*, this avoidance seems natural. In his study (p. 193), Kramers made an effort to persuade his readers that Wang Su did not forge the *K'ung-tzu chia-yü* but rather overhauled a collection of Confucian lore that already existed before his time. Kramers' suggestion was based, among other things, on the testimony of Wang Su himself, who stated in his preface to the *K'ung-tzu chia-yü* that his former disciple, K'ung Meng,

Confucius's descendant of the twenty-second generation, gave him the manuscripts of the *K'ung-tzu chia-yü*.[42] Now, assuming that Wang Su himself wrote the *KTT*, and provided, for reasons I shall discuss later, that the *KTT* is earlier than the *K'ung-tzu chia-yü*, how could Wang Su's own testimony about the way he uncovered the K'ung family manuscripts be credible? Kramers (p. 193) suggests that Wang Su's testimony should not be considered completely fictitious. However, how can we accept Kramers' suggestion, if Wang Su claimed that he somehow managed to get possession of the K'ung family's manuscripts, when he already had finished writing a similar version, the *KTT*?

Before I suggest an answer to the problems that emerge from the supposedly identical authorship of these two works, let me first recapitulate Wang Su's preface to the *K'ung-tzu chia-yü* and imagine that we are recapitulating a hypothetical preface to the *KTT*.

Wang Su expresses his objection to the line of classical learning advocated by the school of Cheng Hsüan. The *KTT*, as seen above, clearly rejects the line of classical learning advocated by the school of Cheng Hsüan.

Wang Su describes himself as a man who is forced into controversies with the scholars of his time. Many of the *KTT*'s protagonists, such as Tzu-kao and Tzu-yü, share the same view of themselves.

Wang Su declares that the Way of the K'ung family is obstructed and should be opened by him. The *KTT* is the anthology of that very family, an anthology which expresses the identical aspiration, that is, to feature the true heritage of the K'ung family.

Wang Su claims that K'ung Meng, Confucius's descendant of the twenty-second generation, gave him the manuscripts of the K'ung family. The *KTT* ends with Chi-yen, Confucius's descendant of the twenty-first generation, who was mistakenly said to be the father of K'ung Meng.[43]

Wang Su claims that his work on the *K'ung-tzu chia-yü* is for the purpose of handing down the truth about the heritage of the K'ung family for the *chün-tzu* of future generations. To see how the *chün-tzu* of the future is also embedded in the *KTT*, and to reinforce the point that the *K'ung-tzu chia-yü*'s preface can be seen as a hypothetical preface to the *KTT*, I shall examine one of the final passages in the *KTT* (B, 64a8–65b6). In this passage the last protagonist of the *KTT*, Chi-yen, reveals in a lengthy monologue his insights into such problems as current scholarship, classical learning, and the duty imposed on a K'ung family member to transmit his family heritage. The following is a precis of this passage:

Chi-yen, like Wang Su, is frustrated because his generation adopts a different line of classical learning than the one advocated by the K'ung family. Like Wang Su, he takes the transmission of the true heritage of the K'ung family to be his own duty. Like Wang Su, Chi-yen feels all alone in his effort to advocate the true heritage of the K'ung family. Like Wang Su, he assumes a future virtuous *chün-tzu* who would identify himself one hundred years later with his, Chi-yen's, intellectual enterprise.

One may now ask: Is there a concrete example of a virtuous *chün-tzu* who, as Chi-yen (d. A.D. 124) assumed, was to live one hundred years later and would suffer from not having lived during the same period as Chi-yen? In other words, who, in the neighborhood of A.D. 224, can be considered a *chün-tzu* with an identical frame of mind to Chi-yen?

I believe that Wang Su's (A.D. 195–256) preface to the *K'ung-tzu chia-yü* provides a suitable candidate, that is, Wang Su himself. To state this hypothesis more bluntly: Wang Su's preface to the *K'ung-tzu chia-yü* is a revised version of Chi-yen's monologue in the *KTT*, which Wang Su had previously written.

Regarding the dating of the two works, I have argued above for certain specific reasons that the *KTT* is earlier than the *K'ung-tzu chia-yü*. First, the fact that the *KTT* records Tzu-ssu's discussions with both Confucius and Mencius shows that at the time of its composition the author of the *KTT* had not mastered the historical sources that specify the dates of birth and death of various members of the K'ung family. The *K'ung-tzu chia-yü* to the best of my knowledge does not bear many anachronisms, and whenever an anachronism occurs, Wang Su immediately corrects it in his subsequent commentary.[44]

Second, the *KTT*'s systematic correction of Kung-sun Lung's thesis "A white horse is not a horse" to "A white horse is not a white horse" indicates an overenthusiastic writer who is not aware of the limit of his philosophical knowledge.

Third, the *KTT* is a more philosophically and less exegetically oriented work than the *K'ung-tzu chia-yü*. This is congruent with the development of Wang Su's scholarly interests as they unfold in his preface to the *K'ung-tzu chia-yü*.

Fourth, the unsubtle way in which the *KTT* states its ideas, the shortcuts and the hasty manner that mark the style of its arguments, and its enthusiasm to encompass an excessive number of problems, personalities, and periods indicate, to my mind, that the writer was indeed young and inexperienced.

Finally, one of the *KTT*'s unique features is its generally individualistic tone, which seems to accentuate the solitariness of its protagonists. This tone represents a state of mind typical of frustrated young writers who live in a psychological atmosphere of solitude. In the *K'ung-tzu chia-yü* this tone becomes indistinct. Confucius is now surrounded by many disciples and his words are more maturely formulated. Confucius is delineated in terms of someone who has emerged from the state of loneliness as portrayed in the *KTT* to become a central figure of a group of followers in the *K'ung-tzu chia-yü*.

It is because of the above characteristics, I suggest, and mainly because of discrepancies, anachronisms, and flaws, that Chu Hsi labeled the *KTT* a worthless forgery. On the other hand, Chu Hsi considered the *K'ung-tzu chia-yü*, an extremely balanced and cautiously written text, at least partly authentic.[45]

Before concluding this study I must again remind the reader of the hypothetical nature of this exercise. In the initial statement of the problem of the *KTT*'s authorship, I suggested that this problem cannot be definitely settled as long as the evidence continues to be largely speculative. I have also alluded to another individual from Wang Su's circle, his daughter, suggesting that such a gifted textual scholar could have written the *KTT* as a tribute to her father's scholarship. If this latter possibility is true then the discussion of the problems that emerge from the identical authorship of the *KTT* and *K'ung-tzu chia-yü*, although textually verified, is almost meaningless. The idea that Wang Su himself wrote both works is, however, a reasonable suggestion based on a large degree of probability. The acceptance of this suggestion remains a matter of personal choice.

But if Wang Su was indeed the author of both works, as the above discussion implies, then the earlier questions concerning the place of these two works in his intellectual development must be both raised and resolved satisfactorily. To recapitulate, why did Wang Su embark on the compilation of a work like the *K'ung-tzu chia-yü*, which is similar in character and shares many parallels with the *KTT*? And why did he explicitly identify himself with the ideas expressed in the *K'ung-tzu chia-yü*, for which he even wrote a commentary, while never referring to the *KTT*?

A hypothetical explanation might be formulated as follows: During Wang Su's formative years he found himself in total disagreement with the line of classical learning advocated by the followers of the school of Cheng Hsüan. He was also very distressed by the fact that the scholars of his time increasingly turned their backs on Confucianism, looking for answers to the crucial problems of the time in the non-Confucian schools that flourished in the pre-Han era. As a young and individualistic philosopher, and as a beginning student of the Classics, Wang Su did not have many opportunities to change the intellectual tendencies and directions of his contemporaries. One way open to him, however, was to utilize the old Confucian notion of "transmitting and not innovating," that is, to appeal to the early authorities using their name as a shelter in his philosophical combat. He therefore extracted from many works, such as the *Shih-chi, Han-shu, Lun-yü, Mencius, Hsün Tzu, Li-chi, Ta-tai li-chi, Tso-chuan, Lü-shih ch'un-ch'iu, Kuo yü, Chan-kuo ts'e, Yen-tzu ch'un-ch'iu, Shuo-yüan, Hsin-hsü, Han-shih wai-chuan,* and *Shang-shu ta-chuan,* whatever material he considered relevant and suitable for his case. He then renovated and overhauled this material, giving it a framework and infusing it with some of his own ideas, which he considered identical with the

Confucian philosophical heritage. It is my conviction that his decision to adopt a contextual framework of an historical anthology for his work took place only in the last stage of the formation of the *KTT*. The following list suggests that while compiling his anthology he was thinking of several *Han-shu I-wen-chih* titles that were no longer extant in his time, but which could therefore be used as titles for various parts of his work.

Han-shu i-wen-chih Title	KTT *Chapter*
The *Book of Tzu-ssu* (p. 1724)	1–10
The *Hsiao Erh-ya* (p. 1718)	11
The *Ju-chia yen* (p. 1725)	12–21
The *K'ung Tsang's Ten Chapters* (p. 1726)	22

In any event, at some stage, as his scholarship became more refined, he may have realized that the scope of his enterprise was too broad, and that the work itself was flawed. He may have conjectured that the whole project might evoke purely negative responses. He therefore decided to put aside his juvenile work. Then, mature and quite confident, he applied himself once again, for the same reasons as before, to the making of another, more reliable and balanced compendium. He therefore compiled the *K'ung-tzu chia-yü*, using only those parts of his former work, the *KTT*, that he considered of great value. He claimed credit for the discovery of the *K'ung-tzu chia-yü* and used it to advance his standing in the intellectual battleground of his time. As for the sketch of the *K'ung-tzu chia-yü*, namely, the *KTT*, he probably kept it, and when he became director of the Department of the Imperial Library in A.D. 236,[46] he or one of his closest assistants circulated it among other works.

K'ung-ts'ung-tzu

PART A, CHAPTERS 1–10, 12–14

Translator's Note

The following is a translation of chapters 1–10 and 12–14, which form the first of the two parts of the *KTT* in the *Ssu-pu ts'ung-k'an* edition. This edition is a facsimile reprint of a Ming reproduction of a Sung copy in a two-part, seven-*chüan* edition without commentary. For a detailed description of the *Ssu-pu ts'ung-k'an* edition of the *KTT* see figure 1, p. 40.

As noted earlier, the eleventh chapter of the *KTT* is a word gloss, in which one term is shown as equivalent to others. A translation of this Chinese-Chinese vocabulary would be otiose because of the absence of the linguistic and cultural context necessary for its comprehension. I have therefore decided to give this glossary a context by including equivalences drawn from it in the notes of my translation, where the reader can best appreciate the lexical views exemplified in the *KTT* itself. References to the equivalences given in chapter 11 are always in accord with their pagination in the *Ssu-pu ts'ung-k'an* edition of the *KTT*.

In translating the *KTT*, I have made use of other editions, all of which are referred to in the bibliography. The only two commentaries that cover the bulk of the seven *chüan* of the *KTT* are *Sung Hsien* and *Tsukada Tora*. I have used both extensively, as my notes show. For a description of these two commentaries see figures 3, p. 42, and 15, p. 54.

CHAPTER 1

WORDS OF PRAISE[1]
(Chia-yen)

1.1 (A, 6a3)   When the Master[2] went to Chou he met Ch'ang Hung.[3] When their conversation[4] was over he retired. Ch'ang Hung then said to Duke Wen of Liu: "To me K'ung Chung-ni[5] seems to have the outward manifestations of a sage. The flowing shape of his eyes[6] and the rise of his forehead make him look like the Yellow Emperor.[7] His long arms and arched back,[8] along with his nine-foot six-inch stature,[9] give him a stature like Ch'eng T'ang.[10] Yet in his speech he is deferential to the former kings, and his personal bearing is extremely modest. He is a man of broad learning and retentive memory, and his general knowledge is inexhaustible. Shouldn't these things account for the advent of a sage?"

Liu Tzu said: "At present there is a fierce struggle between the feudal lords[11] at the very time when the royal house of Chou is in decline. K'ung Ch'iu[12] has no official title;[13] so where would sagehood be manifested?"

Ch'ang Hung said: "The Way of Yao, Shun,[14] Wen, and Wu[15] is most likely to be reached at the point of total ruin. Rites and music are collapsing. All he can do is to try to rectify the moral foundations of orderly rule and nothing else."

Later the Master heard what they had said, and he remarked: "I could never be so presumptuous as to do this, though I am, after all, one who devotes himself to rites and music."

1.2 (A, 6b4)   It was for the purpose of fortifying his city wall that Duke Hui of Ch'en[16] built the Ling-yang tower.[17] Before the project had reached its final stage, he had already put to death several tens of workers and imprisoned three supervisors, whose death he decreed. When the Master came to Ch'en,[18] he heard about it. Then he came to see the Marquis of Ch'en and both of them climbed to the tower and took in the view. "O what a magnificent tower," said the Master. "Since antiquity, when the Sage Kings built their city walls and towers, an achievement of similar magnitude has never been brought about without any bloodshed."

The Marquis of Ch'en retired without a reply. Hurriedly, without fanfare, he pardoned the three supervisors and then, upon meeting the Master, he asked him: "Formerly, in Chou, when marvelous towers[19] were built, was there also bloodshed?"

The Master answered: "At the time of King Wen's rise to power, six of the nine provinces were brought under unified rule.[20] All the people of these six provinces came traveling to join him, bringing their own children along with them.[21] Therefore the project of building a tower of limited size was accomplished in less than the allotted time. How could there be any occasion for killings? It is only a ruler such as you who is able to realize such a great achievement with so few people."

1.3 (A, 7a5) Tzu-chang[22] asked: "Why must a girl approach[23] the age of twenty before she is allowed to get married?"[24]

Confucius said: "A girl is engaged to be married at the age of fifteen and only afterward can she follow her husband.[25] This is analogous to the principle of yin's response to the $yang^a$'s stirring,[26] and the female following the male's call. The tasks of an unmarried girl consist of reeling, spinning, and weaving. The beauty of the variously colored figures embroidered on robes are the great achievements of a married woman. She must be past the age of fifteen and approaching the age of twenty before she can master these activities. It is only afterward that she can, first, treat her parents-in-law filially and, then, serve her husband and raise her children."

1.4 (A, 7b4) When Tsai-wo[27] returned from his mission to Ch'i he appeared before the Master and said: "Liang-ch'iu Chü[28] was bitten by a poisonous snake and after thirty days he recovered. He then came to pay court to the Prince of Ch'i, who assembled his counsellors and many other guests to celebrate the occasion. I, your disciple, was one among the guests. Both counsellors and guests submitted their own prescriptions for curing a snakebite. I, your disciple, said to them: 'Usually the reason for submitting a prescription would be for the sake of curing an illness. Liang-ch'iu has by now been cured, but all of you submitted your prescriptions. Where could these prescriptions be applied? Do you actually wish that Counsellor Liang-ch'iu should be injured again by a snake, and then use your prescriptions?' The various guests sat silently and uttered no word. What do you think of these words of mine?"

The Master said: "What you have said was wrong. The healing of a broken arm in three places,[29] or Liang-ch'iu's cure after a poisonous snakebite—those who suffer from such an affliction will surely ask for a prescription with which to end it. It is for this reason that the various guests submitted their

Words of Praise

prescriptions. Each one described his own prescription, hoping to have it adopted in order to cure people's afflictions. The presentation of a prescription is made through reference to its virtues. Moreover, it is through such presentations that one can verify what it is that makes a prescription aimed to cure people's afflictions superior to another.''

1.5 (A, 8a8) When the Master came to Ch'i, Yen Tzu[30] came to see him in his guest house during a feast. After the banquet Yen Tzu met with him alone and said: "The current situation in Ch'i is so dangerous that it may be compared to riding down an enormously deep valley[31] in a chariot without linchpins. Surely it would be unreasonable to hope that this chariot will not turn over. You are my very heart;[32] if you will make Ch'i your headquarters for your traveling and resting it will be possible to save the situation. I hope you will not evade my request for assistance.''

The Master replied: "There is no way of effecting a cure for a fatal illness. Governmental orders are the bridle and reins with which the ruler controls those under his command. It has been a long time since the Prince of Ch'i has lost control of the situation. Now, even if you wish to pull the chariot pole under your arm,[33] and to push its wheel, it will probably be to no avail. It seems that this state of things will last as long as the Prince of Ch'i and you live, but afterward Ch'i will become the possession of the T'ien clan.''[34]

1.6 (A, 8b8) Tung-kuo Hai of Ch'i[35] wanted to attack the T'ien clan. Carrying an introductory present, he appeared before the Master and asked for his advice. The Master said: "Your intention is righteous, but I, Ch'iu, am not in a position to join you in planning this matter.'' The Master introduced Tzu-kung,[36] allowing him to reply to the plan.

Tzu-kung said to Tung-kuo Hai: "The present situation is that you are a Gentleman.[37] This means that your status is low though your ambitions are great. People do not tend to join forces with those of low status, and they are intimidated by men of great ambition. It is probably not your duty to attack the T'ien clan. Why don't you abandon the plan? Think of a man who ties a heavy weight[38] with one thread, hangs it on an extremely high post, and suspends it over an immeasurably deep abyss. All the bystanders are apprehensive that the thread will snap, but the one who did this fails to recognize the approaching danger.[39] Is this case not analogous to that of yours? When you strike a drum and scare an already startled horse, when you add weight and overload a rope that is on the verge of snapping, the horse bolts and the chariot overturns. When the six reins are unloosened, and when the rope on the high peak snaps and the weight falls into the abyss, the danger is unavoidable.''

With a visibly frightened look on his face Tung-kuo Hai kneeled down and said: "I will not go on, and I wish you to say no more.'' Then the Master said to Tzu-kung: "Tung-kuo Hai's intention was righteous. If you had merely told him about how difficult or easy it was, it would have been enough. Why did you have to frighten him?"

1.7 (A, 9b4)   Tsai-wo asked: "Does the superior man[40] set the highest value on using the right expressions?"[41]

Confucius answered: "The superior man regards principle[42] as of high value. He ignores extensive arguments that do not focus on essentials and turns a deaf ear to intricate arguments and extravagant doctrines. It is only the intelligent who avoids losing sight of the principle."

Confucius said: "As for Yü,[43] I approve of the way he argues by convincing analogy, while in the case of Ssu,[44] I approve of the way he adheres to the facts of the situation. Convincing analogy is enough to make people grasp the application to their own situation, while adherence to the facts of the situation is enough to frighten them."

CHAPTER
2

DISCUSSION OF THE *BOOK OF DOCUMENTS*
(Lun-shu)

2.1 (A, 10a2) Tzu-chang asked: "When the sage receives the mandate[1] he must receive it at Heaven's bequest. Why, then, does the *Book of Documents*[2] say: 'Shun received Yao's retirement in the temple of the Accomplished Ancestor'?"[3]

Confucius answered: "As examples of those who received the mandate from Heaven we have T'ang[4] and Wu. Those who received it from men include Shun and Yü.[5] If one is not versed in the *Book of Odes*,[6] the *Book of Documents*, the *Book of Changes*,[7] and the *Spring and Autumn Annals*,[8] then not only does one not understand the mind of the sage, but one also has no means of distinguishing between Yao and Shun, who received the mandate by peaceful succession, and T'ang or Wu, who received it by force of arms."

2.2 (A, 10a7) Tzu-chang asked: "According to the rites, a man gets married at the age of thirty,[9] and yet, in the days of old, Shun was summoned to employment at the age of thirty,[10] as when the *Book of Documents* made the following reference to him:

There is an unmarried man among the people called Shun of Yü.[11]

How so? Previously I received from you, Master, the teachings that when a sage holds sway and the superior man occupies his rightful position, there are neither resentful women within the inner chambers nor unmarried men abroad.[12] While Yao ruled as the Son of Heaven,[13] how could there be an unmarried man among the people?"

Confucius answered: "When a young man reaches the age of twenty he undergoes the capping ceremony,[14] and only then is he allowed to take a wife. This is a universal principle that has been accepted by all people from the

79

earliest times down to our own day. Shun's father was stupid and his mother deceitful.[15] Neither of them could maintain proper order in their family. For this reason he reached the age of thirty and was still in the category of unmarried person. The *Book of Odes* says:

> How does one take a wife? By first seeking approval from one's parents.[16]

If one's parents are alive, then the parents should make the proper arrangements for the marriage. But when one's parents are already gone, then one takes a wife by oneself and one announces the marriage in the ancestral temple. In this case, the reason why Shun was unmarried was that his parents were stupid and deceitful. How could Yao, even as the Son of Heaven, have had an effect on Shun's case?''[17]

2.3 (A, 11a1) Tzu-hsia[18] asked what were the most fundamental ideas of the *Book of Documents*. The Master answered: "In the 'Canon of the Emperors'[19] I see the sagehood of Yao and Shun. In the 'Great Yü,'[20] the 'Counsels of Kao-yao,'[21] and the 'I and Chi,'[22] I see the loyalty, diligence, accomplishments, and merit of Yü, Chi, and Kao-yao. In the 'Announcement Concerning Lo,'[23] I see the virtue of the Duke of Chou.[24] Therefore one may observe excellence in the 'Canon of the Emperors,' implementations in the 'Counsels of the Great Yü' and the 'Tribute of Yü,'[25] government in the 'Counsels of Kao-yao' and the 'I and Chi,' ordering of society in the 'Great Plan,'[26] righteousness[27] in the 'Speech of the Duke of Ch'in,'[28] benevolence in the 'Five Announcements,'[29] and admonishment in the 'Punishments of the Prince of Fu.'[30] If one thoroughly masters these seven items,[31] then the fundamental ideas of the *Book of Documents* will become evident."

2.4 (A, 11a8) Confucius said: "The attitude of the *Book of Documents* toward events is this: It goes far without a sense of detachment; it gets close without exerting pressure. It fully expresses its intended meaning without indulging in grievance. Its words are agreeable, yet not to the point of sycophantic praise. In the 'Day of the Supplementary Sacrifice of Kao-tzung'[32] I see how rapidly virtue is rewarded.[33] If one follows his proper Way and extends his benevolence to others, then people from far away will submit their wills to his, and fulfill their reverence toward him. In the 'Great Plan,' I see that the superior man cannot bear words concerning other people's vices but fosters examples of human perfection. It arises from the depth of the mind and is expressed in external formulation, thus forming this piece of literature: this is surely the case of the 'Great Plan.' "

2.5 (A, 11b6) Tzu-chang asked: "In the age of Yao and Shun the world was ordered without a single man being punished.[34] How was this possible? Because their moral teaching was grounded in truth and their concern for the people was deep. According to Lung-tzu,[35] however, all teachings were uniformly enforced by the threat of the five punishments.[36] Might I ask the meaning of this statement?"

Confucius answered: "It is not so. The five punishments are only to be used as a prop to basic moral teaching.[37] As for Lung-tzu, he could never be considered someone who was able to engage in the study of the *Book of Documents*."

2.6 (A, 12a2)   After Tzu-hsia had concluded his study of the *Book of Documents*,[38] he appeared before the Master. The Master said: "What have you attained in your study of *Book of Documents*?"

Tzu-hsia replied: "The manner in which the *Book of Documents* discusses events is as brilliantly illuminating as the sun and the moon in their alternating illumination,[39] and as distinctively arranged as the stars in their overlapping paths of movement. It ranges[40] from the virtue of Yao and Shun in remote antiquity, down to the righteousness of the Three Kings[41] in later times. Whatever I, Shang,[42] have learned from you about the *Book of Documents* is firmly imprinted in my mind. Could I ever allow myself to forget it? Even if I were to retire and live in poverty between the Ho and the Chi channels,[43] or in the depths of the mountains,[44] if I were to build a mud hut with a door of plaited grass[45] and spend my days there unceasingly strumming my lute, as I sang the praises of the Way of the former kings—even there I could still express my pent up indignation,[46] sigh for lost glory, and forget my own poverty and destitution. Therefore, whether I am in the company of others or not, I always find delight in the Way. Whenever I contemplate the virtue of Yao and Shun in remote antiquity and the righteousness of the Three Kings in later times, I immediately lose all thought of sorrows, troubles, and death."

Changing his countenance, the Master said: "Ah! You are apparently a man with whom I can speak about the *Book of Documents*.[47] Nevertheless, you are still approaching it from the exterior alone; you have not yet viewed the interior. If one peers through the gate without entering the chamber, how can one view the inner recesses of the ancestral temple or the splendor of the hundred officials?"[48]

2.7 (A, 12b6)   Tsai-wo asked for instruction in the *Book of Documents*, asking what was meant by the words:

> Although sent to the great foothill forest[49] he was not led astray by violent winds, thunder, and rain.[50]

Confucius said: "These words refer to the correspondence between Heavenly phenomena and human deeds. When Yao had already gained the service of Shun, he repeatedly examined him by many difficult tasks. Later he recruited him for honorable and prestigious office, appointing him as Grand Recorder[51] to exercise governmental control over numerous contingencies. Therefore the *yin* and the *yang*[a] were purified and harmonized, the five planets[52] made their regular appearance, and violent winds, thunder, and rain responded in proper accord, with neither error nor imbalance. The harmony between Shun's conduct and Heavenly phenomena was thus clearly manifested.''

2.8 (A, 13a4) Tsai-wo asked: "May I ask what was meant by the Pure Sacrifice to the Six Honored Ones?''[53]

Confucius answered: "The Honored Ones are six in number, to all of whom the pure sacrifices are offered. By burying a small animal at the Altar of Shining Splendor, they sacrificed to the four seasons.[54] By offering prayers of greeting to the departure of Cold and to the arrival of Heat[55] in the pit and on the altar, they sacrificed to the winter cold and summer heat. When sacrifice was performed on the Altar of the Border-Palace,[56] they sacrificed to the sun; on the Altar of the Night-Light, they sacrificed to the moon; on the Altar of Honored Gloom, they sacrificed to the stars; and on the Altar of the Honored Rain, they sacrificed to the flood and drought. This is what was meant by the pure sacrifice to the Six Honored Ones.''[57]

2.9 (A, 13b) The *Book of Documents* says:

> When I offer the great sacrifices to the former kings, your forefathers join in to share the sacrificial feast.[58]

Chi Huan-tzu[59] asked: "What is the meaning of this line?"

Confucius answered: "Under the rule of the kings of ancient times, when ministers of great achievement died, sacrifices were always offered to them in the ancestral temple, to distinguish the ministers marked by meritorious deeds, exhortations, loyalty, and devoted service. P'an Keng[60] singled out these activities in order to motivate the ministers whose families had been in service for many generations. That is why he made a laudatory reference to forefathers in his speech.''[61]

Huan-tzu said: "When the Son of Heaven has ministers with great merit, this is certainly true; but is it also applicable to the feudal lords and their meritorious ministers?"

Confucius answered: "If by his laborious toil a minister is able to stabilize the country, and if his achievements have an effect on the people, or if a high minister dies a martyr's death for the country,[62] it is permissible to sacrifice to these ministers even in the ruler's temple.''

Huan-tzu said: "How are positions ranked in such cases?"

The Book of Documents 83

Confucius answered: "During their lifetimes, the ministers of the Son of Heaven and of the feudal lords occupy their places in accordance with their ranks at court. If they die, they are given a proper position in the temple. The order is the same in both cases."

2.10 (A, 14a2) The *Book of Documents* says,[63]

It was Kao-tzung[64] who offered the *pao*[65] sacrifice to Shang-chia Wei.[66]

Duke Ting[67] said: "What is the meaning of this line?"

Confucius answered: "This relates to the fact that when the familial relationships are exhausted the temple is destroyed, so that meritorious ancestors and virtuous forefathers are not honored in their respective halls in the temple.[68] That is why every year during the autumn sacrifice the *pao* sacrifice was performed in order to throw light on the ancestors' merits and virtues."

The Duke said: "Could I offer a sacrifice for my forefather Duke Hsi,[69] whose merits and virtues were first in rank?"

Confucius answered: "I have heard that formerly there were cases in the Yü,[70] Hsia, Shang, and Chou when these rituals were performed by emperors and kings. From that time on, however, I have not heard of it."

2.11 (A, 14a8) Duke Ting asked what was meant by the following words from the Book of Chou:

He employed the employable and revered those worthy of reverence. He showed his power to those who deserved to be put in fear. He revealed himself clearly to the people.[71]

Confucius replied: "The meaning of these words is that the ruler did not lose the Way and made the people see this very clearly. If the ruler is able to employ those who are worthy of employment, government will be rectified. If he is able to respect those who are deserving of respect, the wise will be highly valued. If people stand in awe of those worthy of awe, then punishments will be imposed compassionately.[72] There has never been a case of a ruler who paid close attention to these three points and used them to instruct the people, whose state did not flourish."

2.12 (A, 14b5) Tzu-chang asked for instruction in the *Book of Documents*, asking what was meant by the line:

Yü determined the high mountains.[73]

Confucius said: "This line refers to the five sacred mountains.[74] Yü determined their order and degree in reference to the sacrifices offered to them."[75]

Tzu-chang asked: "What were the rites of these sacrifices?"

Confucius replied: "They used bullocks and silks as sacrificial objects. The five sacred mountains received sacrificial honors like those paid at court to the three dukes,[76] while other famous[77] mountains of lesser status received sacrificial honors like those paid at court to the barons and counts."

Tzu-chang asked: "Why does the benevolent person find delight in mountains?"[78]

Confucius answered: "Mountains are majestic in their height."

Tzu-chang said: "But why delight in height?"

Confucius replied: "Mountains are places where grass and trees grow and birds and beasts multiply. Wealth is produced from the mountains in a manner that is straightforward and shows no preferential treatment. From all around people come to cut down their vegetation yet they remain straightforward and show no preferential treatment. They stir up and spew forth winds and clouds, which pervade the space between Heaven and Earth. They are the place where the *yin* and the *yang* are harmoniously united, and where the rain and dew are bounteous, through which all creatures are formed and all people are nourished. That is why the benevolent person finds delight in the mountains."

2.13 (A, 15a6) Meng I-tzu[79] asked for instruction in the *Book of Documents*, asking what was meant by the line: "Be reverent you Four Neighbors."[80]

Confucius replied: "In front of the kings there used to be the Solver of Doubts, and behind them, the Chief Aid. To their left there was the Guide, and to their right the Corrector. They were referred to as the Four Proximate Ministers.[81] That means that the king's Proximate Ministers, who surrounded him from all sides, inspired awe and reverence for him, so that none could oppose his personal authority. The Four Neighbors of King Wen of Chou were the Bringer-near of the Distant, the Expeditious Assembler, the Advancer of Those in the Back, and the Defender Against Insult. They were the ones who delivered King Wen from harm in Yu-li."[82]

I-tzu said: "Do you, the Master, also have 'four neighbors'?"

Confucius said: "I have four friends instead.[83] Ever since I have taken on Hui[84] my disciples have become more intimate with me; is he not my Bringer-near of the Distant? Ever since I have taken on Ssu,[85] scholars from distant places have come flocking to me day after day; is he not my Expeditious Assembler? Ever since I have taken on Shih,[86] I have light ahead and radiance behind; is he not my Advancer of Those in the Back? Ever since I have taken on Yu,[87] evil words do not reach my gate; is he not my Defender from Insult?"

2.14 (A, 15b7) When Confucius was visiting Duke Ching of Ch'i,[88] Liang-ch'iu Chü arrived from abroad. The Duke said: "What kept you that long?"

Liang-ch'iu Chü answered: "The head of the Ch'en clan was going to punish⁸⁹ one of his petty subjects, and I had to argue for his defense. That is what kept me so long."

The Duke looked at Confucius and said with a smile: "What the *Book of Chou* says about illuminating one's virtue and exercising great care in punishment⁹⁰ can be applied to the illustrious virtue of Ch'en-tzu.⁹¹ The fact that, in applying a punishment to someone, he gave the opportunity to have arguments presented in his defense cannot be considered contrary to a careful use of punishment."

Confucius said: "Formerly, when K'ang Shu⁹² was enfeoffed in Wei, he united the land of the Three Inspectors⁹³ and became the chief prince. It was in accordance with King Ch'eng's⁹⁴ command that the Duke of Chou⁹⁵ made the 'Announcement of K'ang'⁹⁶ regarding this issue. There he recounted with admiration the virtue of King Wen and turned it into a literary piece of a rectifying and admonishing nature.⁹⁷ It reads:

> It was your greatly glorious father King Wen who was able to illustrate his virtue and take great care in the application of punishment.⁹⁸

The person who is able to illustrate his virtue is one who can prominently employ men of virtue, singling them out and appointing them to office. One who takes great care in the application of punishment is one who is constantly preoccupied with this issue to the exclusion of all other concerns. Only after the numerous relevant points are settled should one put it into practice. The fullest extent of punishment involves many restrictions.⁹⁹ These words mean that with those he employs he does not lose sight of their virtues, and with those he punishes he does not lose sight of their crimes. They do not mean the illumination of one's personal virtue."

The Duke said: "If I had not gone too far in my statement,¹⁰⁰ how would I have had an occasion to hear my Master's teachings?"

2.15 (A, 16b2) The *Book of Documents* says:

> Regarding Tsu-chia's¹⁰¹ unrighteous behavior as a king. . . .¹⁰²

Kung-hsi Ch'ih¹⁰³ said: "I have heard from Yen-tzu that T'ang,¹⁰⁴ T'ai-chia, Tsu-i,¹⁰⁵ and Wu-ting¹⁰⁶ were great sovereigns of all under Heaven. However, while T'ai-chia had been a king, he acted unrighteously during his period of mourning.¹⁰⁷ Why, therefore, was he included in such an exalted company of sovereigns?"

Confucius answered: "The attitude of the superior man toward other people is that he tries to account for their merits and extirpate their faults. When T'ai-chia assumed the throne he did not have a clear idea of the rites concerning the mourning period, and so he offended the government of the great minister.¹⁰⁸ I-yin banished T'ai-chia to T'ung. For three years he was occupied with remorseful thoughts regretting his past misconduct. Then he emerged and reassumed his position. For this he was called an enlightened king. Seen from this angle, although he is a fourth with the other three kings, is it not indeed proper?''[109]

2.16 (A, 17a1)   Duke Ai of Lu[110] asked: "What was meant by the *Book of Documents*' laudatory reference to K'uei?'':

> Oh! When I strike or tap the stone, all kinds of animals dance in unison, and all the chiefs of officers become truly harmonious.[111]

Confucius replied: "These words refer to the transforming influence of good government. When the Ancient Emperors and Kings had accomplished their deeds, they composed music. When their achievements were good, the music was harmonious. And if the music was truly harmonious, it seemed as if Heaven and Earth were resonating with it. How much more so was the reaction of the various kinds of animals? K'uei was the Director of Music in Emperor Shun's court. He was truly able to use music to bring the true essence of well-ordered principles of government to their full realization."

The Duke said: "If this is so, then with regard to the great basis of the government is there anything more exalted than music?''[112]

Confucius answered: "Music is only the means by which the accomplishments of the government are extolled; it is not the basis of government itself. Only when all the government officials are already functioning in perfect harmony as a whole can music be truly harmonious."

The Duke said: "I heard that K'uei had only one foot whereby he was distinguishable from other men; is this true?''[113]

Confucius answered: "Formerly, when Chung and Li[114] recommended K'uei and he was promoted at the court, they were also looking for other men to be his assistants. Shun's response was as follows: 'Music is the essence of Heaven and Earth.' It is only the sage who can tune the six pitch-pipes and adjust the five notes.[115] He harmonizes music in its basic structure and thereby fully masters the eight winds.[116] One man with K'uei's qualifications would be enough to accomplish all these. That is why the saying 'one is enough' does not mean 'one foot.' ''[117]

The Duke said, "I approve."

CHAPTER
3

RECORD OF RIGHTEOUSNESS
(Chi-i)

3.1 (A, 18a2) Chi Huan-tzu gave the Master a formal gift of a thousand measures of grain.[1] The Master accepted it without a word of decline and then divided the grain between those of his disciples who were destitute. Tzu-kung came forward and said: "Chi-sun[2] has presented the grain to you because of your poverty and you have accepted it and given it away to others. Isn't your act contrary to Chi-sun's intention?"

The Master said: "How so?"

Tzu-kung replied: "The intended purpose of Chi-sun's gesture was generosity."

The Master said: "That is correct. My acquisition of the thousand measures of grain and the reason why I have accepted it without a word of rejection were for the sake of Chi-sun's generosity, which I have regarded as an act of special favor as well. One does not accept goods from others in order to become rich. Is it not better that the generosity that Chi-sun has shown to one person benefit a great many other people?"

3.2 (A, 18b1) Ch'in Chuang-tzu[3] died. Meng Wu Po[4] presented the following question to Confucius: "Did colleagues observe mourning for each other in antiquity?"

Confucius answered: "Yes, the requirements of honorable behavior between mutual friends did apply among colleagues. Collegiality was not affected by the distinction drawn between the honorable, the low, and the other different ranks.[5] I have heard it from Lao Tan:[6] Formerly Shu of Kuo,[7] Hung Yao, T'ai Tien,[a8] San I-sheng, and Nan-kung K'uo were five colleagues who assisted kings Wen and Wu by merging their own virtues. When Shu of Kuo died the four remaining men mourned for him with the mourning ritual for a friend. Those among the ancients who fully understood the rites put them into practice."

3.3 (A, 18b7) When Kung-fu Wen-po[9] died some of the ladies of his chamber followed him in death.[10] His mother was furious and did not weep. When his chamberlains protested, she replied: "Confucius was the wisest man under Heaven. But when he was denied an office in Lu he retired. My son, who has always venerated him, was not able to follow him. Now my son is gone, and two of his wives have followed him in death. This shows that he cared little for his master while caring greatly for women."

Later, when the Master heard about this, he said: "Mr. Chi's wife[11] indeed sets the highest value on wisdom."

Changing his countenance, Tzu-lu[12] said: "Is the Master after all a man who, like others, is fond of people's praise? A mother cannot be considered compassionate if she does not weep over her son's death; so why have you approved her attitude?"

The Master said: "By responding in fury to her son's inability to follow the wise, she showed herself to be a person who placed the highest value on the wise. How can I myself have any involvement in the matter? Surely my remark was in reference to this aspect of her response and nothing else."

3.4 (A, 19a8) Duke Ch'u of Wei[13] sent a messenger to Confucius, posing the following question: "When I assign people to official service I pay no attention to their status; I personally inquire and examine each one of them. And still it seems that I repeatedly misjudge people. Why is this so?"

Confucius answered: "It is precisely because of what you have said that you keep losing them. People are really very difficult to assess. This is something that verbal inquiries cannot achieve and observations cannot fully cover. Moreover, the ruler's concerns are legion. When there are many worries, then his mind is not attentive. When a ruler whose mind is not attentive examines people who are hard to assess, it is only natural that he loses some of them. Haven't you heard that formerly, when Shun was in the service of Yao, he was given the job of selecting men of talent and employing gentlemen for service, and Yao invariably agreed with Shun's choices. People in Yao's company said: 'In employing gentlemen, the ruler himself should be the one to assign them to act as his Ears and Eyes[14] and grasp the extent of a candidate's sincerity. Is any other way possible?' Yao said: 'By nominating Shun, I have already got him to act as my Ears and Eyes. Now Shun himself has nominated others. If I myself have to reassign them, then the assigning of people to act as my Ears and Eyes will be endless.' If a ruler delegates authority to those worthy of it, then he himself is not overextended, nor are the wise and the talented lost."

3.5 (A, 20a2) Tzu-kung asked: "Formerly Sun Wen-tzu[15] was able to discern that Wei was going to ruin, on the basis of the fact that while the Marquis of Wei, the appointed successor,[16] was weeping over the death of the Duke of Wei, he did not show true grief. As a result, Sun Wen-tzu, while traveling, did not dare to leave his valuables in the capital of Wei, but deposited them all in the city of Ch'i, and assiduously cultivated the friendship of twenty counsellors of Chin.[17] Some people praised his foresight. What do you think of this?"

Confucius answered: "I think he was criminal, not foresighted."

Tzu-kung said, "May I ask what you mean?"

The Master said: "An official who draws a salary must realize that he is obligated to be steadfast in his duties unto death. Nevertheless Sun-tzu, while aware of the fact that the ruler of Wei would eventually act in violation of the standards of kingship, did not consider sacrificing his own life to oppose him, but was, for a long time, preoccupied with the dilemma of his potential environments. He was just seizing upon his own advantage, demonstrating disloyalty. He was not acting in accordance with what one expects from one's minister. A minister who does not make his heart subservient is someone whom a wise ruler cannot pardon. It was indeed sheer luck that Sun-tzu escaped severe punishment for this conduct."

3.6 (A, 20b2)   Confucius sent Tsai Yü[18] on a mission to Ch'u. King Chao of Ch'u[19] wanted to take advantage of Tsai Yü's presence to send a gift for Confucius of a luxurious carriage with ivory decorations.

Tsai Yü said: "The Master will have no use for this carriage."

The King said: "What is the reason for this?"

Tsai Yü replied: "I have noticed what sort of things he uses, and so I have a sense of where his true feelings lie. By observing this, I have the means of understanding what he is like."

The King said, "Please elaborate."

Tsai Yü replied, "Ever since I became a retainer of the Master I have humbly noticed that his words never depart from the Way, and his acts never violate the dictates of benevolence. He cherishes righteousness and places a high value on virtue. He is of pure integrity and is fond of frugality. When he is in an official, salaried post, he does not manipulate his position to make a fortune for himself. When things are not in accord he leaves office and willingly forgets the prerogatives of office. His wives do not dress in varicolored silks, nor do his concubines wear fine silks. The equipment of his carriage is not decorated in red,[20] and his horses are not fed on millet. If the Way is put into practice, he delights in the fact that the world is properly ruled; if the Way is not put into practice, he delights in the fact that his own selfhood practices it. Such is the basis of the Master's standing. For example, if there is a gaudy sight or an alluringly suggestive voice, the Master passes it by without looking or encounters it without listening. Therefore I know that the Master will have no use for this carriage."

The King said, "If so, then what can fulfill the Master's wishes?"

Tsai Yü replied: "At present the Way and virtue are in a state of dormancy in the world. The Master's ambition is to restore them and make the world practice them. If there were truly a ruler who wished to exercise proper rule and was able to put the Way into practice, then even if it required the Master, walking on foot, to pay court to the ruler, the Master would surely be willing to do it. Why must the Master be forced from afar to slight the ruler's excessive gifts?"

The King said: "From this moment on I will understand that Confucius's virtue is great."

Tsai Yü returned and reported to Confucius. Confucius said: "What do you, my disciples, think of Yü's words?"

Tzu-kung replied: "He did not fully display the Master's excellence. The Master's virtue, if put in terms of height, would match Heaven; if put in terms of depth, it would match the sea. Yü's words seem to represent the reality of practical behavior."

The Master said: "Words in which reality is valued influence people to believe in them. If reality is abandoned, what is left to be praised? Ssu's[21] flowery words are not as good as Yü's, which are real."

3.7 (A, 21b6) When Confucius came to Ch'i, Duke Ching wanted him to lead the way as they were going up into the hall. The Master, however, kept one step below the Duke. The Duke made three gestures of yielding and only afterward led the way up the steps. When he was seated, the Duke said: "You, the Master, humbled your virtue and accepted inferior status in order to pay me court. I take this as a great honor. Still, you have cut yourself off from me by keeping the distance of a step below me. I do not know how I have offended you."

Confucius replied: "When a ruler graciously bestows his attention on a minister from outside, his court is showing favor. Nevertheless, an ordinary person must not dare to act as if he were the ruler's equal. Even if the ruler himself allows intimacy, we must keep in mind how this affects righteousness."

3.8 (A, 22a4) Yen Ch'ou[22] was good at serving his parents. Tzu-lu considered him a righteous person. When Ch'ou was held captive in Wei and condemned to death for a crime he had not committed, Tzu-lu offered to ransom him with gold, which the people of Wei were inclined to accept. Then a few of Confucius's disciples collected gold for Tzu-lu to take to Wei. Someone said to Confucius: "Can the acceptance of gold from others for the sake of ransoming a personal friend be considered righteous?"

The Master said: "It is because of his righteousness and the fact that he was a man of limited means that he was ransomed with funds collected from his friends. What is this if not righteousness? To be niggardly of one's gold to the point of allowing an innocent man to suffer punishment is something that even common people could not bear. How much more true is this of my disciples' attitude toward a man whom Yu[23] has befriended? The *Book of Odes* says:

> Could he have been redeemed, we should have given a hundred lives for him.[24]

If by spending gold one can save a person's life, then even a hundred times' greater expense would not have been considered excessive by the ancients. It is for the sake of the fulfillment of Yu's righteous mission that my disciples wanted to help him. This is something that you have failed to understand."

3.9 (A, 22b5) When Confucius studied the *Book of Odes* and reached the "Hsiao ya"[25] section, he said with a deep sigh: "In the books of 'Chou nan'[26] and 'Chao nan'[27] I see why the Way of Chou flourished. In 'Po chou'[28] I see how an ordinary person holds on to his principles unshakably. In 'Ch'i ao'[29] I see that learning can make a superior man. In 'K'ao p'an'[30] I see that the Gentleman is not melancholy when forced to live in seclusion. In 'Mu kua'[31] I see the ceremony of sending presents with something as simple as bundle of rushes.[32] In 'Tzu i'[33] I see the utmost expression of the attitude that cherishes the worthy. In 'Chi ming'[34] I see that the superior men of ancient times did not forget to show reverence. In 'Fa t'an,'[35] I see that the wise put the ideal of service before their personal needs. In 'Hsi shuai'[36] I see how great was the virtue of self-restraint of the Prince of T'ao and T'ang.[37] In 'Hsia ch'üan'[38] I see the longing of a world in chaos for an enlightened ruler. In 'Ch'i yüeh'[39] I see how the dukes of Pin[40] consolidated the realm of Chou. In 'Tung shan'[41] I see how the Duke of Chou put public affairs before personal matters. In 'Lang po'[42] I see that it was the farsighted vision of the Duke of Chou that made him a sage. In 'Lu ming'[43] I see how rites prevail between ruler and subject. In 'T'ung kung'[44] I see that a man of accomplishment gains his proper recompense. In 'Wu yang'[45] I see that good government has a good response. In 'Chieh nan shan'[46] I see how a loyal official worries about the state of the world. In 'Lu o'[47] I see how a filial son is longing for parental nourishment. In 'Ch'u ts'u'[48] I see how a filial son is concerned with the sacrifices. In 'Shang che hua'[49] I see why the wise in ancient times, throughout the ages, maintained their prerogatives of office. In 'Ts'ai shu'[50] I see how the enlightened kings of ancient times showed respect to the feudal lords."

3.10 (A, 23b5)   Once Confucius was taking his daily rest in his room. As he played his lute,[51] Min Tzu[52] heard the music from outside and said to Tseng Tzu:[53] "Formerly, the music produced by the Master was very pure and penetrating, harmonizing and submerging into the perfect Way. Today, however, his music has become gloomy and somber. If music is gloomy it expresses the outpouring of personal desires. If music is somber it manifests covetous cravings. I wonder what it was that brought the Master to such an emotional state? Let us both go in and ask him about it."

Tseng-tzu said: "I agree." The two disciples stepped in and put the question to Confucius.

Confucius said: "Yes, What you say is true. I do have such feelings. While I was playing just now, I saw a cat about to catch a mouse, and I wanted the cat to get it. That is why I produced such a tone. Which of you two noticed it?"

Tseng Tzu replied: "It was Min Tzu."

The Master said: "He is a man with whom you can share the appreciation of music."

CHAPTER

4

ON PUNISHMENT
(Hsing-lun)

4.1 (A, 25a2) Chung Kung[1] asked Confucius to compare the use of punishment[2] in the education of ancient times with that of the present.[3]

Confucius said: "Punishment in ancient times was scarcely used, but in our age punishment is highly prevalent. As for education, in ancient times there were the rites, and only later was there punishment. That is why punishment was used so sparingly. In our age there are no rites to teach with, and the people are kept in line by means of punishment. That is why punishment is so prevalent. The *Book of Documents* says:

> Po I[4] sent down the regulations, for restraining the people there were the penal laws.[5]

The meaning of these words is that Po I first[6] attempted to edify the people by means of the rites,[7] and only afterward did he use punishment to restrain them. When there are no rites the people have no sense of shame, and thus punishment must be used to rectify them. Consequently, the people are preoccupied with shirking responsibilities and avoiding punishment."[8]

4.2 (A, 25b1) When Confucius came to Wei, the commander of Wei, Wen-tzu,[9] asked him: "I have heard that Kung-fu[10] of Lu was not fit to hear litigation.[11] Is this true?"

Confucius answered: "I do not know of any such unfitness. When Kung-fu heard a case the guilty were afraid and the innocent ashamed."

Wen-tzu said: "That the guilty were afraid was because his hearings uncovered all the evidence and the punishments meted out were fitting; but why were the innocent ashamed?"

Confucius answered: "If the people are kept in line by means of the rites, then they all will have a sense of shame.[12] When punishment is applied with the object of ending the need for punishment,[13] then the people will be intimidated."

Wen-tzu said: "It seems that at present the method of keeping the people in line by means of punishment is no longer sufficient to control them, so how could the rites be applied for that purpose?"

Confucius answered: "If one were to take a charioteer to illustrate the method of keeping the people in line by means of the rites, then it is an instance of the use of reins. If one were to take charioteering to illustrate the method of keeping the people in line by means of punishment, then it is an instance of the use of a whip.[14] To make the horse move one way while just holding the reins in the other direction is the mark of a fine charioteer. When the charioteer uses the whip without working the reins, the horse loses its way."

Wen-tzu said: "Drawing on the same metaphor, I should say that a horse will surely be quicker if the right hand of the charioteer holds the reins and his left hand holds the whip. Is it not so? If the charioteer uses reins alone without a whip, how would the horse be intimidated?"

Confucius answered: "I have heard that the excellent charioteers of old times held the reins like silk ribbons and the outside horses moved like dancers;[15] there was no need for the assistance of the whip. That is why the ancients placed great emphasis on rites and tended to deemphasize punishment. For this reason the people followed their commands. At present the rites have fallen into desuetude and punishment is highly valued; therefore the people have become wayward and violent."

Wen-tzu said: "So how is it that the customs of Wu and Yüeh[16] include no rites at all, yet their people are well governed?"

Confucius answered: "According to the customs of Wu and Yüeh, males and females are not kept apart; they all bathe together in the river,[17] and they harass one another at the slightest provocation. Therefore punishment there is severe and yet unsuccessful due to the absence of the rites. The teaching of the Central Kingdoms is to distinguish the exterior from the interior in order to separate male from female, and to differentiate utensils and clothing in order to distinguish ranks and classes. Therefore the people were sincere and law-abiding. Their punishment is lenient and yet successful because they possess the rites."

4.3 (A, 26b3) Confucius said: "Clothing and food are the means by which people sustain life. But if the superiors do not teach the people, the people will fail to earn their livelihoods.[18] They will suffer the ravages of famine and cold, and there will be few who will not slip into misdeeds. Therefore the ancients felt hatred toward brigands but would not kill them. In our day, however, rulers do not take the time to teach first, but kill at once. That is why penalties are exacted without good results, punishment is widely extended, yet crime does not diminish. Newborn babes sense the affection for their parents because of their parents' solicitous concern for them. How much more is this true if those who govern promote those who are worthy and discard those who are not, and thereby transform the people for the better. If these two approaches[19] are thoroughly grasped, then the worst type[20] of brigandage is the first to cease.''

4.4 (A, 27a2) The *Book of Documents* says,

> Follow the penal laws of Yin[21] that are based on principles.[22]

Tzu-chang asked: ''What does this mean?''
Confucius answered: ''The meaning is not losing the principle. At present the feudal lords do not share the same virtue, and every ruler follows different laws. Legal decisions display the absence of norms, and personal opinion becomes the frame of reference for court decisions. That is why there is difficulty in understanding the law.''[23]

Tzu-chang asked: ''Is there a difference between those who were versed in law in ancient times and those of the present?''

Confucius answered: ''Those who were versed in law in ancient times managed to avoid litigation, while in our age they concentrate on holding the guilty captive.[24] The method of holding the guilty captive shows little consideration for others, while the avoidance of litigation displays a far-reaching method of crime prevention. Displaying little consideration for others is just one step removed from an excessive use of punishment, while a far-reaching method of crime prevention results in a perfectly ordered foundation. The *Book of Documents* says, 'Reverently apply the five punishments, so as to fulfill the three virtues.'[25] The meaning of these words is that paying careful attention to punishment leads one to become virtuous.''

4.5 (A, 27b2) The *Book of Documents* says,

> Examine the arguments that should be followed, and those that should not be followed.[26]

Confucius said: ''In dealing with people, the *chün-tzu* avoids speaking to some, but there are none to whom he does not listen. How much more true is it the case in hearing litigation? One should examine the arguments to their fullest.[27] Among those who hear litigation, there are some who go according to the actual evidence and some who go according to the arguments.[28] One cannot decide a case according to the arguments but rather in accordance with the actual evidence.[29] The *Book of Documents* says,

> When men commit small crimes which are not mischances, but purposed, themselves doing what is contrary to the laws, intentionally, though their crimes be but small, you may not but put them to death. But in the case of great crimes, which

are not purposed, but from mischance and misfortune, accidental, if the offenders confess unreservedly their guilt, you may not put them to death."[30]

4.6 (A, 27b7) Tseng Tzu asked about the art of hearing litigation.

Confucius answered: "It has three major rules: when handling a case, one must be lenient. The art of handling a case leniently rests in the examination of the facts. The art of the examination of facts resides in righteousness. Therefore a hearing conducted without leniency is a disordered hearing. A lenient hearing that does not make use of examination is a neglectful hearing. A hearing that makes use of the examination of facts and still does not reach the core of righteousness is a partial hearing.[31] If hearings are partial, the people become resentful. Therefore those who excel at hearing litigation do not let the case go beyond the arguments. The arguments do not go beyond the actual evidence, and actual evidence does not go beyond righteousness. The *Book of Documents* says,

> In graver and lighter cases, you should compare the offenses. Do not admit false and disorderly arguments."[32]

4.7 (A, 28a6) The *Book of Documents* says:

> With compassion and reverence settle the cases.[33]

Chung Kung asked: "What does this mean?"

Confucius answered: "Those who heard litigation in ancient times paid special attention to the poor and the low. They felt sorry for the fatherless, the childless, the widowers and widows, the old and weak, the abnormal, and those who had no one to speak in their behalf. Even after they have established the actual evidence, they could not help pitying them. The dead cannot be brought back to life, nor the amputated parts of the body be rejoined.[34] If the old are punished it is considered unconscionable.[35] If the weak are punished it is considered cruelty. If accidental misdeeds are not pardoned it is considered arbitrary. Treating mistakes as minor offenses is considered harmful.[36] Therefore, forgiving misdeeds and pardoning minor offenses so that the old and the weak are spared from punishment is the Way of the former kings. The *Book of Documents* says: 'When capital punishment is doubtful and remitted.'[37] And again it says: 'Rather than put to death an innocent person you will run the risk of irregularity and error.' "[38]

4.8 (A, 28b5) The *Book of Documents* says:

> Deal with them as if you were protecting infants.[39]

Tzu-Chang asked: "Is it possible to hear litigation in this manner?"
Confucius answered: "Of course. Those who heard litigation in ancient

On Punishment

times detested the criminal intent but not the criminals themselves. They used to look for good reasons to keep criminals alive, and only when they failed did they punish them, and then the ruler had to review the case together with his ministers[40] to show that he loved the people and that he considered it a grave step to abandon them. Those who hear litigation nowadays do not detest the notion of crime but the criminals themselves. They look for good reasons to kill them, which is the opposite of the Way of the ancients."

4.9 (A, 29a2) A subject of the Meng clan rebelled. Wu Po[41] asked Confucius: "What do you think of it?"

Confucius answered: "The world does not tolerate a rebellious subject. Wait for a while and he will return by himself." Thirty days later the rebel came back to the Meng clan. Wu Po wanted to seize him and presented the case to the Master.

The Master said: "You are wrong! Your attitude toward your subjects is found wanting in terms of the rites with which one shows personal respect. That is why he ran away from you. Now he has returned by himself, so that his guilt might be wiped out by his return. What, then, is the point of seizing him? If you treat your subjects with cultivated rites, then even if any of your subjects runs away, where would he go?"[42] Wu Po therefore desisted.

CHAPTER
5

RECORDED QUESTIONS
(Chi-wen)

5.1 (A, 30a2)   Once while the Master was at leisure, he sighed audibly. Tzu-ssu[1] bowed to the ground twice and begged leave to ask a question: "Is it because you are thinking of uncultivated descendants who will eventually disgrace their ancestors that you sigh, or is it because you regret that you have not attained the revered Way of Yao and Shun?"

The Master answered: "You are just a child; how could you fathom my frame of mind?"

Tzu-ssu responded: "While serving your meals I have often heard you teaching that the son who is unable to carry the firewood chopped by his father[2] is called unworthy.[3] I have often pondered this, and it is a cause of great anguish and malaise for me."

The Master laughed with delight and said: "Indeed so. I need no longer worry. A generation that does not abandon its mission will most probably become prosperous."

5.2 (A, 30a8)   Tzu-ssu asked the Master: "Why is it that all rulers realize that it is best to put the worthy into service, yet they fail to employ the worthy?"

The Master answered: "It is not because rulers are not willing to employ the worthy. The reason why they keep losing capable people is that the manner in which they appoint officials is not clear-sighted. These rulers respond to praise with reward and to criticism with punishment. The worthy cannot maintain their position in such an atmosphere."

5.3 (A, 30b4)   Tzu-ssu asked the Master: "I[4] have heard you proclaiming that the best method of rule for rectifying customs and transforming people is by means of rites and music. Kuan-tzu,[5] however, made law supreme, ruled the state of Ch'i with it, and was dubbed a benevolent man by all under

Heaven. The meaning of this is that although law functions differently than rites and music, it brings about the very same results. Why must you, then, insist on rites and music?"

The Master answered: "The transforming influence of Yao and Shun has endured unbroken for a hundred consecutive generations, because benevolence and righteousness have a long-lasting moral force. Now concerning Kuan Chung's making the law supreme, when he himself died, his law passed into disuse. It was strict but lacking in mercy. If one possesses Kuan Chung's knowledge, it is sufficient to establish the law; but if one's capacity is less than that of Kuan Chung and one makes the law supreme, misrule must set in."

5.4 (A, 31a3)   Tzu-ssu questioned the Master: "Things have their inherent forms and their applied categories. Events have their truthfulness and their falsity. By what path should one explore the necessary distinctions between them?"

The Master answered: "It should derive from one's own mind. The essential spirit of the mind is what is called[6] sagacity. To deduce the underlying patterns of phenomena and to pursue the principle to the end, and not to be perplexed by any particular that does not fit, and to generalize the outcome of the examination, is something that even the sage is hard put to do."[7]

5.5 (A, 31a6)   Chao Chien-tzu[8] sent a messenger to invite the Master to the court. The Master was on his way, but when he reached the Yellow River, he heard that Tou Ming-tu and Shun Hua[9] had been put to death.[10] He thereupon turned his carriage around and went immediately back to Wei, making a stop in Tsou.[11] At that point he strummed his lute and sang:

> The Way of Chou has declined,
> Rites and music have deteriorated,
> The tradition of Wen and Wu has fallen.
> What, then, is there for me to follow?
> Everywhere you go under Heaven
> There is no land in which to find a refuge,
> The phoenix[12] goes unrecognized,
> And owls[13] are cherished as treasures.
> I was anxiously concerned,
> And my heart was deeply grieved
> When the Master of the Royal Chariots[14] ordered me to ride
> As I made my way to T'ang.[15]
> The Yellow River lay vast before me,
> With its inexhaustible fish.
> I approached the ford and did not cross it,
> But turned my carriage-shaft away, stopping at Tsou.

Pained by the dissipation of the Way,
And lamenting the plight of this injustice,[16]
Soaring from Wei,
I Returned to my former hut,
Doing as I pleased,
At last, oh! what happiness.

5.6 (A, 31b8) Duke Ai sent a messenger with presents to go to Wei and invite the Master. But, as it turned out, he was not able to give the Master any office. The Master therefore wrote the following "Song of the Hill and Mound":[17]

I climb the hill and
Steep are its slopes,
The Way of Benevolence is close at hand,
Yet seems far when it is sought.
And so I strayed irretrievably,
Becoming entangled of my own accord in straitened circumstances,
Deeply sighing I turned back to ponder
On T'ai Mountain,[18]
Dense and solid in its loftiness.
At its side stands Liang-fu Mountain;[19]
Brambles fill its paths.
I climb its paths, there are no roads,
I would cut a path, but I have no ax.
My worries are endlessly entangled,
There is nothing but to sigh forever,
Stream of drumming tears.

5.7 (A, 32b6) The King of Ch'u[20] sent a messenger with presents of gold and silk to invite the Master to the court. Tsai Yü and Jan Yu[21] remarked: "From now on our Master's Way will be put into practice." And so they requested an appearance before the Master and asked him: "T'ai Kung[22] was diligent but his ambition had been unfulfilled for eighty years when he finally met King Wen.[23] When compared with Hsü Yu,[24] which of the two was more worthy?"[25]

The Master answered: "Hsü Yu was a man who perfected himself in isolation, while T'ai Kung extended benefit to all under Heaven. In our time, however, there is no ruler of King Wen's caliber; so even if a T'ai Kung were alive today, what ruler could appreciate him?" The Master thereupon composed the following song:

> When the Great Way is dormant,
> The Rites are[26] the only foundation,
> The wise run for cover,
> Prepared to wait for the right moment.
> All under Heaven is the same,
> So where would I go?

5.8 (A, 32b5) Ch'u-shang, one of Shu Sun's[27] charioteers, gathered firewood in the countryside and caught a creature that none of his men could identify.[28] Because Shu Sun thought that the creature was inauspicious, he threw it away in Wu-fu Lane.[29] Jan Yu told the Master about it, saying: "This creature has the body of a hornless deer, but with a fleshy horn. Surely it is an evil creature not come from Heaven?"

The Master said: "Where is this creature now? I have to see it." Then he went to see it and said to Kao Ch'ai[30] his charioteer: "Judging from what Ch'iu[31] has said, this creature is probably the *lin*."[32] And when they arrived there and looked at the creature, it was in fact so.

Yen Yen[33] asked: "Among the creatures that fly and those that run, the phoenix and the lin are respected but rarely seen. May I ask, was the appearance of the lin at this time a reflection of any individual in particular?"

The Master answered: "If the Son of Heaven manifests virtue everywhere and the state of great peace is within reach, this is preceded by the good omens of the lin, the phoenix, the turtle, and the dragon.[34] At present the venerated house of Chou is facing extinction and there is no real ruler under Heaven. So by whose influence would the lin come?" The Master then continued in tears: "I am to human beings what the lin is to other beasts. The lin appeared and immediately died, just as my Way is reaching its end." And so he sang the following song:

> In the age of T'ang and Yü[35]
> The lin and the phoenix roamed about.
> Today is not their time,
> What would they come to seek?
> Ah lin, ah lin!
> Sad is my heart.

CHAPTER

6

THE VARIOUS DOCTRINES AND THE TEACHINGS[1] OF THE SAGE
(Tsa-hsün)

6.1 (A, 34a2) Tzu-shang[2] asked about the practice of the various doctrines.[3] Tzu-ssu answered: "It was my late Master's[4] instruction that learning depends upon the sage's teaching to fulfill the student's inherent capacity, just as sharpening depends on the whetstone to bring out the perfection of the blade. Therefore the teaching of the Master has its point of origin in the study of the *Book of Odes* and the *Book of Documents*, and its culmination in rites and music.[5] The various doctrines do not partake of this fundamental learning, so what is the point of asking about them?"

6.2 (A, 34a6) Tzu-ssu said to Tzu-shang: "Po, I was once submerged in deep thought, but I could not fully grasp the meaning of it. However, when I applied myself to study, I gained a sense of awakening. Once I was standing on tiptoes and gazing off afar, but I failed to see what I was looking for. However, when I climbed to a higher place, I was able to see it. In this sense, although we possess our basic nature, we have to improve upon it through study in order to avoid falling into error."[6]

6.3 (A, 34b2) Hsien-tzu[7] asked Tzu-ssu: "I have heard that people who possess an equal reputation seek each other out, and that those whose personal aspirations are the same are fond of each other. Now when your late Master[8] met Tzu-ch'an[9] he served him like an elder brother. Yet the people of that time called Tzu-ch'an a benevolent man, while reserving the term 'sage' for the Master. Does this mean that the Way of the sage was subservient to that of benevolence and love? Since it is not clear to me which of these two figures was superior to the other, I pose the question to you."

Tzu-ssu answered: "Right. Your question is like that formerly posed by

Chi-sun to Tzu-yu.[10] The answer of Tzu-yu to this question was: 'To compare the virtues of benevolence and love of Tzu-ch'an with the qualities of the Master is like comparing irrigation water with abundant rain.[11] Is this not so?'

"K'ang-tzu[12] said: 'When Tzu-ch'an died the men of Cheng threw their jade pendants from their girdles, and the women, their pearls. The weeping in the streets lasted for three whole months and the lute lay idle. Nevertheless, I have not heard that the people of Lu acted in the same manner when the Master died. What is the reason for this?'

"Tzu-yu answered: 'When irrigation water reaches a place, it quickens life there. Places where it does not reach remain lifeless. That is why all people know what it brings them. Nevertheless, there is nothing greater than the power of abundant rain to life, because the bounty bestowed upon the people by it is all-pervasive. Yet no one seems to recognize the source of it. A man of the highest virtue does not display his virtue, that is why he is considered to have no virtue.'[13] Chi-sun agreed with that."

Hsien-tzu concluded: "This is indeed so."

6.4 (A, 35a7) When Meng Tzu-chü[14] was still young he asked to appear before Tzu-ssu. Tzu-ssu met him and took great pleasure in his ideals and aspirations. Then he ordered Tzu-shang to attend to Meng Tzu-chü with all due forms of respect. Tzu-shang was reluctant to do so and when the visitor withdrew he ventured: "I have heard the saying that a gentleman would not see anyone who was not properly introduced, and a proper woman would not get married without the due form of matchmaking. This youngster, Meng, was not introduced, and still you let him appear before you. For a great man like yourself to take pleasure in his company and bestow respect upon him is beyond my comprehension. May I ask for an explanation?"

Tzu-ssu answered: "Quite so. Formerly, when I was accompanying the Master on his way to T'an, we met Ch'eng-tzu[15] on the road. Under the inclined canopies of their carriages, they conversed all day long, and when they parted the Master ordered Tzu-lu to bring a bundle of silk as a present for Ch'eng-tzu. He did so because he considered Ch'eng-tzu's Way the same as that of a superior man. Now, Meng Tzu-chü is a youngster; nevertheless, in his speech he is deferential to Yao and Shun, and his joy in benevolence and righteousness seems to be part of his nature. This is a very rare thing in our generation. To serve him, therefore, seems possible—how much more so to bestow respect upon him. This is quite beyond your capability."

6.5 (A, 35b8) When Tzu-ssu was in Lu he sent a messenger with a letter to inquire after Tzu-shang in Wei. After bowing twice facing north, Tzu-shang accepted the letter, which he then read in a respectful manner. After having read the letter, he gave the messenger a formal dinner, wrote a letter of reply, returned to the courtyard, and, facing north, bowed twice and gave the letter to the messenger. Immediately after the messenger received the letter, Tzu-shang retired. The messenger returned to Lu and asked Tzu-ssu: "Master, you gave me the letter addressed to Tzu-shang while standing in the hall facing south. After completing that formality you then saw me off. Tzu-shang, however, gave me the letter addressed to you with a simple bow in the courtyard and did not see me off. Why so?"

Tzu-ssu answered: "To bow and not see someone off is a sign of respect. To see someone off who has come as a messenger is to treat him according to the courtesy of host to guest."[16]

6.6 (A, 36a6) There was a man in Lu who failed to observe the proper condolence ritual for a deceased clansman. Someone said to him: "According to the rites: 'There was an officer who punished neglect of the rules pertaining to the removal of the cap during mourning, and neglect of the rules pertaining to condolence among relations.'[17] In the light of this, how should we deal with your failure to condole over your relative?" The man answered: "I acted on the basis of the fact that he was only a very distant relative of mine."

When Tzu-ssu heard about it he said: "This is an extreme case of denial of one's debt to ancestral bounty. Formerly Chi-sun presented the following question to the Master:[18] 'Can a clan that has lasted for a hundred generations be extinct?'

"The Master answered: 'The honorable heritage of that clan cannot be extinct if its various members maintain their clan roots intact. Therefore people of the same family roots formed a clan whose members were united through the various degrees of their kinship.[19] Even someone as exalted as the ruler could not renounce his blood relations, and so he treated them with reverence and affection. He used to associate all his clan members in the feasting, defined their places, and made distinctions between them by their order of descent,[20] so that even after ten thousand generations there could be no marriages of clan members with one another. Such was the Way of unswerving faithfulness.' "[21]

6.7 (A, 36b6) Once when Duke Mu of Lu[22] paid a visit to Tzu-ssu he said: "I am not virtuous. It has been three years since I have succeeded my late father in his grand undertaking, and in all that time I have not been able to establish a good reputation of my own. Moreover, I would like to conceal my late father's evils by making public his good deeds, and bring it about that those who discuss such things will transmit something about him. I would like to receive your instruction on this matter."

Tzu-ssu answered: "I have heard that it was not that Shun and Yü's attitude toward their fathers did not express such a wish; they just did not consider

Teachings of the Sage   105

the pettiness of private sentiment to be as worthy as the eminence of public righteousness. This, it is said, is why they did not dare to act selfishly. So if you think that my responsibility is to teach for appearance's sake, you will certainly not find it in my words.''

The Duke said: ''But to ponder such things may be of benefit for the people.''

Tzu-ssu said: ''If you wish to have a heart that is generous to the people, then nothing is better than the elimination of all unlawful activities. Dismantle the palaces in which nobody lives and give their material to the destitute among the people. Confiscate the salaries of your favorites and relieve the poor and oppressed. Do not let people become sorrowful and resentful, and your fame will live on for future generations. Is this not another way to accomplish your aim?''

The Duke said: ''That is true.''

6.8 (A, 37b1) Hsien-tzu asked Tzu-ssu: ''When Yen Hui asked the Master about the governing of a state, the Master answered: 'Follow the calendar of the Hsia.'[23] If so then were both the Yin and Chou dynasties wrong in choosing a different first month[24] of the year?''[25]

Tzu-ssu said: ''The Hsia method of calculation was in accord with Heaven.[26] It was identical with that of Yao and Shun. The kings of the Yin and Chou, however, attacked their predecessors and changed the mandate in response to the decree of Heaven. Consequently they changed the previous calendar in order to make the point that this represented a new beginning in the time of Heaven, and therefore they refused to follow the system of their predecessors. When one succeeds a ruler through abdication, one adopts the previous system of rulership. But when one receives a mandate directly from Heaven, then one changes the previous system, instilling inspiration into his activities, just like the Way of Heaven in its own process of transformation. Among the most righteous systems adopted by the three dynasties, that of Hsia was the most correct. That is why the Master said what he did.''[27]

6.9 (A, 37b8) Duke Mu asked Tzu-ssu: ''Are there constant regulations concerning the installation of the crown prince?''

Tzu-ssu answered: ''There are such regulations in the Canons of the Duke of Chou.''[28]

Duke Mu said: ''Formerly King Wen ignored his first rightful heir and installed his second son as his heir.[29] The Viscount of Wei[30] ignored his grandson and installed his younger brother as heir. What was the legal principle governing these cases?''

Tzu-ssu answered: ''Since the people of Yin were men of inner substance, they honored those worthy of honor. That is why the Viscount of Wei installed his younger brother as heir. Since the people of Chou were men of cultural refinement, they treated their relatives with proper deference. That is why they installed their sons as heirs. Each dynasty acted in accordance with the rites. But since men of cultural refinement and men of inner substance are not the same, their rites were also different. Now, the case of King Wen, who ignored his first rightful heir and installed his second son instead, was a case of expediency.''

Duke Mu said: ''If indeed we persist in acting according to expediency, it would not be the sage alone who could install heirs, but only those whom he considered worthy or those whom he loved.''

Tzu-ssu said: ''The principle of expediency is not the basis for the sage's teaching. That is why the sage establishes his rule and hands down the laws. Those who follow his system do so because they are honored. Now, as for those who are unable to refrain from transgression, what difference would any system make to them?''

The Duke said: ''What do you think of a system of installing heirs in which the worthy are set aside for the sake of the sage, and the stupid are set aside for the sake of the worthy?''

Tzu-ssu answered: ''It is the sage alone who installs another sage as his heir. This was no doubt the case with King Wen. However, if kings are not of the same caliber as King Wen, then each would consider those he holds dear to be worthy and thus equivalent to his legal heir. So how can they be expected to distinguish between candidates? When there is absolutely no way for the king to discern the worthy from the stupid, his elders and entire staff should be consulted, and prognosticators should look for a guiding sign in the ancestral shrine. In such cases, expediency, as well, is admissible.''

6.10 (A, 38b4) Meng K'o[31] asked *what ought to be given priority in shepherding the people.*

Tzu-ssu said: ''First and foremost so that they will profit.''

Meng K'o said: ''What is the point of mentioning the word 'profit' when all that matters is that the superior man teaches the people that there is benevolence and righteousness and nothing more.''[32]

Tzu-ssu said: ''Benevolence and righteousness are certainly the means of causing the people to profit. If superiors are not benevolent then those below them will not find their proper stations. If superiors are not righteous, then those below them will be inclined to cause disorder. These are extreme cases of not profiting. That is why the *Book of Changes* says: 'Profit is the result of the harmony of righteousness.'[33] And again it says: 'Function profitably and calm the self in order to exalt virtue.'[34] These are extreme cases of profiting.''[35]

CHAPTER 7

LIVING IN WEI
(Chü Wei)

7.1 (A, 41a2) When Tzu-ssu was living in Wei he spoke to the Prince of Wei¹ about Kou Pien² and said: "This man's capacity is sufficient to lead five hundred chariots. If you entrust your troops and armies to the command of this man you will have no match under Heaven."

The Prince of Wei said: "I know that his capacity is sufficient to command my troops and armies. Nevertheless, once when he was a commissioner in charge of collecting taxes from the people, he took two eggs from someone and ate them. This is why I do not wish to employ him."

Tzu-ssu said: "The manner in which the sage appoints officials is similar to the way a master carpenter uses lumber by selecting the good portion and discarding the bad. Therefore the excellent craftsman does not discard an excellent piece of timber of an arm's girth simply because a few feet of it are rotten. Why? Because he knows that the unusable parts are negligible, and that eventually the tree may become a utensil of immeasurable value. Now you, although you live in an age of warring states, select men of limited accomplishments, and because of two eggs you discard a general who can be the defender of your country. This decision of yours had better not become known in the neighboring states."

The Prince of Wei bowed twice and said: "I respectfully accept your teaching."

7.2 (A, 40b4) When Tzu-ssu arrived in Ch'i he was standing in attendance next to the favorite minister of the Prince of Ch'i,³ who had a beautiful beard and eyebrows. The Prince of Ch'i pointed at his minister and said to Tzu-ssu with a laugh: "If external appearances could be exchanged I would not hesitate to let you have my minister's beard and eyebrows."

Tzu-ssu said: "That is not my wish. My only wish is to find a ruler who cultivates the rites and righteousness, and who makes the people prosper. In that case I will have to send my wife and children to his territory, to join the line of those who come to him with their children strapped on their backs.[4] This will be enormously rewarding. Now if we refer to my lack of a beard and moustache, it is no cause of grief to me. Yao of old was ten feet tall and his eyebrows were of eight colors. He was truly a sage. Shun was slightly more than eight feet and his face was beardless. And he, too, was a sage. Yü, T'ang, Wen, Wu, and the Duke of Chou were diligent in their thinking and industrious in their physical activities: among them one had a twisted arm, so that he could only look upward, and another had hairless legs and a hunched back. And they, after all, were all sages.[5] It is not because of one's beard, eyebrows, or beautiful moustache that one is referred to with deference. The wisdom or sagehood of a man consists in his virtue, not in his external appearance. Furthermore, the fact that my late Master lacked a beard and eyebrows was due to the natural constitution of his body, and even so the kings and feudal lords in the entire world did not diminish the respect they had for him because of his appearance. To argue from this point of view, I would be troubled only by the imperfection[6] of my virtue. I will not be distressed because I do not have luxuriant hair.''

7.3 (A, 41a8) Tzu-ssu said to Tzu-shang: "It is not only ideals and aspirations that can motivate one to avoid the honor bestowed by dukes and lords and the wealth and reverence that is bestowed by the people. Should not the idea of desirelessness alone guide the formation of such ideals and aspirations? Wearing colorful silk and luxurious dress does not serve any purpose other than that of warming of the body. Eating the three sacrificial animals[7] or cattle does not serve any other purpose than that of filling the belly.[8] If one knows how to take what is proper, then one will know contentment and not consider one's ideals and aspirations to be a heavy burden.''

7.4 (A, 41b5) Tseng-tzu said to Tzu-ssu: "In the days when I followed the Master on his travels among the feudal lords, he never failed to observe the rites befitting a subject, and yet the Way of the sage did not prevail. Now I observe that you have the attitude of one who lives in contempt of temporal rulers. Is this not unacceptable behavior?''

Tzu-ssu answered: "Times change, generations differ, everyone has his way of adjusting to the standards of his age. At the time of my late Master, although the institutions of Chou were in ruin, the relative status of rulers and subjects was still very firmly established. Superior and inferior officials upheld each other like a single unified body. When anyone wished to put his own Way into effect without observing the rites in pursuing this goal, he did not gain admittance into any court service. Nowadays, all the feudal lords under Heaven want only to engage in violence and vie to enlist champion warriors to serve as their personal protectors. In these circumstances, whoever gains the services of gentlemen prospers, and whoever loses them perishes. If I do not value myself highly, in such times people will look down upon me. If I do not hold myself in esteem, people will treat me as worthless. Shun and Yü yielded power, while T'ang and Wu mustered troops. These examples are not contradictory, but are rather a reflection of the period in question."

7.5 (A, 42a7) When Tzu-ssu was in Ch'i, Yin Wen-tzu[9] begot a son who was not worthy of his father. Once Yin Wen-tzu became furious and teased and flogged him. Then he said to Tzu-ssu: "This is not my son. My wife has probably violated her wifely honor. I will send her away."

Tzu-ssu said: "If we adopt your point of view, then the imperial consorts of Yao and Shun would also have been held under suspicion. These two emperors represented the flowering of sagehood, and still their sons, Tan Chu and Shang Chün,[10] fell short of the level of even ordinary men. This example shows that you cannot think of your son in terms of his worthiness of you. In most cases, sons take after their fathers, and this is a constant principle of human experience. When a wise father happens to have a stupid son, it is a matter of Heaven's design. It is not the fault of your wife."

Yin Wen-tzu said: "That is enough, Master, I beg you to say no more words. I will keep her with me."

7.6 (A, 42a7) Meng K'o asked: "Can the Way of Yao, Shun, Wen, and Wu be attained through concerted effort?"

Tzu-ssu answered: "They were men, and I am a man. If one deferentially cites their words and follows in their footsteps, meditating on their examples at night and acting in their light during the day—just like the farmer following the seasons, and just like the merchant seeking profit in the most unrelenting and attentive manner—how could one fail to reach the goal?"

7.7 (A, 43a3) Tzu-ssu said to Meng K'o: "One who considers himself great and still does not cultivate that which makes him great is not great. One who considers himself unique and still does not cultivate that which makes him unique is not unique. Therefore if the superior man exalts his own conduct, no one is able to match him; and when he sets his aspirations distant, no one is able to reach him. When the rites are observed in intercourse with people, they will not dare be negligent. When proper speech is used in communicating with people, they will not be offended. These, perhaps, are the means by which one exalts and sets distant."

7.8 (A, 43a8) Shen Hsiang[11] asked: "The people of Yin ruled by virtue of their lineage from Hsieh[12] to T'ang.[13] The people of Chou ruled by virtue of their lineage from Ch'i[14] to King Wu.[15] Both of these persons[16] were the descendants of Emperor K'u.[17] The people of Chou honored King T'ai,[18] King Chi,[19] and King Wen[20] with the posthumous title of 'King,' while the people of Yin were the only ones who did not honor their founders in this way. What was the reason for that?''

Tzu-ssu said: "It is due to the difference between inner substance and cultural refinement. The people of Chou initiated their imperial enterprise by honoring King T'ai with the posthumous title of 'King.'"

Shen Hsiang went on and said: "When King Wen received the mandate, he put an end to the dispute between the states of Yü and Jui.[21] He launched a punitive expedition against the state of Ch'ung[22] and forced the Ch'üan tribes to retreat.[23] For this he was posthumously titled 'King.' But why were King T'ai and Chi posthumously titled 'King'?"

Tzu-ssu answered: "When the Ti tribes[24] attacked King T'ai,[25] King T'ai summoned the elders and asked them for their counsel: 'Why do the Ti tribes come upon us?' The elders replied: 'They want our food and property.' King T'ai said: 'Give it to them.' The elders gave them so much that nothing was left. But the Ti tribes did not cease their attacks. King T'ai asked the elders once again: 'What do the Ti tribes want?' The elders replied: 'They want our land.' King T'ai said: 'Give it to them.' The elders said: 'Aren't you going to act on behalf of the altars of the gods of earth and grain[26]?' King T'ai answered: 'These altars were meant for the sustenance of the people; one cannot turn what was meant for the sustenance of the people into a source of their destruction!' The elders said: 'Even if you give up the altars of the gods of earth and grain, are you going to give up your ancestral temples as well?' King T'ai answered: 'The case of my ancestral temples is a private matter. I cannot turn my private matters into a source of harm for the people.' And without further ado, he set out, holding the whip in his own hands. He crossed the Liang Mountains and stopped at the foot of Mount Ch'i. The people of Pin packed their belongings and ran after King T'ai with three thousand chariots. Once they stopped, they built the City of Three Thousand Chariots.[27] This is a basic principle of the Way of a true king. King Ch'eng[28] thereupon honored King T'ai with the posthumous title of 'King.' King Chi was King T'ai's son. He received the patrimony and broadened the foundations of rule that his father had established. The fact that he, too, was honored in the same way by the posthumous title of 'King' seems quite reasonable."

7.9 (A, 44b1) Yang K'e[29] asked Tzu-ssu: "The ancient imperial rulers[30] divided[31] all under Heaven into two halves, which they entrusted to the two dukes[32] to rule. The two dukes were referred to as the two counts.[33] Now the rule-sequence of the generations of the Chou's royal line that begins after Hou-

Living in Wei

chi³⁴ had been granted the title of King, through the times his descendants took possession of states, and up to the period of King T'ai, King Chi, and King Wen, is the sequence of generations of the feudal lords. So how could King Wen be considered the Count of the West?"³⁵

Tzu-ssu said: "I have heard it from Tzu-hsia: when the Yin ruled, during the time of Emperor Ti-i,³⁶ King Chi, having made himself worthy of the rank of the ninth emblematic figure,³⁷ attained the title of 'Count.' He also received the Jade Libation-cup and the Black Millet Herb-wine as special grants.³⁸ Therefore King Wen followed him and was given the right to attack on his own initiative. This is what a 'Count' was taken to be in the time of the feudal lords. It is similar to the function the Duke of Chou and Duke Shao filled while they held the status of rulers."

7.10 (A, 44b8) When Tzu-ssu was sixteen³⁹ he arrived in Sung. Yüeh Shuo,⁴⁰ a counsellor in Sung, talked with him about learning and said: "In the *Book of Documents*, each of the four chapters that make up the *Book of Yü*⁴¹ and the *Book of Hsia*⁴² is excellent. But then all the following chapters, which end with the chapters 'The Speech at Pi'⁴³ and 'The Speech of the Duke of Ch'in,'⁴⁴ are mere imitations of the words pronounced by Yao and Shun, and they are not of the same caliber."

Tzu-ssu answered: "Historical events change and have their own limits; what is right is determined by the context of the event. Suppose you could make the Duke of Chou exchange times with Yao and Shun; his book⁴⁵ would be the same as theirs."

Yüeh Shuo said: "The writing of books seeks to edify the people. Simplicity is the highest literary principle, and still there are writers who deliberately include difficult terms in their books⁴⁶ and thereby force complexity upon the reader. Is this not true?"

Tzu-ssu answered: "The basic ideas of the *Book of Documents* are structured with profound mystery, and its textual meaning is based upon the explanation of ancient words. That is why the ancients considered the book canonical. Now your words, sir, are similar to those previously pronounced by a commoner in the narrow lanes of Lu. My answer to him was as follows: 'The Way is transmitted to those who have the ability to comprehend. The Way would be disgraced if it were transmitted to those who do not share this ability.' The similarity between you and that man, sir, is amazing."

Yüeh Shuo left in displeasure and said, "That youngster has insulted me."

One of his followers said: "Even though Sung is the K'ungs' old home,⁴⁷ they have been hostile to us for generations. Let us strike him." Consequently they surrounded Tzu-ssu. When the Prince of Sung heard this, he intervened to save Tzu-ssu.

When Tzu-ssu was free of danger he said: "When King Wen was hard-pressed in Yu-li[48] he wrote the *Book of Changes*. My forefather,[49] while humiliated in Ch'en and Ts'ai,[50] wrote the *Spring and Autumn Annals*. In Sung, while hard-pressed, how could I avoided writing?" He thereupon wrote the *Doctrine of the Mean* in forty-nine chapters.[51]

CHAPTER

8

IMPERIAL TOURS OF INSPECTION
(Hsün-shou)

8.1 (A, 3, 46a2)   When Tzu-ssu was traveling to Ch'i, Ch'en Chuang-po[1] joined him in climbing Mt. T'ai. They looked at some stone inscriptions engraved by an emperor of ancient times during a tour of inspection. Ch'en-tzu said: "I am not fortunate enough to live in an age in which emperors and kings perform the Feng and Shan sacrifices."[2]

Tzu-ssu said: "That is because you do not truly wish it. Nowadays, the royal house of Chou is declining, and the feudal lords do not have an overlord. If the kind of righteousness shown in Ch'i becomes a model for her neighboring states, and if, accordingly, the virtuous among the descendants of kings Wen and Wu are upheld, the exploits of Duke Huan of Ch'i and Duke Wen of Chin[3] can be disregarded."

Ch'en-tzu said: "It is not that I am not pleased with this Way, but rather that my capacity is insufficient for it.[4] You are the descendant of a sage, and therefore I am eager to learn from you. May I ask about the rites with which the sage emperors and the enlightened kings of old performed their tours of inspection?"

Tzu-ssu said: "In most cases when one wants to learn, the intention is to put one's learning into practice. Now your intention[5] could not possibly be actualized, so what is the point of your request?"

Ch'en-tzu said: "Even though I am not quick-witted I take delight in the Way of the former kings. So what fault have you found in me that you deny me your words?"

Tzu-ssu thereupon informed him: "In ancient times, when the Son of Heaven was preparing his tour of inspection, he would first announce his impending departure in person in the shrines of his ancestors and fathers. Then he would order the scribe to announce it in the various temples, at the altars of the gods of earth and grain, and at the famous mountains and great rivers within his domain. The circuit of announcements took seven days. In the case of personal announcements, offerings of bullocks were made. When the announcements were made by the scribe, the offering was that of silks. Then he once again gave instructions to the prime minister and, after the sacrifice to the gods of the road[6] had been made, set forth and began his tour. Sometimes he would remove the tablets of the royal ancestor from the temple and carry them along in the sacrificial carriage of purity,[7] at every stop offering libations to his royal ancestor.[8] When in the course of his tour he reached one of the five sacred mountains or one of the four rivers,[9] sacrifices of bullocks and silks were made to them without fail. In the second month of the year, he made his tour of inspection to the East, up to the venerated Mt. Tai[10] where he offered the burnt-offering to the Supreme Ancestor[11] and the *wang*[b] sacrifice to the mountains and rivers, in their proper order.[12]

"Whenever he passed through the territories of the feudal lords, each one waited for him at the border of his territory. The Son of Heaven first asked the whereabouts of those who were a hundred years old, and then he paid them a visit of inquiry.[13] Afterward he had an audience with the feudal lord of the mountain-quarter.[14] If the feudal lord was meritorious and virtuous, noble rank was conferred on him and he was honored with robes, in compliance with the principle of *yang*.[15] If a feudal lord was without merit, then he would be demoted and he would be deprived of some of his territory, in compliance with the principle of *yin*. Then the Son of Heaven ordered the scribe to collect folk songs, in order to observe the people's disposition. Then he ordered the director of markets[16] to obtain a list of current prices. In this way, by becoming aware of the likes and dislikes of the people,[17] he could fathom their frame of mind.[18] He then ordered the superintendent of rites to rectify the system of laws, to adjust the weights and measures, to examine the various grades of clothing, and to put the cycles of seasons, months, and days into accord. When the Son of Heaven entered a domain of a ruler whose land was neglected, where the old were forsaken, the wise overlooked, and clutching men were in positions of power, the ruler of that place was degraded. In cases in which a ruler did not personally attend all the altars of the gods of the mountains, rivers, and earth and grain, he was degraded and deprived of some of his territory. In cases in which a ruler's land was neglected and his people were wandering about idly, acting without moral discipline—because of the absence of moral teaching—the ruler was dismissed. In cases in which the people were licentious and usurped authority, acting unlawfully—because of unlawfulness—the ruler was treated as a criminal. If, however, the Son of Heaven entered a domain of a ruler whose land was cultivated and opened for settlement, if the old were cared for, if the wise were honored, and if men of distinction were in a position of authority, then that ruler was rewarded.[19]

"Then the emperor went to inspect the South, in the fifth month getting as far as the Southern Mountain.[20] He then continued to inspect the West, in the eighth month, getting as far as the Western Mountain.[21] He then continued to inspect the North, in the eleventh month getting as far as the Northern Mountain.[22] The rites of all these tours of inspection were similar to those performed by the Son of Heaven in his tour toward the sacred Mt. Tai. Upon his return, the Son of Heaven lodged outside his court for three days. Then, in person, he reverently announced his return at the shrine of his ancestors and made an offering of bullocks. He then ordered the government officials[23] to announce his return in the various temples, at the altars of the gods of earth and grain, and at the famous mountains and great rivers in his domain, and only afterward did he appear in formal audience at the royal court. These were the rites performed by the enlightened kings in ancient times."

Ch'en-tzu said: "When feudal lords paid court to the Son of Heaven, or when they were to join in alliance under the feudal overlords of the domain, did they, too, announce their departure in their forefathers' temples, and at the mountains and rivers?"

Tzu-ssu replied, "They did."

Ch'en-tzu said: "If the king, during his tour of inspection, did not reach one of the four mountains, or if the feudal lords, while assembling with each other, did not cross their neighboring state, then were the same rites performed, or were they different?"

Tzu-ssu replied: "The royal domain of the Son of Heaven consisted of a thousand square li^b.[24] The territory of a duke or a marquis amounted to a hundred square $li,^b$ that of the earl to seventy square $li,^b$ and that of a viscount or baron to fifty square li^b.[25] This was a constant system applied by the Yü, Hsia, Yin, and Chou. If any one of the above nobles went beyond his specified territory, then the rites performed were not different from those of the tours of inspection, those of paying court, or those of the assembling of the feudal lords. As long as one did not cross the boundaries of his own territory, even while traveling, he was considered to be in his own state."

Ch'en-tzu said: "This is the righteous practice of the ancients. From now on I will acknowledge the fact that one who does not set his mind on learning is someone whose process of cultivation is superficial."

CHAPTER 9

THE MINISTER KUNG-I
(Kung-i)

9.1 (A, 48b3)   Among the people of Lu there was Kung-i Hsiu.¹ He polished his moral integrity and perfected his conduct. He was delighted in the Way and took deep pleasure in the study of antiquity. He was unmoved by glory and gain, and refused to serve the feudal lords. Tzu-ssu had friendly relations with him. Duke Mu, seeking Tzu-ssu's support to make Kung-i his chief minister, said to Tzu-ssu: "It is essential that Kung-i assist me. Tell him that I am ready to divide the state of Lu into three parts and let him have one."

Tzu-ssu replied: "If I deliver this message of yours, sir, then Kung-i will have all the more reason not to comply. If you are eager to recruit the worthy and are ready to adopt their plans, then even if you were to offer a meal of plain vegetables and water, I, too, would like to be under your influence. Nevertheless, you are only trying to lure a superior man with a distinguished position and substantial salary, and you do not intend to make true use of him. If Kung-i's intelligence were like that of a fish or a bird, then this plan of yours could be put into effect. But since this is not the case, then he will never in his life set foot in your court. Moreover, I am not a lackey and I am not obligated to hold a fishing rod for you and lower the hook in order to dislodge a gentleman who holds fast to his moral integrity."

9.2 (A, 49a5)   Lü-ch'iu Wen² foresaw that it was inevitable that the T'ien clan would surely endanger the state of C'hi. He therefore thought of rebelling and fleeing with the people of his town to Lu. When Duke Mu learned about this he said to Tzu-ssu: "If you can win his loyalty, I will cede you from my territory a town similar to the one he has."

Tzu-ssu replied: "Even though I am capable of winning his loyalty, this is something that by righteousness I cannot do."

The Duke said: "Why so?"

Tzu-ssu answered: "He was a minister in a state whose ruler was about to

The Minister Kung-i

fall. He found himself unable to support his ruler and instead chose to rebel. When treacherous ministers regulate states they are incapable of sacrificing themselves while among the defending forces, and so they desert their ruler. They are criminals deserving capital punishment. Now, I am not only in a position to punish this villain, and I am offered a reward to recruit him! This is something I cannot bear to do."

9.3 (A, 49b4)   Duke Mu asked Tzu-ssu: "I have heard that the sons of the P'ang Lan[3] clan are not filial. What do you think of their conduct?"

Tzu-ssu answered: "I have heard that the enlightened sovereign honors the worthy in his rule and thereby exalts virtue; he promotes the good and thereby encourages the people to act properly. If so, then who could resist this moral influence within the boundaries of his domain? As for minor infractions, these are matters that only small people pay heed to. It is beyond me why some people, instead of having full control over fundamentals, inquire after minor faults."

The Duke said: "I agree."

9.4 (A, 50a1)   Duke Mu said to Tzu-ssu: "There is someone who suspects that the Master's sayings which are recorded in your book are actually your very own words."

Tzu-ssu replied: "Among the sayings of my grandfather, which are recorded in my book, there are some that I have personally heard, and there are some that were brought to my attention by others. So even though my book consists of words that are not precisely the Master's, it does not fall short of the Master's ideas. So what was it in my book that led you to harbor doubts about it?"

The Duke said: "What the book undertakes is flawless."

Tzu-ssu said: "It has no errors because it consists of my forefather's ideas. Assuming that what you have previously said was correct, and the words in my book were actually all mine; and if, as well, these words were without errors, they would still be worthy of honor. But since the case is not so,[4] what is the point in doubting the nature of the book?"

9.5 (A, 50a8)   Duke Mu said to Tzu-ssu: "According to Hsien-tzu, you do not wish to be praised by people for doing good. Is this really so?"

Tzu-ssu replied: "This is not my true feeling. When I cultivate goodness I want people to be aware of it, and subsequently praise me for it. This would indicate that my doing good carries some moral influence. This intent of mine, however, cannot be actualized. Now if I were to cultivate goodness without anyone realizing it, then I would suffer defamation. In that case I would be defamed while trying to do good. This is something that I do not desire, but still it would be unavoidable. One who crows like a rooster all day long that he assiduously does good and says, 'I do not want people to realize what I am doing, I am afraid that people might praise me,' is what I would call either a hypocrite or a fool."

9.6 (A, 50a8)   Hu Wu-pao[5] said to Tzu-ssu: "It is because you are overly fond of greatness that no one in the world is able to accept you.[6] Don't you think you should, after all, go along with the standards of our age?"

Tzu-ssu replied: "I am not troubled by the question of greatness. What I am troubled by is the lack of greatness. The reason one seeks the acceptance of the world is that one wants to put the Way into effect. But if one has to destroy the Way in order to be accepted, then what is left to be put into effect? When greatness is not accepted, this is a matter of Destiny. To destroy greatness in order to seek acceptance is to be condemned. I will not change."

9.7 (A, 51a5)   While Tzu-ssu dwelt in poverty, a friend sent him a present of millet from which he accepted two cartloads. At the same time he found unacceptable a gift of a jar of wine and ten pieces of dry meat given by another man. That man said: "You, sir, accepted your friend's millet and rejected my wine and meat. That is, you rejected the lesser quantity and took the greater. This is entirely contrary to righteousness, and what you took to be your due indicates a failure to be satisfied. What was the basis for your action?"

Tzu-ssu replied: "This is true, but I was unfortunate that my poverty reached the point that my property was nearly destroyed and I was afraid I might have to cut off the sacrifices to my forefathers. The taking of millet meant alleviating the situation. Wine and preserved meat provide the wherewithal for feasting. With respect to my present lack of food, feasting is something contrary to righteousness. I was definitely not thinking of the matter in terms of portions. My act was based on righteousness." The man put his wine and meat on his shoulders and left.

9.8 (A, 51b5)   Duke Mu said to Tzu-ssu: "Is my state capable of flourishing?"

Tzu-ssu replied: "Yes."

The Duke said: "What would you suggest that I do about it?"

Tzu-ssu replied: "If both you and your counsellors take the ruling methods of the Duke of Chou and Po-ch'in[7] as a model to admire, if you put into effect their government and moral influence, if you open the doors to public welfare and shut them to private gain, if you instill gratitude in the people and cultivate proper behavior in your neighboring states, then your state will flourish with remarkable speed."

The Minister Kung-i

9.9 (A, 52a1) Tzu-ssu said: "Wealth and honor are very easy for me to achieve, and yet it seems that other people are unable to achieve it. Not to take from others is what I call wealth; not to take offense at the acts of others is what I call honor. To do these two things means that wealth and honor are at hand."

CHAPTER 10

HOLDING FIRM TO PERSONAL IDEALS
(K'ang-chih)

10.1 (A, 53a2)   Tseng Shen[1] said to Tzu-ssu: "What is preferable, to bend oneself while extending the Way, or to hold firm[2] to personal ideals while living in poverty and destitution?"

Tzu-ssu replied: "It is my wish that the Way be extended. But who among the kings and lords of our age is able to achieve that aim? It is better to hold firm to personal ideals and live in poverty and destitution than to bend oneself for the sake of wealth and honor. If one bends oneself, one will be controlled by others; while if one holds firm to one's personal ideals, one will never be ashamed of one's practice of the Way."

10.2 (A, 53a6)   When Tzu-ssu lived in Wei, there was a man there who caught a *kuan* fish[3] in the river. The fish was so big that it could fill a cart. Tzu-ssu asked the fisherman: "The *kuan* is a kind of fish that is rarely caught, so how did you manage to catch it?"

The fisherman answered: "I started by lowering the hook on which I put a bream as bait. Nevertheless, the *kuan* passed it by without noticing the bait. I again baited the hook, this time with half the body of a pig, and the fish swallowed it."

Tzu-ssu sighed audibly and said: "Though it was hard to catch the *kuan*, its craving led it to the fatal bait. Even though gentlemen cherish the Way, their greed leads them to die for the sake of salaries."

10.3 (A, 53b3)   While Tzu-ssu was living in Wei, Duke Mu of Lu died.[4] Hsien-tzu, who was on a mission to Wei, heard about the bereavement and wore the mourning dress. He then said to Tzu-ssu: "Though you do not occupy any official position in Lu, it is, all the same, your native land and the

Holding Firm to Personal Ideals 121

place where your ancestral shrines are located. Why would you not dress in mourning clothes?"

Tzu-ssu answered: "Surely it is not that I am overly concerned with their cost; it is just that I am prevented from doing so because of the mourning rites."

Hsien-tzu said: "May I hear about this?"

Tzu-ssu replied: "When a minister is forced to leave a state, and the ruler of the state does not obliterate the minister's ancestral shrine, then, upon the death of that ruler, the minister wears mourning because the ruler refrained from obliterating the ancestral shrine. If a duke has been sent into forced residence[5] in another state, he wears mourning for the ruler in whose state he resides, so as to conform with the state in which he has residence. Since I no longer have official rank in Lu, and my sacrifices are performed in Wei, how, then, could I wear mourning? If a minister, who has been sent into forced residence in another state wears mourning for the ruler in whose state he has taken refuge, then it is no longer possible to wear mourning for the ruler he once served. By acting so, the minister clearly manifests the righteous rejection of double loyalty."

Hsien-tzu said: "I approve. This thought has never occurred to me."

10.4 (A, 54a3) The Prince of Wei discussed the rights and wrongs of his strategic planning with his ministers, and their unanimous agreement sounded as if expressed by a single voice. Tzu-ssu said: "In my view, what in Wei is called 'a ruler' is not a true ruler, and 'a minister' is not a true minister."[6]

Kung-ch'iu I asked, "Why so?"

Tzu-ssu replied: "If a ruler presumes his plans to be good, the plans of his court officials will not be presented. In cases when the plans turn out to be correct in practice, the very fact that they have been presumed good seems to eliminate the presentation of all other plans by the court officials. The case is much more serious when wrong plans inspire unanimous agreement and evil is thereby magnified. When a ruler does not examine the rights and wrongs of a case, and he is pleased by praise, ignorance reaches its apex. There is no greater sycophancy than to fail to have a precise grasp of principle and to seek acceptance by means of flattery. When those in charge are ignorant rulers and sycophantic ministers, the people will not cooperate with them. Should this state of affairs not end, the country will dissolve."

10.5 (A, 54a2) Tzu-ssu said to the Prince of Wei: "The affairs of your state are going to become worse every day."

The Prince said: "What is the reason for that?"

Tzu-ssu replied: "There is a cause from which this situation emerges. Whenever you speak, you presume that what you say is right, so there is none among your counsellors who dares to rectify your errors. Your counsellors, too, presume that everything they say is right, so there is none among the gentlemen and commoners who dares to rectify the counsellors' errors. When a ruler and ministers presume themselves wise and all their subordinates unanimously agree with them, then those who consider them worthy are thought to be pliant and are therefore rewarded, while those who try to rectify matters are considered obstructionists and therefore troubles are inflicted on them. That is what makes them act as they do. If this is the state of things, then from where can goodness arise? The *Book of Odes* says:

> They all say: 'We are sages.' But who can tell the difference between the male and the female of the raven?[7]

Is this not analogous to the Prince and the ministers of Wei?''

10.6 (A, 55a1) The Prince of Wei asked Tzu-ssu: "What do you think of my rule?"

Tzu-ssu answered: "No criticism."

The Prince said: "Since I have not been aware of any disreputable behavior, I was hoping that this would be the case."

Tzu-ssu said: "When someone has common aims with you and curries your favor, you put him in a position of intimacy. But when an upright person tries to rectify your faults, you keep him at a distance. It is the ruler who has the power to bring people wealth and honor or poverty and destitution. So who among the gentlemen in the court would choose to forget that which would gain him a position of intimacy and choose instead that which would lead you to neglect him? For such reasons gentlemen vie in gaining your good graces, and no one dares to condemn your faults. This is what I meant when I said 'no criticism.' "

The Duke said: "I suppose that is so. From now on I will know how to change my faults."

Tzu-ssu answered: "You are incapable of doing so. If one gives lip-service to an idea he disapproves of in his heart, then when it comes to putting that idea into effect, he will surely find it as useless as a wart. So even if you command me, I will not dare to obey."[8]

10.7 (A, 55b2) When Wen-tzu,[9] the minister of education,[10] reburied his uncle in another grave, he asked Tzu-ssu about the mourning dress appropriate for such an occasion. Tzu-ssu said: "According to the rites, when one reburies one's parents in another grave one wears the mourning dress of *ssu*.[11] Once the reburial is over, one removes the mourning dress. It is unthinkable to part from one's nearest kin without wearing the mourning dress. If, however, one reburies someone other than one's parents, one should wear, instead of a mourning dress, a dress for condolence, and one should don a hemp fillet."[12]

Wen-tzu said: "What type of cloth should one wear in cases in which a burial takes place only after the mourning dress has already been removed?"

Tzu-ssu answered: "During the period of three-years' mourning[13] one does not change one's mourning dress if the burial has not yet taken place, so how could there be a possibility of removal of the mourning dress? As to the mourning periods of one year, or of nine months, in these cases, during burial one wears the mourning dress that had been taken off. As soon as the burial is over, one removes the mourning dress. As for the performance of the Sacrifice of Repose,[14] one should wear a robe for festive occasions with which one attends to one's sacrificial duties."

10.8 (A, 56a1) Kung-shu Mu[15] said to Shen Hsiang: "I regard Tzu-ssu with affection and respect but he does not pay attention to me." Shen Hsiang brought the case to Tzu-ssu's attention and said to him: "People try to express their affection and respect for you; why do you have to insult them?"

Tzu-ssu answered: "It is a question of righteousness."

Shen Hsiang said: "May I hear more about this?"

Tzu-ssu answered: "This son of the Kung-shu clan loves people who agree with him. He is morally lax and does not recognize the worthy. His affection and respect are not authentic, he simply sees that currently it is worthwhile to display affection and respect for me. He is doing so because of current opinion,[16] and he will surely discard me when current opinion changes."

Shen Hsiang said: "And why can he not recognize the worthy?"

Tzu-ssu answered: "Take the case of Lung Mu,[17] a man who is merely fond of decorative manipulations and rhetorical flourishes. From his seat he observes people's precise expressions in order to act in conformity with their expectations. He is the most frivolous man under Heaven, yet Kung-shu continues to have dealings with him. Now take the case of Ch'iao Tzu-liang.[18] He pursues the cultivation of substance and not reputation. His doings are intrinsically good; they are not aimed at attracting the recognition of others. But he is like a huge bell: unless you strike it, it makes no sound. He is the most profound man of all under Heaven, and even though Kung-shu lived with him in the same town, he was unable to recognize his talent. That is why I said that Kung-shu loved people who conformed to him and that he was unable to recognize the worthy."

10.9 (A, 56b5) When Tzu-ssu returned to Wei from Ch'i, the Prince of Wei paid him a visit in his inn and asked him: "Though you are a gentleman from Lu, you have not considered the smallness of Wei as no more than a route for your gracious footsteps, thereby giving us comfort and a reason to exist. I wish to request that you grant me your favor."

Tzu-ssu replied: "I have abused your dignity by my sojourn here, and the visits you have paid my humble home are a source of great honor. I would like to return the favor by giving you valuable gifts, but your treasury is already overflowing and, moreover, I am a man of few means. Or, if I wanted to return the favor by giving you good advice, I am afraid that my words might not be in keeping with your own aspirations and they would be useless words and would go unheeded. So there is no way in which I can return you a favor, except to teach you the way of advancing[19] the worthy in government."

The Prince of Wei said: "The treatment of the worthy is indeed something I desire."

Tzu-ssu said: "I do not fully understand what you have in mind. Can you tell me what you plan to do?"

The Prince replied: "The worthy must be employed in the orders of government."

Tzu-ssu said: "You will not be able to do that."

The Prince said: "Why so?"

Tzu-ssu replied: "By no means is Wei lacking in worthy and talented gentlemen. Yet, you have never had good government. The reason is therefore your failure properly to employ the worthy and the talented."

The Prince said: "That may be true, but I would like to hear your own definition of what constitutes 'worthy.' "

Tzu-ssu replied: "Are you going to select gentlemen according to their reputations or according to their real achievements?"

The Prince said: "They must be chosen according to their real achievements."

Tzu-ssu said: "On the eastern border of Wei there is a certain Li Yin, a worthy person by virtue of real achievements."

The Prince asked: "What did his ancestors do?"

Tzu-ssu replied: "They have been tillers for generations."

Bursting into great laughter the Prince said, "I am not fond of tillers and I have no use for their sons. Moreover, I have been unsuccessful in giving proper employment to even the sons of hereditary ministers in official service."

Tzu-ssu said: "I made my laudatory reference to Li Yin in deference to his worth and talent. Although the Duke of Chou was a great sage and K'ang Shu a great worthy, the contemporary princes cannot be assumed to be the equals of their ancestors. It cannot be assumed that Li Yin would make an excellent tiller even though his ancestors were tillers of such capacity. If you admit that even the sons of hereditary ministers are not fit for official service, then what I have stated, to the effect that you are merely not making proper

Holding Firm to Personal Ideals   125

use of the worthy and talented, is confirmed. Now the question I have just addressed to you intended, indeed, to suggest that the way you select gentlemen fails to rely on their achievements. In the case of Li Yin, you are not interested in finding why he is worthy and talented, but pay heed only to his tiller's lineage. If for that reason you laughed and rejected him, then it is certain that you select gentlemen in accord with their reputation and not in accord with their real achievements."

The Prince of Wei was taken aback and remained without a word of reply.

10.10 (A, 58a5) The Prince of Wei said: "The Way is great and difficult to understand. It is beyond me. In my own circumstances, I would rather devote myself to learning political methods.[20] What do you think of that?"

Tzu-ssu replied: "I advise you not to do so. One who fully grasps the Way is free from care and is never exhausted. One who exercises political methods labors without attainment. In times of old, the superior men who immersed themselves in the Way did not regard life itself as sufficient for happiness, so how could they regard mere gain to be sufficient to motivate them? Death itself was not enough to intimidate them, so how could they possibly be afraid of any other kind of harm?[21] Therefore, if one clearly understands the relative status of life and death,[22] one fathoms the changes that interrelate benefit and harm.[23] Then one's sense of purpose will not be affected even by the offer to exchange the world for a single hair of his shin.[24] Therefore, living with a sage will make a poor gentleman forget his poverty and destitution and will make kings and dukes regard their wealth and honor lightly. You, Sir, should not devote yourself to political methods."

The Prince said: "I agree."

10.11 (A, 58b5) The King of Ch'i said to Tzu-ssu: "At present all under Heaven is in turmoil and the feudal lords have no overlord. My state is big and its population is vast. What do you think of my prospects for assuming imperial authority?"

Tzu-ssu answered: "It is impossible, for you are unable to rid yourself of your inclination toward greediness."

The King said: "What harm can this do?"

Tzu-ssu replied: "Water is clear by nature and a clod of soil makes it turbid. Man's nature is calm and desires unsettle him. Therefore he who is capable of possessing all under Heaven must be one who is indifferent to it. He who is able to acquire fame and reputation must be one who can do without it. If one reaches this point, then one's greedy heart becomes extrinsic."

10.12 (A, 59a3) The principal wife of Wen-tzu, the commander of Wei, died. The Summoner of Spirits, in a long wailing sound, chanted: "Beautiful,[25] come back." Tzu-ssu heard about this and said: "This was this lady's personal name in her own clan, not the name given her in her husband's clan. According to the rites, when a woman is in her husband's clan she is deferentially referred to by her family clan-name."

10.13 (A, 59a6) Pi Tzu-yang[26] said to Tzu-ssu: "Whenever I contemplate the impending fall of the venerated house of Chou I cannot help weeping."[27]

Tzu-ssu said: "Yes, your intentions are good I am sure. However, someone who is able to learn the knowable by means of his intelligence, but is unable to learn that there are unknowable things, is on a precarious course. Now, for a single individual to be deeply concerned about the misrule of the world and weep helplessly about it, is similar to being deeply concerned over the muddiness of the water of the river and trying to clear it with tears. There is nothing more ineffective. Therefore the Viscount of Wei,[28] who abandoned Yin, and the young brother of the Marquis of Chi, who took refuge in Ch'i,[29] were outstanding examples of understanding the proper time to act. It is only the one who can refrain from concern over the disorder of his time, but who is distressed, instead, with his failure to preserve order in his own life, with whom I can engage in conversation about the Way."

10.14 (A, 59b5) The King of Ch'i once executed one of his subjects without cause. Later he said to Tzu-ssu: "I knew he was innocent, but at that moment he aroused my anger and so I executed him. I think that this case does not deserve to be considered a violation of righteousness."

Tzu-ssu said: "When King Wen buried the dry bones,[30] all under Heaven realized that he was benevolent. When Chou of Shang[31] cut off the feet of those who waded across the water,[32] all under Heaven called him cruel. A righteous man does not necessarily have to spread benefits to all under Heaven. A cruel man does not necessarily have to make tyranny pervade throughout the entire realm. It is rather the perception of one's basic intention viewed in the context of his practices that leads the people to join or abandon him. In your case, your wrathful impulse made you execute an innocent man, but you believe that this case does not deserve to be considered a violation of righteousness. This is a conclusion I would be hesitant to draw."

The King said: "I am truly at fault. Now, having heard your authoritative words, I would like to correct it."

10.15 (A, 60a5) Chiao, the son of the Duke of Wei, appeared before Tzu-ssu and said to him: "You, Sir, are the descendant of a sage, and you have maintained your lofty integrity so that the superior men under Heaven all bow to your great reputation. Even though I am not quick-witted, I would be presumptuous to aspire to your moral influence, and wish to learn your ideas on proper conduct. I would be grateful if you considered my request with sympathy."

Tzu-ssu replied: "You are not suited for this. Those whose moral integrity is lofty do not allow themselves to be encumbered by the prospect of private gain. Nor do they let the desire for profit confuse their intentions. They seek out the perfect Way and walk along the correct path of all under Heaven. Your case, sir, is that you are carrying on the traditional line of K'ang Shu,[33] but you live in an age of strife. You should rather concentrate on recruiting great warriors to protect your territory. This is not a time for either probing what underlies good[34] and bad, or setting up various standards, or improving the conduct of a given individual."

10.16 (A, 60b5) Chiao, the son of the Duke of Wei, offered Tzu-ssu a gift of four teams of horses, saying: "I would not presume to curry your favor and defile your purity with this gift. It has been quite long since you have graced our humble territory with a visit, so it is on this occasion that gifts[35] will be exchanged between host and guest."

Tzu-ssu replied: "Ever since I have entrusted my life to Wei, I have clothed my body in the dress of Wei and determined my capacity for food according to the millet of Wei. And, furthermore, morning and evening I have received grants of wine, preserved meat, and sacrificial meat. With cloth and food in such fine supply,[36] my mind and spirit have become truly settled. But since I have not put into effect my personal ideals, I dare not consider myself deserving of the gift of these carriages and horses. Now, according to the rites, though one possesses a rank, one should not take precedence over one's father or elder brother in the granting of favors.[37] But by my evident rejection of your munificence, I would also be guilty of a breach of the rites. What should I do?"

The Duke's son said: "I have already discussed my offer with the ruler."[38]

Tzu-ssu replied: "It would be wrong to accept it. Whenever a son receives the three gifts, he declines the carriage and the horses."[39]

The Duke's son said: "I had never heard about this. I respectfully accept your teaching."

10.17 (A, 61a7) Duke Mu wanted to appoint Tzu-ssu as his senior minister. Tzu-ssu was reluctant and was thinking of leaving Lu. The Prince of Lu[40] said: "All the other rulers under Heaven are like me, so where can you possibly go?"

Tzu-ssu replied: "Let me explain: I have heard that the superior man is like the Phoenix: when it is discomfited,[41] it flies[42] away.[43] In me, you lack confidence.[44] But when you also judge all rulers under Heaven in accord with your own failings, with all due respect, I think that your words are fallacious."

10.18 (A, 61b3) The King of Ch'i said to Tzu-ssu: "You, sir, have a towering reputation throughout the land. Whenever you make the slightest utterance, all the gentlemen of all under Heaven pay heed. Now, I would like to appoint Liang Ch'i[45] as a senior minister, but since he has such a petty reputation, I would like you to speak persuasively on his behalf."

Tzu-ssu replied: "The reason why the gentlemen of all under Heaven pay heed to me is that they regard my words as standards of right and wrong. Now suppose you bid me to make groundless statements about Ch'i, then the gentlemen of all under Heaven will have to change their attitude toward me. If they change their attitude, Ch'i would gain no benefit, and so there would be a double loss. That is why I dare not accept your command."

The Prince of Ch'i[46] said: "What makes you think that Ch'i is not good?"

Tzu-ssu answered: "You have surely heard that one who overvalues wealth and sex will always undervalue virtue. This is the natural course of events. Now when the fact that Ch'i's wealth resulted from his greed becomes known among the feudal lords, no kindness will be shown to those in need. When the fact that Ch'i overindulged himself in sex becomes known within the state of Ch'i, the proper distinction between male and female will not be manifested. If one had only one of these two vices,[47] one could be regarded as a man of evil destiny. Can Ch'i, who incorporates them both, be able to avoid suffering the consequences?"

The King said: "My words were truly flawed. I beg you, Sir, to pardon me."

10.19 (A, 62a7) Tzu-ssu appeared before Lao Lai-tzu.[48] At that time Lao Lai-tzu heard that Duke Mu was going to appoint Tzu-ssu as senior minister. Lao Lai-tzu said to Tzu-ssu: "If you decide to serve him, how do you intend to act?"

Tzu-ssu answered: "If I follow my own native character and aid him in the Way, I will not meet my death."

Lao Lai-tzu said: "You cannot follow your nature because it is too hard, and you invariably defy the unworthy.[49] Furthermore, one who is not ready to face death in service cannot be considered a true official."

Tzu-ssu replied: "It is precisely because some people are unworthy that they deserve to be defied by others. Now if in serving one's prince, the Way is put into effect and one's words are listened to, what reason will there be to die? If one's Way is not put into effect and one's words are ignored, then one is not able to serve that prince. This is what I meant when I said that I will not meet my death."

Lao Lai-tzu said: "Haven't you ever looked at teeth? They are hard and firm but they ultimately perish, grinding each other down completely.[50] The tongue is soft by nature and it does not wear out till the end."

Tzu-ssu said: "Since I am not able to take on the nature of the tongue, I will not be able to serve a prince."

CHAPTER 12

THE PHILOSOPHER KUNG-SUN LUNG
(Kung-sun Lung)

12.1 (A, 72a3) The man called Kung-sun Lung[1] was a retainer of Prince P'ing-yüan.[2] He devoted himself to the discussions of forms and names,[3] and he held a white horse not to be a white horse.[4] Someone said to Tzu-kao:[5] "By petty distinctions, he slanders the great Way.[6] Why do you not go and put him right?" Tzu-kao replied: "The flouting of the great Way is commonplace everywhere. Why should I be troubled by it?"

Someone said: "In spite of this, since you are concerned with the world, you ought to go."

Thereupon Tzu-kao went to Chao, met Lung in the house of Prince P'ing-yüan, and said to him: "During my sojourn in Lu, I heard of your fame and admired your conduct. I have long desired to receive your noble teaching. However, the only thing I do not accept in your teaching is your assertion that you hold a white horse not to be a white horse. If you could, in fact, discard your teaching of 'not a white horse,' I would like to become your disciple."

Kung-sun Lung replied: "What you say, sir, is contrary to reason. My teaching focuses precisely on the assertion that a white horse is not to be held a white horse. Now, if you were to make me discard this, I would have nothing left to teach. If I were to have nothing to teach and you still wanted to learn from me, could this not be regarded as contrary to reason? Moreover, anyone who seeks my teaching must be inferior to me in wisdom or scholarship. If you now come to instruct me to discard my thesis of 'a white horse is not a white horse,' this would mean that you would be trying to teach me first[7] and take me as your teacher later. This is implausible.

"Now what[8] you are trying to teach me reminds me of the questions the King of Ch'i put to Yin Wen.[9] The King of Ch'i said: 'Even though I am decidedly in favor of gentlemen, Ch'i has none.'

The Philosopher Kung-sun Lung

"Yin Wen replied: 'Suppose there was a man here, loyally serving his prince, filially serving his parents, trustworthy to his friends, and conducting himself in harmony with the local practices of his place of residence. Would you call a man who manifests these four characteristics a gentleman?' The King replied: 'Definitely, this is precisely what I call a gentleman.' Yin Wen continued: 'Assuming you gained the services of such a man, would you be willing to appoint him a minister?' The King replied: 'That is what I am looking for, but I cannot get the service of such a man.'

"Yin Wen said: 'Now, suppose this man were publicly humiliated in the middle of the great square, and yet did not dare to retaliate. Would you still consider appointing him a minister?' The King replied: 'It is a disgrace for a gentleman to be humiliated without retaliating. I would not consider appointing such a man a minister.'

"Yin Wen said: 'Even if he were humiliated and, indeed, did not retaliate, he would not necessarily have lost what made him a gentleman. And if you still would not consider appointing him a minister, then what you have just called a gentleman is not a gentleman, is it? Now, according to your laws, a murderer receives the death penalty, and one who assaults people is given corporal punishment. Because of this, people stand in awe of your laws. Therefore, one who allows oneself to be humiliated and continues to refrain from retaliating is one who fulfills your system of law. You, however, would not consider appointing him a minister, that is, you penalize him. Furthermore, to consider disgraceful someone who does not retaliate must imply that you would consider the willingness to retaliate to be a mark of honor. That is, what the King rewards, his commissioners penalize, and what the ruler regards as right, his law considers wrong. When reward and punishment, right and wrong, negate one another, then even ten Yellow Emperors could not possibly establish order.' The King of Ch'i had no reply.

"Furthermore, my thesis of 'a white horse is not a white horse' was adopted by your late Master, Chung-ni.[10] I have heard that the King of Ch'u stretched the *Fan-jo* bow, cocked the *Wang-kuei* arrow, and shot a dragon and a rhinoceros in the Yün-meng park.[11] When he returned his bow was missing. His companions wanted to look for it. The King said: 'Stop! A man of Ch'u lost the bow, a man of Ch'u will find it. What is the point of looking for it?'

"When Chung-ni heard about this, he said: 'The King of Ch'u was a man of benevolence and righteousness but did not carry these to their complete conclusion. The King could have said: "A man will find it," and nothing else. Why did he insist it would be a man of Ch'u?' If this is the case then Chung-ni differentiated a man of Ch'u from what is called 'a man.' Accepting as correct Chung-ni's differentiation of a man from Ch'u from what is called 'a man' while still regarding as wrong my differentiation of a white horse from what is called a horse is contrary to reason. You, sir, devote yourself to the

Confucian way,[12] and still you reject what Chung-ni approved. You want to learn from me and yet you would have me discard the core of my teaching. Even if my intelligence were multiplied a hundredfold it would not be able to challenge you."

Tzu-kao did not answer. He withdrew and told his followers: "Lung's words are flawed and excessive, cunning, and unprincipled. This is precisely why I did not answer him."

Another day, Prince P'ing-yüan assembled many guests and invited Tzu-kao. The Prince said: "You, sir, are the descendant of a sage. You did not consider a distance of a thousand *li* too far and came here to honor Kung-sun Lung with a visit. You wanted to discard his white horse teaching. But, without waiting for the right and the wrong of the case to be determined, you hastily withdrew into aloofness. Is this proper?"

Tzu-kao answered: "When the principle of right and wrong[13] is in its purest form, it is self-evident. How could my own withdrawal have any bearing on the case?"

Prince P'ing-yüan said: "May I hear more about this doctrine of the 'purest'?"

Tzu-kao said: "This doctrine is entirely based on the Classics and their commentaries. I dare not regard this as my own idea. The *Ch'un-ch'iu* records:

> Six fish-hawks flew backward.[14] Glancing at them you see six, examining them you see fish-hawks.[15]

The term 'fish-hawk' is like the term 'a horse.' The term 'six' is like the term 'white.' Glancing at it you perceive its whiteness; on examining it, you realize it is a horse. When a color of an object is specified by a name, and when the inner essence of that object is clearly manifested through the object's appearance, then the reference to that object as a 'white horse' indicates that the applied term fits the object in question. It is the same as when silks or linen are made by women dyers into black, white, blue, and yellow colors. Although the names are different, the basic material is unchanged. This is why the *Book of Odes* has 'white silk';[16] it does not say 'silk white.' The *Book of Rites* has 'black cloth';[17] it does not say 'cloth black.' 'Black ox,'[18] 'dark warrior,' and other similar examples are abundant. First the color is specified and then its essence is named. Whatever is common to all things is considered constant by the sage. When the superior man engages in discourses he values the underlying principles of things; he does not value intricate arguments[19] such as Yin Wen's, who criticized the King of Ch'i's words because they failed to correspond to his laws. The reason why I engaged in discourse with Master Kung-sun was that I value his wisdom highly and took delight in his conduct. Had he discarded his doctrine of a white horse, his wisdom and con-

The Philosopher Kung-sun Lung

duct would surely have been preserved, and in that case I would never have caused him to lose what made him a teacher in the first place. But he insisted on his routine till he completely lost the principle.

"This was exemplified in the case he brought up about the King of Ch'u, who said: 'A man of Ch'u lost the bow; a man of Ch'u will find it.' My forefather, the Master, sought out the King's basic idea, which was that he wanted to demonstrate his breadth, but in fact the King constricted himself. That is why the Master said: 'It would be better just to say "A man will find it."' Thus the Master's differentiation of the word 'Ch'u' referred to the 'Ch'u' in the King of Ch'u's words, not to the 'man.' If you argue by this analogy, my argument conflicts dramatically with the case brought up by Kung-sun Lung. Whenever we say 'man,' we generalize about man, just as when we say 'horse,' we generalize about horses. Ch'u is in itself a state, white is in itself a color. If one wishes to broaden the meaning of 'man,' one should omit the term 'Ch'u.' If one wishes to be accurate in naming colors, one should not leave the term 'white' out. If you truly examine all my reasoning you will find the distinctions made by Kung-sun are refuted."

Prince P'ing-yüan said: "Your words in respect to principle are excellent." Then he turned to the audience of guests and asked: "Will Master Kung-sun be able to answer these arguments?"

A retainer from Yen by the name of Shih Yu replied: "As for rhetorical arguments he will have an answer, but as for the underlying principle he will not have an answer."

12.2 (A, 76a5) Kung-sun Lung and Tzu-kao met once more for a general debate at Prince P'ing-yüan's palace.[20] While they were debating the principle of right and wrong,[21] they came across the case of "Tsang has three ears."[22] Kung-sun Lung presented the case of Tsang's three ears in a perfected style of eloquence. Tzu-kao did not answer and abruptly left. The next day he had another audience with Prince P'ing-yüan. The Prince said: "Yesterday, Kung-sun Lung's words were truly well argued. What do you, sir, really think of them?"

Tzu-kao replied: "Indeed, he was almost able to show that 'Tsang has three ears.' Nevertheless, it is really difficult. I should like to ask you another question. To make Tsang have three ears is extremely difficult and in fact wrong. To say Tsang has two ears is very easy and in fact right. I do not know if you would rather take the easy way and be right, or take the difficult way and be wrong." The Prince P'ing-yüan was unable to answer.

The next day he said to Kung-sun Lung: "Do not ever argue with K'ung Tzu-kao. In his character, principle prevails over words; in yours, words prevail over principle. When one's words prevail over one's principle, one will always be defeated."

12.3 (A, 76b7) Li Yin[23] spoke about Ts'ao Liang[24] with Prince P'ing-yüan, who wanted to appoint him an official. Prince P'ing-yüan asked Tzu-kao for his opinion. Tzu-kao said: "I do not know him."

Prince P'ing-yüan said: "Liang has already made an appearance before you; that is why I venture to ask for your opinion."

Tzu-kao said: "Many of the contemporary men praise themselves, claiming that if they were given posts by the ruler, their country would have no troubles. Whenever one wants to employ the intelligent, there is no better way than to observe the candidate himself. If it is likely that the candidate will not be able to avoid troubles in his own life, and if he, nevertheless, is going to be employed in the service of a state, how can troubles be avoided?"

Prince P'ing-yüan said: "The troubles Liang is facing are due to the characteristics of the present time, which are muddled. Since his own household is in a state of order, he could transfer this good management to the government.[25] Liang's ability lies in his talent for commerce; that is why I am considering appointing him."

Tzu-kao said: "One never knows. Suppose we had, on the one hand, a man who perfected his selfhood and whose calculations were brilliant, yet he remained poor, because he did not have the personal ambition to become wealthy. On the other hand, suppose that we had a man who did not cultivate his selfhood and whose plans were ignorant, and he was rich all the same. Unless he was a thief, he would have no way of becoming wealthy."

CHAPTER 13

CONFUCIAN CLOTHES
(Ju-fu)

13.1 (A, 78a2) Tzu-kao trailed the skirt of his robe, fluttered his long sleeves, and appeared in square clogs along with a huge bamboo fan before Prince P'ing-yüan. The Prince said: "My master, are these also the clothes of a Confucian?"[1]

Tzu-kao answered: "These are the clothes of a common man; they are not the clothes of a Confucian. Confucian clothes are not invariable."

Prince P'ing-yüan said: "Would you kindly elaborate, Master."

Tzu-kao responded: "When the Confucian is in an official position and the Way is put into effect, he wears embroidered clothes.[2] When he acts as a general in the field, he wears the dress of armor and helmet. When he is moving about at leisure, he wears clothes like those I am wearing now. Therefore I said that the Confucian clothes are not invariable."

Prince P'ing-yüan said: "From where is the term 'Confucian' derived?"

Tzu-kao answered: "It is derived from the idea of the combination of the various exquisite virtues, and the conjoining of the six arts,[3] such that whether in action or repose he never loses the core of the Way."[4]

13.2 (A, 78b2) Tzu-kao traveled to Chao. Among the retainers of Prince P'ing-yüan there were Tsou Wen and Chi Chieh,[5] who were on friendly terms with Tzu-kao. When Tzu-kao was about to return to Lu and all[6] his old friends had finished bidding him farewell, Wen and Chieh escorted him a distance of three overnight posts. When the time finally came for them to take leave, their tears ran profusely, criss-crossing their cheeks. Tzu-kao, however, merely raised his hand in a waving gesture and nothing more. Then he withdrew and took to the road. His disciples questioned him: "You, sir, were on friendly terms with these two. They, on their part, felt a deep attachment to you. And so, uncertain of when they would have another opportunity to meet you, they were sorrowful and shed tears. But you left in an unsentimental mood and with an aloof gesture. Surely, this is contrary to the idea of demonstrating sympathy effectively for persons who are close to one."

Tzu-kao answered: "Originally I said these two were 'men,' but I know now that they are in fact 'women.' A man is born with personal ideals which stretch to the four corners of the world. He is not like a deer or pig which must always congregate in herds."

His disciples said: "Was the weeping of these two wrong?"

Tzu-kao answered: "These two are fine human beings. They have a heart sensitive to suffering.[7] But as far as a decisive spirit is concerned, they are surely lacking."

His disciples said: "Is weeping undesirable in all cases?"

Tzu-kao answered: "There are two cases that call for it; when great villains try to gain the confidence of others by weeping, or when a woman and a weak man manifest their love in tears."

13.3 (A, 79a6) Prince P'ing-yüan was drinking with Tzu-kao and pressed him to drink more wine, saying: "As the old proverbs had it: 'Yao and Shun could drink a thousand *chung* of wine and Confucius a hundred *ku*.[8] Tzu-lu[9] drank in small sips,[10] but he could still drain ten goblets.'[11] That is to say, among the sages and the worthies of old there was none who was unable to drink. Why are you reluctant to do so?"

Tzu-kao answered: "According to what I have heard, it was by means of the Way and virtue that the worthies and the sages became superior to others; not, as far as I know, through food and drink."

Prince P'ing-yüan said: "If what you say is right, then what is the source of these sayings?"

Tzu-kao answered: "These sayings arise from the people who love to drink, and the sayings are no doubt words of encouragement and provocation. They are not necessarily true."

Prince P'ing-yüan was pleased and said: "Had I not provoked you, I would not have heard these sterling words of yours."

13.4 (A, 79b5) Prince P'ing-yüan said to Tzu-kao: "I have heard that your forefather[12] had an intimate interview with Nan Tzu,[13] the wife of the Duke of Wei. I have also heard that when your forefather was traveling south he passed through A-ku, where he exchanged words with a washerwoman.[14] Did this actually occur?"

Tzu-kao answered: "Gentlemen who are protecting their common interest do not believe malicious gossip when they hear it.[15] Why? Because they view the case in the light of the past[16] activities of those to whom the case is ascribed. Formerly, during my forefather's sojourn in Wei, the Prince of Wei asked him about commanding the troops. But my forefather dismissed the question without a statement, and though the question remained unsettled[17] he seized the reins of his carriage and departed.[18] Since the Prince of Wei's request for an interview with my forefather was apparently not carried out, how could his wife have been able to meet intimately with my forefather?[19] It seems that in the remote past, even when the rites and decorum were on the decline, there were those who put into effect the rule concerning the attendance of women in the great sacrificial feast.[20] To suggest that the wife of the Prince of Wei conducted such a feast with the Master is to think of the Master in terms of those who have lost their grasp of the rites.[21] As to the case of his conversation with the washerwoman in A-ku, this is a fictitious story produced in recent times. Its maker fabricated it in order to carry out his own desires."

13.5 (A, 80a7) When Tzu-kao went to Wei, the Ch'in army was just then approaching.[22] Prince Hsin-ling[23] was alarmed and paid a visit to Tzu-kao at his lodge to question him about the rites of prayer for victory. Tzu-kao said: "When a general of honorable courage and strategy was assigned to resist the enemy, he would first be sent into the path of the oncoming forces. There he would build an altar and pray for victory to the five gods.[24] The color of his clothing was correlated with the color of the direction in question,[25] and the number of his functionaries was correlated to the number of the direction in question.[26] The sacrificial animal was also correlated with that of the direction in question.[27] The Supplication Scribe announced the case at the altars of the gods of earth and grain and in the ancestral temples, as well as within the royal domain, on the famous mountains, and on the great rivers. The ruler used to dress by himself in white silk. Then he swore the following oath in the royal ancestral temple before the multitude: 'Our enemy, who are not men of the Way, have invaded our great country. Gentlemen, may you all do your utmost, with common will and united efforts, to defend this land to your deaths.' The commanding general then prostrated himself and bowed twice in acknowledgment of the command. When the oath was already sworn, the commanding general mustered his captains and men in formation on the right side of the temple. The ruler stood in the courtyard of the royal ancestral temple and the Supplication Scribe stood at the altar of the god of the earth, while all the officials attended to their duties, ministering to the ruler and awaiting for his commands. Then the drums sounded in the gate of the temple and the commanding general was summoned and ordered to take command of the troops. He ordered his men to take three shots with their bows and three sword thrusts. A declaration of warfare against the enemy was made in the temple. The five arms[28] were prepared in full array, then they moved out against the enemy to the sound of drums. These were the rites of the ancient feudal lords in meeting an enemy attack."

Prince Hsin-ling said: "I respectfully accept your teaching."

Prince[29] Hsin-ling questioned Tzu-kao, saying: "Dealing with their troops, the ancients felt it necessary to grant rewards in the ancestral temple and to carry out executions at the altar of the God of Earth.[30] What was the reason for that?"

Tzu-kao replied: "Giving rewards for meritorious service in the ancestral temple amounted to a declaration that the portions of the grants were equal and that there was no favoritism whatsoever. Executing the guilty at the altar of the God of the Earth amounted to a declaration that the hearing of the case, which preceded the death sentence,[31] was impartial."[32]

13.6 (A, 81a8) Ch'en Wang[33] was by nature critical of uncleanness. When he was given wine or food, he would regularly remove the top layer before eating the dish. Tzu-kao said to him: "You should not do this. It gives the impression that you have some ulterior motive. In the old days, when the superior men were given grants of wine and food they were duty-bound to taste it. They shunned the throwing away of food. If the food was suitable for eating, there was no reason to choose between the upper and lower layers. If the food was thought unclean, the lower portion of it was regarded as more so."

Ch'en Wang said: "I know that this behavior of mine is of no value. It is just a matter of personal predilection."

Tzu-kao replied: "One should not indulge in one's personal predilection. A tree that is crooked by nature straightens itself out when supported by a wooden prop. Can it be that a man is less capable than a tree in this regard? Haven't you ever observed a chicken? As soon as it sees a mound of gathered grain, it rushes and pecks at it. If you gave free rein to your personal predilection, what difference would there be between yourself and a chicken?"

Ch'en Wang fell to his knees and said: "From now on I will be aware of that fault, and I will strive to overcome it eventually."

13.7 (A, 82a1) Tzu-kao appointed Ssu-ma I[34] as a commander in Ch'i, and he was defeated in a battle against the state of Yen. The Prince of Ch'i said: "I have put my trust in your recommendation because I thought you were worthy and intelligent."

Tzu-kao replied: "Whom do you consider to be superior, myself or the Duke of Chou?"

The Prince of Ch'i replied: "The Duke of Chou was a sage, and you are a worthy; you are not his match."

Tzu-kao said: "Right, I am indeed not a match for the Duke of Chou. But which do you consider superior, my judgment of Ssu-ma I, or the Duke of Chou's judgment of his brothers?"

The Prince of Ch'i said: "Brothers carefully examine each other."

Tzu-kao said: "What you say is correct. Now he was a sage, and his judgment of his brothers was based on the attentive mutual appraisal characteristic of brothers. Still, he was in a nearly desperate state because of Kuan and Ts'ai.[35] His example shows that it is very difficult to arrive at an accurate judgment of men. When I met Ssu-ma I, I took note of his talent and ambitions. I observed that there was no other gentleman in Ch'i who was able to surpass his course. The *Book of Documents* says:

If one knows man, one is wise. Even the Emperor finds it difficult.[36]

Why should I feel ashamed on this account? Furthermore, Ts'ao Tzu[37] was engaged in battles with Ch'i three times in the service of Lu, and he was defeated and lost territory three times. But later, with the daring of a true man of valor, he seized a three-foot sword and importuned Duke Huan and Kuan Chung at the altar of the alliance, and finally recovered what he had lost.[38] The defeat of a superior man is like an eclipse of the sun or the moon. Every man has his own ability: how could Ssu-ma I be discarded? Now, Yen has defeated and crushed Ssu-ma I through deceit. The meaning of this is that his true ability does not lie in the realm of deception. When I praised him I was referring to his courage in combat and to his accomplished talents. I said nothing of his having the talent to deceive. So even though he was defeated I cannot consider him devoid of what he has been praised for."

The Prince of Ch'i yielded to this argument, and he did not dismiss Ssu-ma I from office.

CHAPTER
14

A DIALOGUE WITH THE KING
OF WEI
(Tui Wei-wang)

14.1 (A, 83a2) The King of Wei[1] asked about the primary causes of concern for a ruler. Tzu-kao replied: "When he installs a high minister and yet does not plan things together with him, and when the ideas of favored sycophantic ministers are put into effect, then the neglect of the wise gentlemen will put them into a state of self-doubt. When wicked ministers meet with fortunate treatment, then they cater to the ruler's wishes inside the court, while outside they openly discuss the ruler's wrongs. This is a great cause for concern in a ruler."

14.2 (A, 83a6) Tzu-kao said to the King of Wei: "When I entered the state of Wei I met two of your strategists. Chang Shu's[2] stratagems went beyond what was necessary, while Fan Wei's[3] cleverness was insufficient to meet the challenge. Yet their merits were considered identical."

The King said: "What do you mean by saying that Shu, whose stratagems went beyond what was necessary, was considered identical with Wei, whose cleverness was insufficient to meet a challenge?"

Tzu-kao replied: "If one were to let an emaciated and a superior horse together pull the shafts of a carriage, then Po-lo[4] would utter a sigh of remorse. If one were to let jade stones and crude stones intermix, then Mr. Pien[5] would sigh audibly. Thus, if the worthy and the unwise are linked together, the able gentleman is forced to conceal his strategic talent. And if men of truth and falsehood are used indiscriminately, the upright gentleman becomes tongue-tied. In this light, even Shu, whose stratagems went beyond what was necessary, is no different from Wei, whose cleverness was insufficient to meet a challenge."

Dialogue with the King of Wei 141

14.3 (A, 83b3) The King of Wei asked what sort of man one must be to be called a great minister. Tzu-kao replied: "A great minister is a man whom all the officials take as their favored choice. He is a man who is able to remonstrate against his ruler's activities despite his angry countenance, while remaining impartial and upright. When his plans are set forth and his deeds accomplished, the ruler decides on the proper reward. When he fails in his deeds, the minister himself must accept the bitter consequences. When the ruler gives him responsibility he feels no doubts about his ability, and he, on his part, fulfills his charge with no evasion. The ruler comprises virtuous qualities,[6] and the minister exercises his righteous duty. In such a case, the ruler does not have uncertainties about his minister, and the minister does not conceal anything from his ruler. Therefore, in his deeds the minister never strays from a fitting plan, and in his undertakings his actions never fail. Hence both gain their respective benefits."

14.4 (A, 84a2) Prince Hsin-ling asked: "The ancients were so skilled at statecraft that they reached a stage in which there was no litigation. As for their Way, what did they follow?"

Tzu-kao answered: "Through government that was good. Superiors and inferiors all strove to act virtuously without any private gain. In their virtues, there were none that were not transformed for the better, and in their customs there were none that did not change. Whatever the multitudes praised, the government regarded as right, and what they denounced, the government regarded as wrong. The reason why there was no litigation was that the people agreed with the government as to what should be praised or denounced, and as to what should be regarded as right or wrong."[7]

14.5 (A, 84a7) The King of Ch'i[8] carried out the punishment in which someone was pulled apart by chariots.[9] And though all his ministers admonished him, he paid them no attention. Tzu-kao met the King of Ch'i and said to him: "I have heard that you carried out the punishment of having someone pulled apart by chariots. This punishment is not in keeping with the Way, and yet you carried it out. With all humility, I think that this was the fault of your subordinates."

The King said: "It was my own decision and nothing else. The reason why the common people quite often break the law is that punishment is too light."

Tzu-kao said: "I see that this is indeed a superlative motive on your part. But mankind's nature consists of the five norms of behavior[10] and is expressed in the feelings of sorrow, joy, pleasure, and anger. None of these feelings can ultimately avoid exceeding its proper degree. When that happens, one's sense of righteousness is undermined.[11] The reason why people often break the law is that the law is so severe that there is no place on which they can set hand or foot without breaking it. At present all under Heaven is in flux, and gentlemen have lost their secure places. If the ruler is a man of virtue, the gentleman retains his position; otherwise he abandons it. When a ruler aspires to establish hegemony—which is a difficult task to carry out in all great countries[12]—and yet simultaneously carries out brutal punishments that intimidate people near and far, then the people within his country will rebel and gentlemen from all corners of the world will not come to his aid. This is the way to lose one's country. Your subordinates, however, are not prepared to learn all this. Their only fear is that by opposing your ideas they may bring sorrow upon themselves; they do not take heed of the approaching doom caused by failure to admonish you. The object of their concern is petty, but what they stand to lose is great. That is why I said that it was the fault of your subordinates. As I see it, it is not merely a case of not remonstrating and nothing more, for deep down in their hearts they realize that this is an inadmissible practice that will eventually draw harsh criticism. So they say: 'Our ruler's indignation is quite substantial; if we remonstrate him we will be struck by the same calamities that Lung-p'ang[13] and Pi Kan[14] brought upon themselves.' This is a futile attempt to assume the standing of a loyal and upright man, which unwittingly pushes the ruler to act like tyrants such as Chieh and Chou. When someone, while exercising the role of a minister, observes the faults of his ruler and does not remonstrate him against them, by not doing so he pushes his ruler into the trap[15] of doom. This is one of the greatest crimes. When a ruler detests ministers who correct him, and hates them for it, and when he evaluates them according to the standards of trustworthiness of the Viscount of Chi[16] and Pi Kan, he creates a high degree of confusion."

The King of Ch'i said: "I respectfully accept your instruction and will rescind the punishment of having someone pulled apart by chariots."

14.6 (A, 85b3) Tzu-kao met the King of Ch'i. The King asked Tzu-kao to suggest a qualified man for the governorship of the district of Lin-tzu. Tzu-kao recommended Kuan Mu[17] for the position. The King said: "The people will not respect Mu because of his appearance, which is so crude."

Tzu-kao answered: "One wins people's respect because of one's virtue. And, furthermore, my recommendation was with respect to his capacities. Have you heard of Yen-tzu and Chao Wen-tzu?[18] Yen-tzu's height did not exceed six feet,[19] his appearance was repulsive, and there was no one in Ch'i, superiors and inferiors alike, who did not venerate him. Chao Wen-tzu's body was too limp to clothe and his speech was inarticulate. His case was just that of a body that was crude, but the manner of his speech was sluggish as well. When he was chief minister in the state of Chin, however, Chin was peaceful, and the feudal lords respected and submitted to him. This was due to the fact that they both possessed virtue. My comparison of Mu's body with the physical forms of these two men means that I consider him completely worthy. Formerly, when I used to travel to the city of Lin-tzu, I met a butcher eight feet high, with a beard that bristled like lances, an upright face, and a complexion of wholesome red and white. Nevertheless, it has never crossed the minds of the men and the women of that city to respect him, since he was devoid of virtue."

The King said: "That man is Tsu Lung-shih. What you say is true. I hereby appoint Kuan Mu a governor of Lin-tzu."

Notes
Glossary
Bibliography
Index

NOTES

Introduction: Section 1

1. The English word "forgery" carries with it a taint that can be untrue to the implications of the Chinese term *wei-shu*. The term represents a corpus of numerous works whose authenticity, title, or ascription is doubtful. The term can be translated into English as "forged book," "spurious text," "fabricated work," "pastiche," or "pseudepigraph," as the context requires. No less than nine different gradations of *wei-shu* are listed in Chang Hsin-ch'eng, *Wei-shu t'ung-k'ao*, vol. 1 (Taipei, 1973), pp. 16–17. His list includes examples of *wei-shu* that are complete forgeries, authentic books that contain some fabricated material, as well as works whose degree of inauthenticity is negligible. He furthermore provides a list of twelve motives underlying the production of such books, ranging from outright deception motivated by the desire for gain, to the innocent writing of a pseudepigraph for the sake of intellectual exercise. Each of these fits a certain gradation of *wei-shu*. It is clearly misleading to translate all these different gradations of *wei-shu* with the same indiscriminate word "forgery." I therefore urge the reader to keep in mind the full spectrum of meanings whenever the term occurs. For an excellent survey of the various categories of literary forgeries in Western culture see W. Speyer, *Die Literarische Fälschung Im Heidnischen Und Christlichen Altertum: Ein Versuch Ihrer Deutung* (München, 1971), pp. 3–106.

For a survey of the various evaluations of the *KTT* in history see the second section of the Introduction. The following paragraphs lay out the general contours of the issue.

2. The study of the *KTT* as a "forgery" might provide an interesting comparative framework for the reexamination of such values and concepts. However, I can do nothing more than suggest the framework. The comparative study of "forgeries" would require a separate study and is beyond anything I can allow myself here.

3. See, for instance, E. Balazs, *Chinese Civilization and Bureaucracy* (New Haven, 1964), p. 195; W. T. Chan, *Source Book in Chinese Philosophy* (Princeton, 1963), pp. 314–318; P. Demieville, "Philosophy and Religion from Han to Sui," in *The Cambridge History of China*, vol. 1, *The Ch'in and the Han Empires 221 B.C.–A.D. 220*, ed. D. Twitchett and M. Loewe (Cambridge, 1986), pp. 826–828; E. Zürcher, *The Buddhist Conquest of China*, vol. 1 (Leiden, 1959), pp. 45–46.

4. For a general characterization of Chinese philosophy at the end of the Later Han and the Wei–Chin eras see Balazs, *Chinese Civilization and Bureaucracy*, pp. 187–254; Ch'en Ch'i-yün, "Confucian, Legalist, and Taoist Thought in Later Han," in *The Cambridge History of China*, vol. 1, *The Ch'in and the Han Empires 221 B.C.–A.D. 220*, pp. 766–807; D. Daor, "The Yin Wenzi and the Renaissance of Philosophy in Wei-Jin China," Ph.D. diss., University of London, 1973, pp. 40–103; H. Goodman, "Exegetes and Exegeses of the Book of Changes in the Third Century A.D.: Historical

and Scholastic Context for Wang Pi," Ph.D. diss., Princeton University, 1985; R. G. Henricks, *Philosophy and Argumentation in Third-Century China* (Princeton, 1983), pp. 3–6; D. Holzman, *Poetry and Politics: The Life and Works of Juan Chi, A.D. 210–263* (Cambridge, 1976); R. B. Mather, trans., *Shih-shuo hsin-yü; A New Account of the Tales of the World* (Minneapolis, 1976); M. Nylan, "Ying Shao's *Feng Su T'ung Yi*: An Exploration of Problems in Han Dynasty Political, Philosophical and Social Unity," Ph.D. diss., Princeton University, 1982; J. Sailey, *The Master Who Embraces Simplicity: A Study of the Philosopher Ko Hung, A.D. 283–343* (San Francisco, 1978), pp. 346–464; Liu Ta-chieh, *Wei-Chin ssu-hsiang lun* (Taipei, 1973); and Yü Ying-shih, "Individualism and the Neo-Taoist Movement in Wei-Chin China," in *Individualism and Holism: Studies in Confucian and Taoist Values*, ed. D. Munro (Ann Arbor, 1985), pp. 121–155.

5. In an earlier work I have said that Confucianism of the beginning of the third century A.D. appears to have been on the whole moribund. See Y. Ariel, "The *K'ung-Family-Masters' Anthology* and Third Century Confucianism," in *Confucianism: The Dynamics of Tradition*, ed. I. Eber (New York, 1986), pp. 40–42. Even though I used the word "appears," I now realize that this judgment may have been exaggerated. I have come to see the exaggerated implications of my judgment as a result of an interchange with Professor Ch'i-yün Ch'en, who pointed out that Confucianism, though outwardly at a low ebb, retained a substantial inner strength, enduring in the form of "Dark Learning" and "Pure Conversation." Hsün Yüeh's admirers, outwardly un-Confucian, non-Confucian, and even anti-Confucian, were, in fact, deeply imbued with Confucian values, as is demonstrated in Professor Ch'en's admirable studies of Hsün Yüeh. See both his *Hsün Yüeh: The Life and Reflections of an Early Medieval Confucian* (Cambridge, 1975), and *Hsün Yüeh and the Mind of Late Han China* (Princeton, 1980).

6. The conventional portrayal of third-century Confucianism was recently challenged by J. Paper, whose study of Fu Hsüan's (A.D. 217–278) *Fu-tzu* (Leiden, 1987) shows that the sinological emphasis on the study of *hsüan-hsüeh* blurred the fact that traditional Confucianism remained a creative force in third-century China.

7. There are some rare cases, such as the headings of chapters 10 and 13, that might be considered exceptions to this rule. The last section of chapter 9 as well as the opening section of chapter 10 are centered on Tzu-ssu's view of the problem of "Wealth and Poverty." The chapter heading of the tenth chapter could therefore be placed one section earlier. The nature of the headings of the last two chapters of the *KTT* is discussed below.

8. In a communication, Professor Wang Yi-t'ung suggested an alternate translation for the title of the *KTT*: *Miscellaneous Notes by Master Philosophers of the K'ung Family*.

9. For references to the variant titles of the *KTT* from the Wei-Chin period through the T'ang see section 2.

10. In the translation I take note of such instances.

11. B, 46a1.

Introduction: Section 2

1. *Sui-shu*, vol. 4, p. 937.
2. See S. Teng and K. Biggerstaff, *An Annotated Bibliography of Selected Chinese Reference Works* (Cambridge, 1971), p. 9.
3. See P. M. Thompson, *The Shen Tzu Fragments* (Oxford, 1979), p. 55.
4. *Po-shih* is also translated "scholar," an official of unique and immense knowledge. For a detailed exposition of this title see "Hucker, *Titles*," #4746.
5. Ch'en Sheng or She (d. 208 B.C.) is sometimes referred to as Ch'en She the King. He was one of the leaders of the rebels against the Ch'in dynasty. For his biography see B. Watson, tr., *Records of the Grand Historian in China*, vol. 1 (New York, 1971), pp. 19–33.
6. The Liang dynasty, A.D. 502–557.
7. *Sui-shu*, vol. 4, p. 937.
8. I.e., the *K'ung-tzu chia-yü*.
9. *Sui-shu*, vol. 4, p. 939.
10. *Shih-chi*, vol. 6, p. 1947.
11. For a discussion of the problem involved with the translation of *ssu yü Ch'en hsia* (he died in [or, under] Ch'en), see R. P. Kramers, tr., *K'ung-tzu chia-yü: The School Sayings of Confucius* [hereafter Kramers, *K'ung-tzu chia-yü*] (Leiden, 1950), p. 105, n. 344.
12. *Shih-chi*, vol. 10, p. 3117; Watson, *Records of the Grand Historian of China*, vol. 2, p. 397.
13. This is the date given by the *Chung-kuo wen-hsüeh-chia ta-ts'u-tien*, vol. 1 (Taipei, 1974), p. 183, which is in agreement with the *Chung-kuo jen-ming ta-ts'u-tien* (Taipei, 1974), p. 1385. Thompson, however, in his *The Shen Tzu Fragments*, p. 52, gives the mid-sixth century as P'ei Yin's date.
14. *Shih-chi*, vol. 10, p. 3117.
15. Kramers, *K'ung-tzu chia-yü*, p. 120, n. 394, suggests that the difference between the (Tzu)-shen in the *Shih-chi*'s reference to K'ung Fu and the *Han-shu*'s (Tzu)-shun is due to the fact that *shen* and *shun* were sometimes confused. In a communication Professor Wang Yi-t'ung has suggested that *shen* and *shun* are variants in T'ang editions and are not necessarily orthographical errors.
16. *Han-shu*, vol. 10, p. 3352; vol. 11, p. 3592.
17. The *Han-shu I-wen-chih* is an abridged version of the *Ch'i lüeh* written by Liu Hsin (d. 23). Liu Hsin was the son of Liu Hsiang (77–6 B.C.), whose *Pieh-lu* was made the groundwork of his son's *Ch'i-lüeh*.
18. The names of the meritorious were engraved on such receptacles. See W. K. Liao, tr., *The Complete Works of Han Fei Tzu*, vol. 1 (London, 1959), p. 279.
19. The legendary Yellow Emperor traditionally ruled in the first half of the third millennium B.C.
20. Emperor K'ung Chia of the Hsia dynasty traditionally ruled between the years 1879 and 1848 B.C.

21. *Han-shu*, vol. 6, p. 1740. Some Chinese scholars mistakenly considered this remark concerning the *P'an Yü* and K'ung Chia to be Yen Shih-ku's and not Pan Ku's.

22. *T'ai-shih*. See Hucker, *Titles*, #6213.

23. For a translation of the *K'ung-tzu chia-yü*'s Postscript see Kramers, *K'ung-tzu chia-yü*, pp. 103–109.

24. Chapters 18–21; B, 24a2–44b5.

25. The first emperor of the Ch'in dynasty (221–210 B.C.).

26. Shu-sun T'ung was an Erudite in the court of both the Ch'in and the founder of the Han. For his biography see the *Shih-chi*, Watson, *Records of the Grand Historian of China*, vol. 1, pp. 291–298.

27. *Shih-chi*, Watson, *Records of the Grand Historian of China*, vol. 2, p. 408.

28. *Han-shu*, vol. 6, p. 1706.

29. Kramers, *K'ung-tzu chia-yü*, pp. 104–105.

30. *Shang-shu*, 2b7.

31. The *Han-chi* in question is probably that written by Chang Fan of the Chin period (A.D. 265–420). It should not be confused with Hsün Yüeh's *Han-chi*. See Yen Shih-ku's commentary to the *Han-shu*, vol. 6, p. 1707. The *Han-chi* is no longer extant; for this reason it is not possible to examine the discrepancy from this angle. The biography of Yin Min, however, appears in the *Hou-Han-shu*, vol. 9, p. 2558. It mentions some Canonical Books but makes no single reference to the hidden anecdote.

32. *Shang-shu cheng-i* (Taipei, 1981), I, 15a7–10.

33. *Sui-shu*, vol. 4, p. 915.

34. *K'ung-shih tsu-t'ing kuang-chi* (Taipei, 1965), p. 5.

35. See Kramers, *K'ung-tzu chia-yü*, pp. 124–125, n. 408. I fail to follow Kramers' arguments. Kramers' discussion attempts the suggestion that Hui was possibly an erroneous form for Hsiang, and that, consequently, Lu Te-ming was in agreement with the *K'ung-tzu chia-yü*'s opinion. After examining Lu Te-ming's *Ching-tien shih-wen*, I, 13a2, I find that a certain Hui is indeed mentioned as the one concealed the books. It is possible, however, that the text might be corrupt, and that the mentioned Hui is none other than Emperor Hui whom K'ung Hsiang served as an Erudite. This would align Lu Te-ming's opinion with that found in the K'ung Ying-ta's version. Second, Lu Te-ming explicitly mentions in I, 13a3, both the *K'ung-tzu chia-yü*'s opinion, according to which K'ung Hsiang hid the books, and the opinion expressed in the biography of Yin Min in the *Han-chi*, according to which K'ung Fu hid the books. I therefore think that Lu Te-ming was uncertain concerning the identity of the K'ung family member who hid the Canonical Books.

36. For a discussion of the nature and the composition of the *Sheng-cheng-lun* see Kramers, *K'ung-tzu chia-yü*, pp. 79–80.

37. See Lo Ken-tse and Ku Chien-kang, eds., *Ku-shih-pien*, vol. 4 (Taipei, 1970), p. 193. See also Kramers, *K'ung-tzu chia-yü*, pp. 98–99.

38. *T'ai-p'ing yü-lan*, vol. 2 (Taipei, 1980), p. 1671 (2a9). See also *Sheng-cheng-lun*, as reconstructed in Ma Kuo-han's *Yü-han shan-fang chi-i-shu*, vol. 4 (Taipei, 1968), p. 1968 (36a9–36b1).

39. *Han-shu*, vol. 6, p. 1728. The "present record" refers to the *Han-shu I-wen-chih*.

Section 2

40. Cf. Huang I-chou, *Tzu-ssu Tzu* (Taipei, 1975), pp. 268–269 (14b3–15a2).
41. For this anecdote see Legge, III, p. 203.
42. I.e., Emperor T'ai Chia.
43. *T'ai-p'ing yü-lan*, vol. 1, p. 390 (6a1). *Ts'ung^a* is a variant form of *ts'ung*.
44. I examined all of Kuo P'o's (A.D. 276–324) works as well as all the Chin era's (A.D. 265–420) works, which are in Ma Kuo-han's *Yü-han shan-fang chi-i-shu*, but I failed to find even one citation of the *KTT*.
45. *Shih-chi*, vol. 10, p. 3259.
46. See *Shih-shuo hsin-yü* under the title *A New Account of Tales of the World*, tr. R. Mather, p. 105.
47. *Shui-ching-chu*, VI, 23a2, and XXV, 3a8.
48. Kao Ssu-sun, *Tzu-lüeh Mu*, by Kao Ssu-sun (Taipei, 1938), pp. 59–63.
49. See *Sui-shu*, vol. 4, p. 937.
50. The *Mencius*, which is one of the Thirteen Classics, was not canonized before the Sung dynasty and was therefore included in the *Tzu-ch'ao*.
51. I am unable to provide a persuasive argument that would explain the omission of the *KTT* from the *Ch'ün-shu chih-yao* (also entitled *Chu-tzu chih-yao*). This anthology, traditionally ascribed to Wei Cheng (A.D. 580–643), consists of various paragraphs from sixty-seven classical, historical, and philosophical works. It is almost inconceivable that the compiler of the *Chün-shu chih-yao* did not recognize the *KTT*. It is possible, however, that he did not think well of the text, or else considered its content an overlap of the other, more celebrated Confucian works.
52. A significant comparison, for instance, was made by Liu Chao (ca. A.D. 510) in his commentary to Ssu-ma Piao's (A.D. 240–305) supplementary sections of the *Hou-Han-shu*. See *Hou-Han-shu*, vol. 11, p. 3185, where he compares the *KTT* with pseudo-K'ung An-kuo's commentary to the *Shang-shu*. This comparison was presented at a much later date by Tsang Lin (1650–1713) as crucial evidence indicating that both of the works were products of the same author. Tsang Lin's discussion of the *KTT* is examined later.
53. Neither the *Pei-t'ang shu-ch'ao* nor the *I-wen lei-chü* refers to any item of chapters 18–21 of the *KTT*, namely, the chapters that portray the life of K'ung Fu. Nevertheless, these chapters did exist in the seventh century's text of the *KTT*, because Li Shan (d. 689) quotes the Tzu-yü (K'ung Fu) of chapter 19 (B, 31a3) in his *Wen-hsüan-chu*. See *Wen hsüan*, vol. 2 (Hong Kong, 1974), p. 984.
54. References to the *I-wen lei-chü* are specified according to their *chüan* and page in the Hong Kong edition of 1973.
55. B, 44b1. A different interpretation of the last passage of chapter 21 of the *KTT* has been suggested in a communication from Professor Chi-yün Ch'en. Professor Ch'en maintains that the passage in question does not refer to the actual death of K'ung Fu but rather to the period when K'ung Fu was "about to die." This interpretation makes it not totally impossible that K'ung Fu himself wrote the last section of the *KTT* proper. I see the point of Professor Ch'en's interpretation but I disagree with him. I therefore leave it to the reader's discretion to decide which reading is more plausible.
56. See *Wen-hsüan-chu yin-shu yin-te* (Peiping, 1935), p. 90.
57. See *Ch'u-hsüeh chi so-yin* (Peking, 1980), p. 172.

58. *T'ang-shu ching-chi I-wen ho-chih* (Shanghai, 1956), p. 48.

59. See *T'ai-p'ing yü-lan yin-shu yin-te* (Peiping, 1935), pp. 212–213.

60. *Ch'ung-wen tsung-mu*, vol. 3 (Taipei, 1969), p. 17.

61. *Hsin T'ang-shu*, vol. 5, p. 1444.

62. This catalogue was circulated under two additional titles: *T'u-shu shih-chih* and *Han-tan t'u-chih*. See Chao Kung-wu, *Chün-chai tu-shu-chih (mu-lu)*, vol. 1 (Taipei, 1979), p. 132, and vol. 2, p. 733. See also Yao Ming-ta, *Chung-kuo mu-lu-hsüeh nien piao* (Taipei, 1971), p. 60.

63. See *Chün-chai tu-shu-chih*, vol. 2, p. 733. This view was later repeated in 1178 by Ch'en K'uei's *Chung-hsing kuan-ko shu-mu* (Peking, 1933), IV, 2b9.

64. Chou Chung-fu (ca. 1800) thought that the *Ch'ung-wen tsung-mu*'s reference to a three-*chüan* edition of the *KTT* was erroneous. See his *Cheng-t'ang tu-shu-chi*, vol. 3 (Peking, 1959), pp. 504–505.

65. For various reproductions of the Sung Hsien edition and commentary see figures 1, 2, and 3, pp. 40–42.

66. See his report to the Secretariat-Chancellor in A, 1a1–3a3.

67. For the Sung Hsien's preface to the *KTT* see A, 4a1–5a2.

68. In this short biography of K'ung Fu, Sung Hsien states (A, 4a3) that when K'ung Fu discovered that his counsel was ignored by Ch'en Sheng the King, he retired from office citing his defective eye as a pretext. Now the circumstances that brought about the retirement of K'ung Fu from office are recorded in the B, 42b3–44a8. Nevertheless, there is no mention there of K'ung Fu's alleged pretext. I have tried to locate the source from which Sung Hsien drew the story of K'ung Fu's pretext but have been unable to do so. It might be suggested that his source for the story was one of the *KTT*'s passages he decided to delete from his commented edition. For an account of his deletions, see the second part of his preface.

69. Sung Hsien's ascription of the seventh *chüan* to K'ung Tsang is adapted from the opening section of the seventh *chüan*, B, 45b4–46a1. This section attributes to K'ung Tsang only the writing of the letters and rhyme prose which are imbedded in the following sections of the seventh *chüan*, and not the composition of the whole *chüan*.

70. Professor Ch'i-yün Ch'en believes that my criticism of Sung Hsien's preface is too harsh and based on too literal a reading. I have previously noted that Professor Ch'en does not regard as absurd the attribution of the whole of the *KTT* proper to K'ung Fu. In the present case, of the attribution of the whole seventh *chüan* to K'ung Tsang, Professor Ch'en's view is that Sung Hsien's preface should be read as saying that K'ung Tsang put his fu^a (rhyme prose) and *shu* (letters) to be "Lien-ts'ung, 'A' (*shang*) and 'B' (*hsia*), in one *chüan*." Professor Ch'en continues that, to him, "A" and "B" refer only to sections 1–7 of the present "Lien-ts'ung-tzu, shang" (chapter 22 of the present *KTT*), originally divided into "A" (fu^a) and "B" (shu^a). As for the last two sections in the present "Lien-ts'ung-tzu, shang" and the material in the present "Lien-ts'ung-tzu, hsia" (chapter 23 of the *KTT*), Professor Ch'en asserts that Sung Hsien considered them to be "later additions." He then concludes that his reading would make Sung Hsien's preface "not as nonsensical" as I took it to be. I see the point of Professor Ch'en's reading very clearly, yet I remain skeptical. I therefore leave it to the reader's discretion to decide which reading is more plausible.

71. See his *T'ung-chih* in *Chung-kuo li-tai ching-chi-tien*, vol. 4 (Taipei, 1970), p. 1291.

72. The *Shu*[b] edition was probably a printed edition of the *KTT*, printed prior to 1188 in one of the printing centers of Ssu-ch'uan.

73. *Jung-chai sui-pi wu-chi*, vol. 2 (Shanghai, 1937), pp. 90–91.

74. *Han-shu*, vol. 8, p. 2359.

75. 1.6 in the translation.

76. *Han-shu*, vol. 6, p. 1726.

77. It must be noted, however, that Hung Mai does not detail the stylistic features of the *KTT*.

78. *Han-shu*, vol. 6, pp. 1716–1717.

79. There are ten references collected in the *Wei-shu-k'ao wu-chung* (Taipei, 1965), *Chu Hsi pien wei-shu*, pp. 64–67. For the context of these references see throughout *chüan* 78 of the *Chu-tzu yü-lei* (Taipei, 1962).

80. K'ung Yüan-ts'o (fl. 1192), for instance, who was a descendant of Confucius of the fifty-first degree, drew various material from the *KTT* for his *K'ung-shih tsu-t'ing kuang-chi* but was cautious to refrain from mentioning it. A second example is provided by the *Sung-shih I-wen-chih*, which coupled its references to the *KTT* to Chu Hsi's derogatory opinion. See *Chung-kuo li-tai ching-chi-tien*, vol. 1, p. 96.

81. I failed to follow Ch'ao Kung-wu's calculation. He explicitly refers to the *KTT* proper as a work of twenty-one chapters. If we deduct, as he suggests, the supposedly six lost chapters of the *P'an Yü* from the supposedly twenty-six original chapters of that work, we will have a *KTT* of only twenty chapters. The possibility that Ch'ao Kung-wu considered the "Hsiao *Erh-ya*" not an integral part of the *KTT* can be easily refuted because he explicitly states the opposite. See IV, 8b7–8, where he lists the "Hsiao *Erh-ya*" as a work of one *chüan* and refers the reader to the "Book of K'ung Fu."

82. *Chün-chai tu-shu-chih*, vol. 2, pp. 733–734.

83. *Tzu-lüeh* (Taipei, 1977) I, 10b–11a.

84. According to the *Shih-chi*, vol. 6, p. 1946, Po, who was Confucius's son and Tzu-ssu's father, predeceased his father Confucius. Therefore his son, the young Tzu-ssu, must already have been alive when his father died.

85. *Chih-chai shu-lu chieh-t'i*, vol. 2 (Taipei, 1979), pp. 604–605.

86. *Chu-tzu pien* (Taipei, 1978), p. 20.

87. The *K'ang Ts'ang-tzu* pretends to be connected to K'ang Sang-tzu, who was, according to the *Lieh tzu*, IV, 2a3, one of Lao Tzu's disciples. The text, however, was written by Wang Shih-yüan (ca. A.D. 745). See J. Needham, *Science and Civilization in China*, vol. 2 (Cambridge, 1956), p. 255.

88. *Shao-shih shan-fang pi-ts'ung* (Shanghai, 1964), pp. 361–362.

89. It is evident, for instance, that Hu Ying-lin did not examine the *Sui-shu ching-chi-chih*'s entry on the *KTT* for he refers to Ch'en K'uei's *Chung-hsing kuan-ke shu-mu* as the first bibliographical list that mentions the *KTT*. See ibid., p. 361.

90. The *Tzu-hui*'s edition of the *KTT* was reproduced by the Taiwan Commercial Press in the 1971 edition of their *Jen-jen wen-k'u* library (see fig. 4). All references to Li Lien's preface of the *KTT* are from this edition.

91. The Ch'ien-an-tzu whose signature appears on six of the twenty-four works of the *Tzu-hui* collection is probably Chou Tzu-i himself. For a more detailed description of the *Tzu-hui* see Thompson, *The Shen Tzu Fragments*, p. 15.

92. Ta-liang is the old name of the district of Ho-nan.

93. For a short biography of Li Lien, and for a list of his works, see *Chung-kuo wen-hsüeh-chia ta-ts'u-tien*, vol. 2, p. 1084.

94. The problem of the authorship of the Li Lien preface is reflected in Yen Ling-feng, *Chou Ch'in Han Wei chu-tzu chih-chien shu-mu*, vol. 3 (Taipei, 1979), pp. 184–185. On page 184 he ascribes the preface of 1577 to Ch'ien-an-tzu, that is, Chou Tzu-i, while on page 185 he ascribes the very same preface to Li Lien. See also Yao Chi-heng, *Ku-chin wei-shu k'ao* (Taipei, 1972), p. 174, where he refers to the second part of the preface as Li Lien's.

95. *Ching-i tsa-chi*, vol. 2 (Taipei, 1967), pp. 711–713.

96. *Li-chi*, ch. 23, XIV, 1b5.

97. J. Legge, tr., *Li-chi*, vol. 2 (New York, 1967), p. 203.

98. Tsang Lin, *Ching-i tsa-chi*, pp. 711–712, cites in full Cheng Hsüan's commentary to the *Li-chi*, XIV, 1b9.

99. Wang Su, *Li-chi-chu*, II, 10a1–2, in Ma Kuo-han, *Yü-han shan-fang chi-i-shu*, vol. 2, p. 925.

100. Tsang Lin briefly pointed out that the *KTT*, pseudo-K'ung An-kuo's *Shu-ching*, and Wang Su's commentary to the *Shu-ching* have identical interpretations for the meanings of the concepts *ta-lu*[a] and *liu-tzung*. See Legge, III, pp. 32 and 34. I discuss these similarities in the next section.

101. For further data on Chiang Chao-hsi see Kramers, *K'ung-tzu chia-yü*, p. 42, n. 116. See also *Ssu-k'u ch'üan-shu tsung-mu t'i-yao*, vol. 3 (Taipei, 1971), p. 76, for a description of Chiang Chao-hsi's commentaries on both the *K'ung-tzu chia-yü* and the *KTT*.

102. See Kramers, *K'ung-tzu chia-yü*, p. 42.

103. See Chiang Chao-hsi's preface, 1a2.

104. Ibid., 1b4.

105. The date 1777 is specified by the *Ssu-k'u ch'üan-shu* edition of the *KTT*. See *Ch'ing-ting Ssu-k'u ch'üan-shu* (fig. 11), vol. 695, p. 308. For their discussion of the *KTT* see ibid., or the *Ssu-k'u ch'üan-shu tsung-mu t'i-yao*, vol. 3, pp. 4–5.

106. *Sui-shu*, vol. 4, p. 939.

107. For the *Ssu-k'u ch'üan-shu tsung-mu*'s discussion of the *K'ung-tzu chia-yü* see Kramers, *K'ung-tzu chia-yü*, pp. 15–22.

108. *Sui-shu*, vol. 4, p. 939.

109. *Ssu-k'u ch'üan-shu tsung-mu t'i-yao*, vol. 3, p. 6.

110. See his *Cheng-t'ang tu-shu-chi*, vol. 3, pp. 504–505.

111. See his *Shang-shu yü lun*, 2b4.

112. See his *Ku-shu-mu san-chung* (Peking, 1963), V, 1a.

113. Yao Chen-tzung was probably not acquainted with Ting Yen's essay because he referred only to Jen Ho (ca. 1850) and Sun Chih-tzu (1737–1801) regarding the connection between Wang Su and the *KTT*. See his *San-kuo-chih i-wen-chih*, in Liu Fu-ch'in's *Erh-shih-wu shih pu-pien*, vol. 3 (Taipei, 1974), p. 3250.

Section 2   155

114. See his *Ku-chin wei-shu-k'ao: K'ao-shih* (Peking, 1924), 25a3.

115. See his *Ku-chin wei-shu-k'ao pu-cheng* (Taipei, 1972), pp. 174–179.

116. See his *Ssu-k'u ch'üan-shu tsung-mu t'i-yao pu-cheng* (Shanghai, 1964), pp. 724–726.

117. The *Ku-shih-pien*, edited by Ku Chieh-kang and others, is a seven-volume collection of critical studies written by famous contemporary scholars.

118. *Ku-shih-pien*, vol. 4, pp. 189–195.

119. See Chao Ch'i's preface to the *Mencius*, 1a5–6.

120. *Ku-shih-pien*, vol. 4, pp. 184–187.

121. *Lü-shih ch'un-ch'iu*, XVIII, 11b10.

122. See his *Ch'ien-Ch'in chu-tzu hsi-nien* (Hong Kong, 1956), vol. 1, pp. 172–176; vol. 2, pp. 455–458, 489–491.

123. See his *Kung-sun Lung-tzu k'ao* (Taipei, 1970), pp. 23–24.

124. *Wei-shu t'ung-k'ao*, vol. 2 (Taipei, 1973), pp. 744–751.

125. *Chung-kuo wen-hua hsüeh-yüan* (Taipei, 1975).

126. *Chou Ch'in Han Wei chu-tzu chih-chien shu-mu*, vol. 3, pp. 177–191.

127. *Ching Chin-ku-wen-hsüeh wen-t'i hsin-lun* (Taipei, 1982).

128. Ibid., pp. 737–767.

129. See Wylie's *Notes on Chinese Literature* (Shanghai, 1867), p. 83, and Legge in his various introductions and notes to his *The Chinese Classics*.

130. See his *Geschichte der alten chinesischen Philosophie* (Hamburg, 1964), pp. 87, 100, 119, 158–159, 436–437.

131. See his "Two Dialogues in the *Kung-sun Lung-tzu*: 'White Horse' and 'Left and Right,'" *Asia Major*, n.s. 11 (1965), pp. 139–140. See also his *Later Mohist Logic, Ethics and Science* (Hong Kong, 1978), pp. 20, 66, 227.

132. Kramers, *K'ung-tzu chia-yü*, pp. 98–99, n. 323.

133. Ibid., p. 121.

134. Ibid. pp. 127, 136–137.

135. *Han-shu*, vol. 6, p. 1724.

136. *Sui-shu*, vol. 4, p. 997.

137. Wang Chuo's *Tzu-ssu Tzu* is incorporated in Huang I-chou, *Tzu-ssu Tzu* (Taipei, 1975).

138. For the *I-lin*'s eight quotations of the *Tzu-ssu Tzu* see 1, 7b4–8a7.

139. See Huang I-chou, *Tzu-ssu Tzu*, pp. 273–309.

140. *Chün-chai tu-shu-chih*, vol. 2, pp. 643–644.

141. For this argument and a discussion of the nature of the *Tzu-ssu Tzu*, see *Ssu-k'u ch'üan-shu tsung-mu t'i-yao*, vol. 3, pp. 37–38.

142. *Yung-lo ta-tien*, vol. 23 (Taipei, 1962), p. 5, *chüan* 2973, duplicates the *KTT*, A, 68b7; vol. 56, p. 20, *chüan* 10309, duplicates the opening section of the *KTT* in A, 6a3. In both cases the reference is made to the *Tzu-ssu Tzu*.

143. For various references and discussions of the *Tzu-ssu Tzu* see Chang Hsinch'eng, *Wei-shu t'ung-k'ao*, p. 733; Yen Ling-feng, *Chou Ch'in Han Wei chu-tzu chihchien shu-mu*, vol. 3, pp. 141–144; Takeuchi Yoshio, "Shi-shi-shi nitsuite," *Shinagaku* (February 1921), pp. 488–494; Fujiwara Tadashi, *Shi-shi-shi* (Tokyo, 1935).

144. For a survey of the most important references to the *Hsiao Erh-ya* see Chang Hsin-ch'en, *Wei-shu t'ung-k'ao*, pp. 543–545.

145. For some of these lexical affinities see ibid., p. 543, which reproduces Tai Chen's (1724–1777) discussion of the *Hsiao Erh-ya*. Liu Shih-heng's *Hsiao Erh-ya i-cheng* (Taipei, n.d.) (preface dated 1821) lists many of the lexical affinities among the *Hsiao Erh-ya*, Wang Su's writings, and various chapters of the *KTT*. See I, 12a7; II, 2b9, 17b8, 36a8; VI, 8a11–8b6; VII, 1b9, 4a2, 4b2–3; XI, 1b–2a; XII, 1a; XIII, 1b, 4b.

146. *Yü-han shan-fang chi-i-shu*, vol. 4, p. 2389. All the editions of the *Yü-han shan-fang chi-i-shu* that I have examined so far list only the *K'ung Tsang shu* but do not contain any of its alleged material.

147. *Han-shu*, vol. 6, p. 1726.

148. *I-wen lei-chü*, vol. 2, pp. 990, 1419, 1610.

149. *Yü-han shan-fang chi-i-shu*, vol. 4, pp. 2415–2421. For a discussion of the alternative pronunciation of *ts'an* see Kramers, *K'ung-tzu chia-yü*, p. 104, n. 342.

150. *Yü-han shan-fang chi-i-shu*, vol. 4, p. 2415.

151. *Han-shu*, vol. 6, pp. 1727 and 1725, respectively.

152. See Kramers, *K'ung-tzu chia-yü*, p. 104.

153. *Han-shu*, vol. 6, p. 1728.

154. We really do not have to consider Ma Kuo-han's argument for the inclusion of the alleged *Ts'an-yen* in his anthology of reconstructed works, because it is clear that he considered the Postscript of the *K'ung-tzu chia-yü* a genuine text, and it did not occur to him that its major part was fabricated later by Wang Su.

155. *Ssu-k'u chien-ming mu-lu piao-chu Tseg-ting* (Peking, 1959), pp. 377–378. See also Yen Ch'in-nan, *K'ung-ts'ung-tzu chiao-cheng*, pp. 4–23 for a discussion of the nature of some of those lost editions of the *KTT*.

156. *Chou Ch'in Han Wei chu-tzu chih-chien shu-mu*, vol. 3, pp. 177–191.

Introduction: Section 3

1. See B. Karlgren, "The Authenticity of Ancient Chinese Texts," *Museum of Far-Eastern Antiquities Bulletin* 1 (1929), p. 167.

2. The *KTT* contains, for example in A, 22b4; B, 5a2–3; B, 5a4; and B, 43a3, four occurrences of the determinative particle *chih*^{a} after pronouns such as *wo* and *ju*^{a}. This is a distinctive late grammatical feature. (See A. C. Graham, "The Date and Composition of Lieh Tzyy," *Asia Major*, n.s. 8 [1961], p. 171). I do not intend to discuss these supposedly late stylistic and grammatical features in full, for two reasons: First, much of the original and early Chou material is not collated, let alone computerized, to allow a definitive conclusion (see Thompson, *The Shen Tzu Fragments*, p. 147). Second, in the case of the *KTT* the stylistic or the grammatical argument can be met by the counterargument that I introduce in the present section.

3. See Chang Hsin-ch'eng, *Wei-shu t'ung-k'ao*, vol. 1, pp. 187–237, for a comprehensive discussion of the forged chapters of the *Ku-wen shang-shu*. See also *Shang-shu ta-chuan*, V, 14b, for Ch'en Shou-ch'i's discussion of the *KTT*'s spuriousness in view of its reference to these two forged *Shu-ching* chapters.

4. For this intriguing case of the "Singlish Affair" see J. DeFrancis, *The Chinese*

Language, Facts and Fantasy (Honolulu, 1984), pp. 1–19, and especially his epilogue, pp. 19–22.

5. See his *Wei-shu t'ung-k'ao*, vol. 1, pp. 16–17.

6. There is no need to enter into a discussion of the dating of the *Shang-shu ta-chuan* here. It can only be stated that the *KTT* was a product of the first half of the third century A.D. while the recorded transmission of the *Shang-shu ta-chuan* started much earlier. See Chang Hsin-ch'eng, *Wei-shu t'ung-k'ao*, vol. 1, p. 246; Kramers, *K'ung-tzu chia-yü*, p. 187, n. 601.

7. *Analects*, Legge, 1, p. 195.

8. For a full exposition of the authenticity of the *K'ung-tzu chia-yü*, see Kramers, *K'ung-tzu chia-yü*.

9. See Chang Hsin-ch'eng, *Wei-shu t'ung-k'ao*, vol. 1, p. 220; Kramers, *K'ung-tzu chia-yü*, p. 155.

10. See Kramers, *K'ung-tzu chia-yü*, pp. 154–156.

11. For the possibility of identifying an unknown author by means of a computer program see J. Tankard, "The Literary Detective," *Byte*, vol. 11, no. 2 (February 1986), pp. 231–238.

12. For a short discussion of the authenticity of symphonies K 16a and K 19a see *Gramophone* (February 1985), pp. 974–975.

13. *Chin-shu*, vol. 4, p. 950; see also H. Goodman, "Exegetes and Exegeses," p. 59.

14. Kramers, *K'ung-tzu chia-yü*, pp. 54–90; Goodman, "Exegetes and Exegeses," pp. 56–65; Li Chen-hsing, "Wang Su chih ching-hsüeh," Ph.D. diss., National Cheng-chi University, 1971, p. 59; Chien Po-hsien, "Chin-ts'un san-kuo liang-chin ching-hsüeh i-chi k'ao," Ph.D. diss., National Taiwan University, 1980, pp. 152–374; and Hsü Ch'un-hsiung, *Wang Su chih Shang-shu hsüeh* (Taipei, 1975).

15. See Kramers, *K'ung-tzu chia-yü*, p. 76.

16. For a summary of the Old Text versus New Text controversy see Tjan Tjoe Som, *Po Hu T'ung*, vol. 1 (Leiden, 1949), pp. 137–145; Saily, *The Master Who Embraces Simplicity* (San Francisco, 1978), esp. pp. 364–365; Wang Yün-wu, ed., *Ching chin ku wen hsüeh* (Taipei, 1967).

17. For the "rehumanization of Confucius" see Kramers, *K'ung-tzu chia-yü*, p. 5. For an anti-apocryphal and mundane portrait of Confucius in the *KTT* see the translation, 1.1. The *KTT*, A, 6a4, and the *K'ung-tzu chia-yü* v, 23b, also use the same metaphors for the description of Confucius's body.

18. See Kramers, *K'ung-tzu chia-yü*, pp. 80–81; Saily, *The Master Who Embraces Simplicity*, p. 313.

19. See Kramers, *K'ung-tzu chia-yü*, p. 81; Saily, *The Master Who Embraces Simplicity*, pp. 313, 353–366.

20. Kramers, *K'ung-tzu chia-yü*, pp. 71, 76–79.

21. See, for instance A, 18b3 (3.2 in the translation) for Confucius's reference to Lao Tan as an authoritative figure.

22. Kramers, *K'ung-tzu chia-yü*, pp. 167–168. See also J. L. Dull, "The Confucian Origins of Neo-Taoism," paper delivered at the Second International Conference on Taoist Studies, Harvard University, 1972, p. 1.

23. Kramers, *K'ung-tzu chia-yü*, pp. 58, 65.

24. See especially chapters 5–10, which contain many discussions of such governmental problems.

25. Kramers, *K'ung-tzu chia-yü*, p. 65.

26. See ibid., p. 95.

27. For a discussion of the authorship of the *Sheng-cheng-lun* see ibid., pp. 79–84. For the nature and the scope of this work see pp. 84–90, 138–154.

28. See Legge, III, p. 34.

29. *Yü-han shan-fang chi-i-shu*, vol. 4, *Sheng-cheng-lun*, 1a6, p. 1951.

30. Ibid.

31. *Li-chi*, XIV, ch. 23, 1a6; Kramers, *K'ung-tzu chia-yü*, p. 140.

32. For a discussion of Wang Su's view of *tsu* and *tsung* see note 68 in chapter 2 of the translation, p. 164.

33. Kramers, *K'ung-tzu chia-yü*, p. 75.

34. For the reconstruction of this lost work of Wang Su see *Yü-han shan-fang chi-i-shu*, vol. 2, pp. 825–826.

35. *T'ung-tien* (Taipei, 1963), *chüan* 102, p. 541.

36. For his commentary to the *Shang-shu* see *Yü-han shan-fang chi-i-shu*, vol. 1, pp. 401–419.

37. Huang Chang-ch'ien, *Ching chin-ku-wen hsüeh wen-t'i hsin-lun* (Taipei, 1982), pp. 737–767.

38. For some of the affinities between the *KTT* and other works associated with Wang Su, such as the *K'ung-tzu chia yü*, the pseudo-K'ung An-kuo commentary to the *Shu-ching*, the *Sheng-cheng-lun*, and his annotations of the various Classics, see in the subsequent translation: ch. 1, nn. 6, 24; ch. 2, nn. 51, 53, 57, 68, 75, 102; ch. 3, n. 32; ch. 4, nn. 13, 29; ch. 5, nn. 10, 28; ch. 6, n. 15; ch. 7, nn. 41, 53; ch. 9, n. 7; ch. 10, n. 32; ch. 12, n. 6; ch. 13, nn. 1, 2, 24, 31.

39. For various opinions on the authenticity and authorship of the *K'ung-tzu chia-yü* see Kramers, *K'ung-tzu chia-yü*, and Chang Hsin-ch'eng, *Wei-shu t'ung-k'ao*, pp. 721–731.

40. See Ting Yen, *Shang-shu yü lun*, 2b4; Kramers, *K'ung-tzu chia-yü*, esp. pp. 361–379; also the index of the present study, s.v. *K'ung-tzu chia-yü*.

41. Kramers, *K'ung-tzu chia-yü*, pp. 98–99, n. 323.

42. Ibid., p. 92.

43. For a discussion of the identity of K'ung Meng and its relation to Chi-yen see ibid., pp. 97–100.

44. See ibid., p. 171.

45. For Chu Hsi's opinion of the *K'ung-tzu chia-yü* see Chang Hsin-ch'eng, *Wei-shu t'ung-k'ao*, pp. 723–724.

46. See Kramers, *K'ung-tzu chia-yü*, p. 62, n. 187.

Chapter 1

1. *Chia-yen*, "words of praise," alternatively, "good words," or "admirable words." Cf. Legge, III, pp. 53, 198.

Chapter 1 159

2. I.e., Confucius.

3. Ch'ang Hung was a counsellor in Chou. He had been in the service of Duke Wen of Liu. References to these two figures are in the *Tso-chuan*, Legge, IV, p. 801, and in the *Kuo-yü*, III, 25b–26a.

4. A reference to a meeting that took place between Confucius and Ch'ang Hung appears in both the *Shih-chi*, vol. 4, p. 1228, and the *K'ung-tzu chia-yü*, III, 2a. In both cases the subject of the conversation was "music."

5. I.e., Confucius. Chung-ni was Confucius's formal name.

6. Lit., "riverine eyes." According to Wang Su, "riverine eyes" are evenly shaped long eyes. See his annotation to an identical description of Confucius's eyes in *K'ung-tzu chia-yü*, V, 23b.

7. Huang Ti, the legendary Yellow Emperor, assumed to have reigned in the first half of the third millennium B.C.

8. Lit., "turtle back."

9. The *Shih-chi*, vol. 6, p. 1909, also has nine-feet six-inches as Confucius's height. The ancient Chinese foot, *ch'ih*, is said to be about three-quarters of the present foot. *Ts'un*, an "inch," is equal to about one-tenth of a foot. See A, 70a6, for a definition of various ancient measures.

10. Emperor Ch'eng T'ang, the first emperor of the Shang dynasty, is traditionally assumed to have mounted the throne in 1766 B.C.

11. Lit., "the various *hou*," usually translated as "feudal lords." See H. Creel, *The Origins of Statecraft in China* (Chicago, 1970), pp. 317–387, esp. p. 323, n. 20.

12. I.e., Confucius. Ch'iu was Confucius's personal name.

13. Lit., "K'ung Ch'iu wears a cloth gown." "Cloth gown" is a symbol of a scholar not in government service. Cf. *Shih-chi*, vol. 6, p. 1947, "Confucius, who had no official title, has been looked up to by scholars for more than ten generations."

14. The legendary model emperors Yao and Shun of the Golden Age of Chinese antiquity, traditionally assumed to have reigned in the second half of the third millennium B.C.

15. The virtuous King Wen (1231–1135 B.C.), whose son was King Wu (1169–1116 B.C.), the first sovereign of the Chou dynasty.

16. Duke Hui ruled in Ch'en between the years 528 and 506 B.C.

17. Lit., "A soaring to the sun terrace."

18. The *Shih-chi*, vol. 5, p. 1583, states that Confucius arrived in Ch'en in the sixth year of Duke Min of Ch'en's reign (496 B.C.). For that reason *Tsukada Tora*, I, 1b6–7, has suggested emending the text by replacing Duke Hui of Ch'en with Duke Min of Ch'en.

19. I follow Legge's translation of *ling-t'ai* as "marvelous tower." See Legge, IV, p. 456; cf. A. Waley, *The Book of Songs* (New York, 1960), p. 259 ("magic tower"); B. Karlgren, *The Book of Odes* (Stockholm, 1950), p. 197 ("divine tower"); and D. C. Lau, *Mencius* (Harmondsworth, 1970), p. 50 ("sacred tower").

20. The six provinces that comprised the Chou realm and constituted two-thirds of China were Ching[b], Liang, Yung, Yü, Hsü, and Yang. The other three provinces, which continued to be subordinate to the Shang dynasty, were Ch'ing, Yen[b], and Chi[b].

For more data on the nine provinces see the *Book of Documents*, Legge, III, pp. 92–151.

21. Cf. the *Book of Poetry*, Legge, IV, p. 456.

22. One of the most prominent disciples of Confucius. For more data on Tzu-chang see Lau, *Analects*, pp. 216–218.

23. Cf. the *chien* hexagram in the *I-ching*, V, 13b.10; J. Legge, tr., *Yi King: Book of Changes* (Oxford, 1899), p. 178.

24. Cf. *Shang-shu ta-chuan*, I, B,4a2. Cf. also *Sheng-cheng-lun*, p. 1954; *K'ung-tzu chia-yü*, VI, 11b; and *Li-chi*, VIII, 26a, Legge tr., *Book of Rites*, vol. 1, p. 479.

25. I.e., she follows her husband's commands and joins his clan.

26. The *yin* and the *yang*ᵃ may be basically defined as the structive and the active aspects of an effective position. They very rarely appear in the entire *KTT*. For excellent discussions of these two fundamental concepts of Chinese philosophy see M. Porkert, *The Theoretical Foundations of Chinese Medicine* (Cambridge, 1974), pp. 9–43; A. C. Graham, *Yin-Yang and the Nature of Correlative Thinking* (Singapore, 1986).

27. One of Confucius's disciples. For more data on Tsai-wo see Lau, *Analects*, p. 204.

28. Liang-ch'iu Chü was a great counsellor of Ch'i. For more data on this figure, see *Tso-chuan*, Legge, V, pp. 683, 716, and 777.

29. Cf. *Tso-chuan*, Legge, V, p. 784.

30. Yen Tzu or Yen Ying, ca. sixth-century B.C., was a famous statesman, philosopher, and economist of Ch'i. The work *Yen Tzu Ch'un-ch'iu* was traditionally attributed to him.

31. Lit., "A valley of a thousand *jen*." A *jen* was an ancient measure of varying lengths. It usually denotes a man's height, about seven *ch'ih*.

32. According to the *Shih-chi*, vol. 6, p. 1911, "rivals" would be a better term to describe the relationship between Confucius and Yen Tzu, whose protest denied Confucius the title to the fief of Ni-hsi.

33. Cf. *Tso-chuan*, Legge, V, p. 33, for the use of the same metaphor.

34. Ibid., p. 589: "Gan-tsze (Yen Tzu) replied: '. . . Ts'e (Ch'i) will become the possession of the Ch'in (Ch'en) family.' " *Shih-chi*, vol. 6, p. 1881: "Yen Tzu said: '. . . Ch'i will eventually yield to the T'ien clan.' " T'ien and Ch'en stand for the same clan. See a discussion of the interchangeability of these two family names in Legge, V, p. 840.

35. There is a certain Tung-kuo Chia (Tzu-fang) in *Tso-chuan*, Legge, V, pp. 838–839, who had been in conflict with the Ch'en, i.e., T'ien clan. *Sung Hsien*, I, 3b5, and *Tsukada Tora*, I, 4a6, have therefore suggested that Tung-kuo Hai was a relative of Tung-kuo Chia.

36. Tzu-kung was one of the most prominent disciples of Confucius. For more data on Tzu-kung see Lau, *Analects*, pp. 204–207.

37. *Shih*, which was the lowest rank of officials, is often translated as a "scholar," a "knight," or a "Gentleman." For a discussion of the various connotations of the term see A. Waley, *The Analects of Confucius* (London, 1938), pp. 33–34; Lau, *Analects*, p. 12; and Hucker, *Titles*, #5200.

38. Lit., "A thousand *chün*," that is, three thousand catties.

39. For the same analogy see *Han-shu*, vol. 8, p. 2359.

40. *Chün-tzu* has been translated as "superior man," "gentleman," "true philosopher," "man of complete virtue," "consummate person," and "profound person." For a discussion of the term see Waley, *Analects*, pp. 34–38; Lau, *Analects*, pp. 14–15. For a philosophical discussion of the term and for bibliographical references to various studies, see Rubin, "The Profound Person and Power in Classical Confucianism" (Taipei, 1981).

41. The term *tz'u* has a broader meaning than "argumentation." It refers to form of expression and rhetorical style as opposed to content. Cf. *Fa-yen*, II, 2a10.

42. *Li* (principle) does not occupy a central place in the philosophical terminology of the *KTT*, as it does in other writings of the third century A.D. For a discussion of various philosophical usages of the term by Han and Wei-Chin philosophers see Wing-tsit Chan, *Neo-Confucianism* (New York, 1969), pp. 54–61.

43. I.e., Tsai-wo.

44. I.e., Tzu-kung.

Chapter 2

1. *Ming*, "mandate" or "ordinance." For an illuminating discussion of the evolution and philosophical significance of the concept of *ming* see T'ang Chün-i, "The T'ien-ming (Heavenly Ordinance) in Pre-Ch'in China," *Philosophy East and West* 11 (1962), pp. 195–218; and 12 (1962), pp. 29–49. See also Creel, *The Origins of Statecraft in China*, pp. 81–100.

2. *Shu*[c], *Shu-ching*, or *Shang-shu*, the *Book of Documents* or the *Classic of History*, is one of the five Confucian Classics.

3. Legge, III, pp. 32–33. See also Legge's discussion of the passage in question.

4. I.e., Ch'eng T'ang.

5. Yü was traditionally Shun's successor and the first ruler of the Hsia dynasty (2200–1800 B.C.).

6. *Shih*[b], or *Shih-ching*, the *Book of Odes* or the *Classic of Poetry*. One of the five Confucian Classics.

7. *I*[a], or *I-ching*, the *Book of Changes*. One of the five Confucian Classics.

8. *Ch'un-ch'iu*, the *Spring and Autumn Annals*. One of the five Confucian Classics.

9. Cf. *Li-chi*, VIII, 26a; Legge, tr. *Li-chi*, vol. I, p. 478.

10. See Legge, III, pp. 50–51.

11. Ibid., p. 26.

12. Cf. ibid., II, p. 164.

13. *T'ien-tzu*, "Son of Heaven," a standard reference to the supreme ruler in China.

14. *Kuan*[a], the capping ceremony that marks a man's coming of age. Cf. *Li-chi*, VIII, 25b–26a; Legge, tr., *Li-chi*, vol. I, p. 478.

15. Cf. Legge, III, p. 26, and *Shang-shu ta-chuan*, I, B,4a. More about Shun's proverbially outrageous parents appears in *Mencius*, Legge, II, p. 346.

16. Legge, IV, p. 156.

17. I.e., Yao, as a *t'ien-tzu*, could not have an effect on the malicious character of

Shun's parents. In practice, though, he gave Shun his two daughters without informing Shun's parents. See Legge, III, pp. 26–27, and II, p. 346.

18. A prominent disciple of Confucius. For more data on Tzu-hsia see Lau, *Analects*, pp. 213–214.

19. I.e., the "Canon of Yao" and the "Canon of Shun." See Legge, III, pp. 15–51.

20. I.e., the "Counsels of the Great Yü." Ibid., pp. 52–67.

21. Ibid., pp. 68–75.

22. Ibid., pp. 76–90.

23. Ibid., pp. 434–452.

24. The Duke of Chou, the Confucian paradigm of culture and statecraft. He was the fourth son of King Wen and the younger brother of King Wu, who was the founder of the Chou dynasty (1111–249 B.C.).

25. Legge, III, pp. 92–151.

26. Ibid., pp. 320–343.

27. Read i^b instead of i^c in accordance with almost all non-*Ssu-pu ts'ung-k'an* editions, and in accordance with *Shang-shu ta-chuan*, V, 14a4.

28. Legge, III, pp. 626–630.

29. The *Book of Documents* in its present form contains eight chapters in which an "announcement," *kao*, occurs in the title. According to the *Tsukada Tora* commentary it is not clear to which five the *KTT* referred. Nevertheless, there is an entry in *Ssu-k'u ch'üan-shu tsung-mu t'i-yao*, vol. 1, pp. 57–58, on a lost book from the Sung entitled *Wu-kao chieh* (An Explanation of the Five Kao), written by Yang Chien (1140–1225). According to the entry the "five *kao*" consist of chapters 37, 38, 39, 40, and 41 of the present *Book of Documents*, i.e., Legge, III, pp. 380–452. The *Shang-shu ta-chuan*, V, 14a3, however, has "the Six Announcements," not "Five Announcements" as in the *KTT*. The *Book of Chou*, Legge, III, pp. 281–630, to which the *KTT* refers in the final lines of the paragraph, has indeed six and not five chapters in which "announcement" occurs in the title. I therefore think that the original text of the *KTT* had "six" and not "five" announcements.

30. I.e., the "Punishments of the Prince of Lü," Legge, III, pp. 588–610. For a discussion of the double title of this chapter see ibid., p. 588.

31. Emend $wang^a$ to $ch'i^a$ in accordance with *Tsukada Tora*, I, 7a3. The seven are: excellence, implementations, government, ordering of society, righteousness, benevolence, and admonishment.

32. Legge, III, pp. 264–266; cf. *Shang-shu ta-chuan*, II, 14b.

33. Cf. *Shang-shu ta-chuan*, II, 15a.

34. Cf. *Shang-shu ta-chuan*, IV, a1, and *Hsün Tzu*, X, 17b6–7.

35. There are almost no available data about Lung-tzu. A philosopher of the same name is quoted twice in the *Mencius*. See Legge, II, pp. 241, 405.

36. The five punishments were tattooing, severing the nose, amputating the feet, castration, and death.

37. Cf. Legge, III, p. 58.

38. Cf. *Shang-shu ta-chuan*, V, 13a–14a, and *Han-shih wai-chuan*, II, 17b; J. Hightower, tr. (Cambridge, 1952), pp. 69–70.

39. Cf. *Chung-yung*, Legge, I, p. 427.

40. Hightower, in his translation, p. 69, renders *shang . . . hsia* as "On the one hand . . . , on the other . . ." but I think that the *shang* and the *hsia* refer to two different periods described in the *Book of Documents*.

41. The Three Kings are the founders of the Hsia, the Shang, and the Chou dynasty, i.e., emperors Yü and Ch'eng T'ang and King Wen. King Wen's son, King Wu, who was the real founder of the Chou dynasty, appears in some sources as a co-king with his father in the distinguished company of the "Three Kings."

42. I.e., Tzu-hsia, whose name was Pu Shang.

43. The Ho cannot designate the Yellow River here. The words are probably, as *Tsukada Tora* suggests, the names of two bodies of water. They are mentioned in the *Shih-chi*, vol. 7, p. 2166, and in Legge, III, p. 99, who discusses the origin of these two bodies of water.

44. A phrase directly borrowed from *Mencius*. See Legge, II, pp. 456–457.

45. For a short discussion of this metaphor see Hightower, tr., *Han-shih wai-chuan*, p. 69, n. 7, and p. 19, n. 3.

46. Cf. *Analects*, Legge, I, p. 201.

47. Cf. ibid., pp. 144–145.

48. For a similar metaphor, see ibid., p. 347.

49. *Ta-lu^a* may mean either "the great plains at the foot of the mountains," as translated by Legge, III, p. 32, or "the great foothill forest," as translated by Karlgren, *Documents*, p. 4. The *Shih-chi* refers to this anecdote twice: In I, p. 22, it has *shan-lin* ("hill-forest") instead of *ta-lu^a*; in I, p. 38, it has the orthography of *ta-lu^a* of the *Book of Documents*.

50. Legge, III, p. 32.

51. Here the *KTT* has a different orthography of *Ta-lu^b*. Following pseudo-K'ung An-kuo's commentary to the *Shang-shu*, 1, 6a, Wang Su's commentary to the *Shang-shu* (*Yü-han shan-fang chi-i-shu*, vol. 1, p. 402 [A, 3b]), and the *Shang-shu ta-chuan*, I, B, 12a–b, it replaces the *Book of Documents*' orthography of *ta-lu^a* ("The great foothill forest") with *Ta-lu^b*—the Grand Recorder.

52. The five planets are Venus, Jupiter, Mercury, Mars, and Saturn.

53. Legge, III, pp. 33–34. Instead of Legge's "Pure Sacrifice," Karlgren's *Book of Documents* (p. 4) has "*yin*-sacrifice." Originally this sacrifice denoted a sacrifice offered with absolute sincerity. See also Legge's discussion of this sacrifice. Cf. *KTT*, A, 63a6; *Shang-shu ta-chuan*, I, B, 5b3; *Shang-shu Wang Su chu*, A, 4b, in *Yü-han shan-fang chi-i-shu*, vol. 1, p. 402; Kramers, *K'ung-tzu chia-yü*, p. 87, n. 284.

54. The Lesser Lao sacrifice used a small animal—either a sheep or a pig. Cf. *Li-chi*, XIV, 1b; Legge, tr., *Li-chi*, vol. 2, p. 203.

55. *Tsu* and *ying* are the names of two separate sacrifices, one for the departure of winter cold and one for the arrival of summer heat. For an analysis of the controversy between Cheng Hsüan and Wang Su concerning this issue see Tsang Lin's discussion on p. 32.

56. The *Li-chi* has, instead of "the border-palace," "the royal palace." See Legge tr., *Li-chi*, vol. 2, p. 203.

57. Cf. *Shang-shu Wang-shih chu*, 1,4a–b, in *Yü-han shan-fang chi-i-shu*, vol. 1, p. 402, and *Sheng-cheng-lun*, 1,a; *Yü-han shan-fang chi-i-shu*, vol. 4, p. 1951.

58. Legge, III, p. 230.

59. Chi Huan-tzu was a counsellor in Lu around the end of the fifth century B.C. See Waley, *The Analects of Confucius*, p. 204, n. 6; W. Soothill, *The Analects of Confucius* (New York, 1968), p. 786.

60. P'an Keng (1401–1374 B.C.) was one of the Shang dynasty emperors.

61. For the whole reference concerning the forefathers' labor and toil see Legge, III, p. 230.

62. Cf. *Li-chi*, 14,3b; Legge, tr., *Li-chi*, vol. 2, pp. 207–208.

63. The fifty-eight chapters of the present *Book of Documents* do not contain the reference in question. It is impossible to determine if this is a case of literary license or a pseudo-epigraphical citation from one of the alleged lost chapters of the *Book of Documents*, which according to tradition comprised one hundred chapters. See Legge, III, pp. 15–46.

64. The "Supreme Ancestor," Wu Ting, one of the virtuous emperors of the Shang dynasty. He ascended to the throne in 1324 B.C. See Legge, III, p. 264.

65. According to *Tsukada Tora*, 1, 10a9, the *pao* sacrifice was a sacrifice offered to remote ancestors. *Sung Hsien*, 1, 7b7, comments that the sacrifice was offered in response to the ancestors' virtuous conduct.

66. Wei[a] was one of Emperor Ch'en T'ang's forefathers, and therefore one of Kao-tzung's ancestors. The *Shih-chi so-yin* quotes Huang-fu Mi to the effect that Wei's formal name was Shang-chia. See *Shih-chi so-yin* in the *Shih-chi*, vol. 3, p. 92.

67. Duke Ting reigned in Lu between the years 508 and 495 B.C. For additional data on Duke Ting see Legge, V, p. 744.

68. *Tsu* and *tsung* may mean here either two kinds of sacrifices or else the halls (*t'iao*) storing the tablets of those ancestors who no longer had temples of their own. The whole of 2.10 can be considered the beginning of Wang Su's attack on Cheng Hsüan's commentary to the *Li-chi*, XIV, ch. 23, 1a6, which took both the *tsu* and the *tsung* as one sacrifice. In the *Sheng-cheng-lun*, 31b–32a, Wang Su forcefully argued that *tsu* and *tsung* denote two different sacrifices. Nevertheless, it was probably the same Wang Su who made the issue the central theme of chapter 33 of the *K'ung-tzu chia-yü*, VIII, 1a–5b. While annotating it, especially in 5a5, he stated very clearly that the *tsu* and the *tsung* have also the meaning of *t'iao*, i.e., the ancestors' tablet hall. Kramers nevertheless maintained that the *tsu* and the *tsung* indicated terms of special sacrifices (see his *K'ung-tzu chia-yü*, pp. 139–140). In any case, in light of Wang Su's annotation, and in light of *K'ung-tzu chia-yü*, IV, 14b, where *tsu* and *tsung* cannot possibly be considered sacrifices but rather the shrines reached and destroyed by a fire in Lu, I tend to believe that the author of the *KTT* takes these two terms as the ancestors' tablet halls, which can no longer store the tablets of the meritorious and virtuous ancestors. It was for this precise reason that the *pao* sacrifice was offered as a substitute.

69. Duke Hsi reigned in Lu between the years 658 and 626 B.C. For further information concerning Duke Hsi see Legge, V, p. 133.

70. Yü is the name given to the regime of Emperor Shun.

71. The present *Book of Documents* consists of four books, the *Book of T'ang*

(chapters 1–5), the *Book of Hsia* (chapters 6–9), the *Book of Shang* (chapters 10–26), and the *Book of Chou* (chapters 27–58). This passage appears in Legge, III, p. 383.

72. Cf. ibid., III, p. 39, and pseudo-K'ung An-kuo's commentary to the *Shang-shu*, VIII, 1b8, which has almost the same wording.

73. Legge, III, p. 92.

74. The five sacred mountains were Mt. T'ai in the East, Mt. Heng in the South, Mt. Hua in the West, Mt. Heng in the North, and Mt. Sung in the Center. For the present locations of the five mountains see Legge, tr., *Li-chi*, vol. 1, pp. 217–218, nn. 1–2, and p. 225, n. 2; Ch'en, *Hsün Yüeh and the Mind*, p. 142, n. 59. See Tjan, tr., *Po Hu T'ung*, vol. 2, p. 502, for another variation of the list of the five sacred mountains. Cf. *Shang-shu ta-chuan*, II, 8a8.

75. Cf. pseudo-K'ung An-kuo's commentary, *Shang-shu*, III, 1a8, which is identical with the *KTT*. See also *Li-chi*, IV, 7b10–11; Legge, tr., *Li-chi*, vol. 1, p. 225.

76. The three dukes are the Grand Tutor, the Grand Assistant, and the Grand Guardian. See Legge, III, p. 527.

77. Some editions emend *erh* for *hsiao*. The sentence then reads: "Other, less famous, mountains."

78. Cf. *Analects*, Legge, I, p. 192; *Shuo-yüan*, XVII, 23a5; *Shang-shu ta-chuan*, V, 11b–12a. See also Hightower, tr., *Han-shih wai-chuan*, p. 106, n. 1, and pp. 107–108.

79. Meng I-tzu is Chung-sun He-chi, a great counsellor in the time of Duke Ting and Duke Ai, i.e., the beginning of the fifth century B.C.

80. Legge, III, pp. 81–82.

81. The *KTT*'s identification of the "Four Neighbors" as the "Four Proximate Ministers" follows both the *Shang-shu ta-chuan*, II, 5a4, and pseudo-K'ung An-kuo's commentary to the *Shu-ching*, II, 11a2. For a discussion of the identification of the "Four Neighbors" see Legge, III, p. 82. The *Li-chi*, VI, 15a12; Legge, tr., *Li-chi*, vol. 1, p. 350, identifies I^d, "Solver of Doubts," and *Ch'eng*, "Chief Aid," as two of the "Four Palace Aides."

82. Cf. Mather, tr., *Shih-shuo hsin-yü*, p. 263. Yu-li was the place where King Wen was held in prison by King Chou of the Shang dynasty. *Shang-shu ta-chuan*, II, 19a9, refers to this also as "escaping from the tiger mouth." Cf. *Shang-shu ta-chuan*, II, 19a2–19b3, for the various versions of that section. Cf. also the *Book of Poetry*, Legge, IV, p. 441, and B. Karlgren, *The Book of Odes* (Stockholm, 1959), p. 190. Cf. also *Han-shu*, vol. 12, p. 4126, for an additional reference to the "Four Friends."

83. There is almost no doubt that the author of the *KTT* had before his eyes the *Shang-shu ta-chuan* version and not the *Book of Odes* version, since the *Shang-shu ta-chuan* also refers to Confucius's four friends as analogous to the four ministers, *ssu-ch'en*, i.e., *ssu-lin*, and not as analogous to the four qualities of the *Book of Odes*. See *Shang-shu ta-chuan*, II, 19a5.

84. I.e., Yen Hui, Yen Yüan, or Tzu-yüan, the favorite disciple of Confucius. For more details concerning Yen Hui see Lau, *Analects*, pp. 201–203.

85. I.e., Tzu-kung.

86. I.e., Tzu-chang.

87. I.e., Tzu-lu, disciple of Confucius. See Lau, *Analects*, pp. 209–212.

88. Duke Ching ruled in Ch'i between the years 547 and 501 B.C. His short biography is in the *Shih-chi*, vol. 5, pp. 1502–1505.

89. *Lu*. Cf. *Analects*, in Soothill, tr., *The Analects of Confucius*, p. 247–248: "death"; Lau, *Analects*, p. 76: "humiliation"; Waley, *The Analects of Confucius*, p. 107: "mutilation"; and Legge, I, p. 173: "disgrace." In any case it is obvious that in the context of the present section *lu* denotes a certain punishment.

90. Legge, III, p. 383.

91. I.e., Master Ch'en.

92. K'ang Shu was one of the ten sons of the founder king of the Chou dynasty, King Wen, and the brother of King Wu, the cofounder of that dynasty. See Legge, III, pp. 381–382.

93. The Three Inspectors were King Wu's three brothers, among whom he divided the conquered land of the Yin (Shang) dynasty. See Legge, tr., *Li-chi*, vol. 1, p. 214, n. 1.

94. King Ch'eng was the son of King Wu.

95. The Duke of Chou was King Wu's brother and King Ch'eng's regent.

96. Legge, III, pp. 381–398.

97. Cf. A, 64b6.

98. Legge, III, p. 383.

99. My translation of *ts'o* follows the *Shang-shu ta-chuan*, IV, 6b3, which reads: "Tzu-hsia said: 'Formerly the Three Kings who sincerely wanted to restrict punishment (*ts'o hsing*) and to refrain from the use of penalties.' " The *KTT*, 66b7, however, has *tsa*, "complexity," for *ts'o*. Therefore the sentence in question might also mean: "The fullest extent of punishment involves many complexities."

100. I.e., he went too far with his attempt to establish a correlation between Ch'en-tzu and King Wen in reference to the careful use of punishment.

101. Tsu-chia (r. 1258–1226 B.C.) was Emperor Kao Tzung's (Wu-ting, r. 1324–1266 B.C.) son; see Legge, III, p. 268. Nevertheless, it was argued in the pseudo-K'ung An-kuo commentary that Tsu-chia was none other than T'ai-chia (r. 1753–1721 B.C.), the grandson of Emperor T'ang. See *Shang-shu*, IX, 9b6–7. The *KTT* obviously follows the pseudo-K'ung An-kuo commentary.

102. Legge, III, p. 467. The clause in Legge's translation reads: "In the case of Tsu-chia, he would not unrighteously be emperor." In any case, my translation follows K'ung An-kuo's reading of the clause according to which Tsu-chia, i.e., T'ai-chia, was unrighteous.

103. Kung-hsi Ch'ih is Kung-hsi Hua, one of Confucius's disciples. See *Analects*, Legge, I, pp. 175–176; Lau, *Analects*, p. 200.

104. I.e., Emperor Ch'eng T'ang.

105. Tsu-i reigned between the years 1525 and 1507 B.C.

106. I.e., Emperor Kao Tzung.

107. For a full account of this anecdote see *KTT*, B, 17a2–17b7; Legge, III, p. 203.

108. I.e., I-yin. See *KTT*, B, 17a2–17b7; Legge, III, p. 203.

109. I.e., T'ai-chia may be included in the category of T'ang, Tsu-i, and Wu-ting.

110. Duke Ai of Lu reigned between the years 494 and 469 B.C. See Legge, V, p. 794.

111. Ibid., III, p. 89. K'uei was the director of state music in Shun's time.

112. Read *k'uei* as *lo* in accordance with Chiang Chao-hsi's edition.

113. For the various versions of these anecdotes see M. Nylan, "Ying Shao's *Feng Su T'ung Yi*: An Exploration of Problems in Han Dynasty Political, Philosophical, and Social Unity," Ph.D. diss., Princeton University, 1982, pp. 361–362; Liao, tr., *Han Fei Tzu*, vol. 2, pp. 71–72, and *Lü-shih ch'un-ch'iu*, XX, 11a3.

114. Chung and Li were supposed to have been two of Shun's ministers. See Legge, III, p. 593, and Nylan, "Ying Shao's," p. 410, n. 12.

115. I.e., the five notes of the pantothenic scale.

116. I.e., the whole cosmos.

117. "One foot" and "one is enough" are written and pronounced identically: *i-tsu*. Hence the pun and Confucius's explanation of it.

Chapter 3

1. Lit., "A thousand *chung*^{a}." *Chung*^{a} was an ancient measure of grain. For the exact definition see *KTT*, A, 7ob5. The *I-wen lei-chü*, vol. 2, p. 1451, reads "ten *chung*^{a}" instead of "a thousand *chung*^{a}." See also chapter 13, note 8, p. 181, in the translation.

2. I.e., Chi Huan-tzu.

3. *Sung Hsien*, I, 11a4; and *Tsukada Tora*, I, 15a7, state that Ch'in Chuang-tzu was a counsellor in Lu. Nevertheless, I could not find any reference to Ch'in Chuang-tzu that would support the *Sung Hsien* and *Tsukada Tora* affirmation.

4. Meng Wu Po was a counsellor in Lu in 481 B.C. See Lau, *Analects*, pp. 242–243.

5. Chiang Chao-hsi's *K'ung-ts'ung cheng-i* omits this sentence. I believe that the sentence implies that Ch'in Chuang-tzu and Meng Wu Po, though colleagues, were not of the same official rank. Hence the argument concerning the irrelevancy of ranks to the requirements of collegial behavior among fellow servicemen.

6. Lao Tan is Lao Tzu, the reputed founder of Taoism.

7. Shu of Kuo was King Wen's younger brother. Hung Yao, T'ai Tien, San I-sheng, and Nan-kung K'uo were in the service of King Wen. See *Book of Documents*, Legge, III, p. 481.

8. T'ai Tien^a is sometimes written T'ai Tien^b.

9. Kung-fu Wen-po was a counsellor in Lu. See *Tso-chuan*, Legge, V, p. 758.

10. This anecdote appears in various sources in slightly different forms. Cf. *Han-shih wai-chuan*, I, 8b; *Shih-chi*, vol. 7, p. 2373.

11. I.e., Kung-fu Wen-po's mother. The Kung-fu and the Chi clans belong to the same family. See *Tso-chuan*, XXVII, 11a,1–2.

12. Tzu-lu was one of Confucius's disciples. For more information on Tzu-lu see Lau, *Analects*, pp. 209–212.

13. Duke Ch'u reigned in Wei between the years 492 and 480 B.C. See *Shih-chi*, vol. 5, p. 1599.

14. For the use of the Ears and the Eyes as a metaphor for entrusted ministers see the *Book of Documents*, Legge, III, pp. 79, 586.

15. Sun Lin-fu (ca. 576 B.C.), the son of Sun Liang-fu, the chief minister of Wei. See *Tso-chuan*, Legge, V, p. 364.

16. Duke Hsien, r. 576–559 B.C.

17. This anecdote appears in the *Tso-chuan*, Legge, V, p. 384.

18. I.e., Tsai Wo, one of Confucius's disciples.

19. King Chao reigned in Ch'u between the years 515 and 489 B.C.

20. *Sung Hsien* and *Tsukada Tora* read *pu-tiao*, "not carved."

21. I.e., Tzu-kung.

22. According to *Mencius*, Yen Ch'ou was Confucius's host in Wei. See Legge, II, p. 365.

23. I.e., Tzu-lu.

24. Legge, IV, p. 199.

25. The "Hsiao ya" forms the second of the four parts of the *Book of Odes*. See Legge, IV, pp. 245–425.

26. The "Chou nan" consists of odes 1–11. It forms the first book of the "Kuo feng," which is the first part of the *Book of Odes*. See ibid., pp. 1–19.

27. The "Chao nan" consists of odes 12–25. It forms the second book of the "Kuo feng." See ibid., pp. 20–37.

28. Ode 26, ibid., p. 38.

29. Ode 55, ibid., p. 91.

30. Ode 56, ibid., p. 93.

31. Ode 64, ibid., p. 107.

32. For the very same words concerning this ode see *Shih-ching*, III, 18b4. See also Legge's remark on this parallelism, IV, p. 108, where he explicitly exposes Wang Su as the fabricator of the *KTT*.

33. Ode 75, ibid., p. 124.

34. Ode 96, ibid., p. 150.

35. Ode 112, ibid., p. 168.

36. Ode 114, ibid., p. 174.

37. I.e., Emperor Yao. See Legge, III, p. 159.

38. Ode 153, ibid., p. 224.

39. Ode 154, see Legge, IV, p. 226.

40. The dukes of Pin were the leaders of the house of Chou between the years 1796 and 1325 B.C.

41. Ode 156, see Legge, IV, p. 235.

42. Ode 160, ibid., p. 242.

43. Ode 161, ibid., p. 245.

44. Ode 175, ibid., p. 278.

45. The sequel of the odes mentioned in this paragraph and the content of Ode 190, Legge, I, p. 307, which refers to the prosperity of the kingdom, make it logical to follow *Tsukada Tora* I, 20b8, with "Wu yang" and not "Kao yang," ode 18, Legge, IV, p. 28, as in the *SPTK* edition.

46. Ode 191, ibid., p. 309.

47. Ode 202, ibid., p. 350.

48. Ode 209, ibid., p. 368.

49. Ode 214, ibid., p. 384.
50. Ode 222, ibid., p. 401.
51. For another version of this anecdote see *Han-shih wai-chuan*, VII, 17a1; Hightower, tr., p. 250.
52. Min Tzu or Min Tzu-ch'ien was one of Confucius's disciples. See Lau, *Analects*, p. 203, for more information on Min Tzu.
53. Tseng Tzu was a prominent disciple of Confucius. For more information on Tseng Tzu see Lau, *Analects*, pp. 214–216.

Chapter 4

1. Chung Kung was one of Confucius's disciples. For more data on Chung Kung see Lau, *Analects*, pp. 203–204.
2. For a philosophical analysis of this chapter and for a comparison between the Western and the Chinese philosophy of punishment see Y. Ariel, "A World with No Punishment: A Third Century Confucian View," *Bulletin of the Chinese Philosophical Association* 3 (1985), pp. 737–754. See also R. T. Ames, *The Art of Rulership* (Honolulu, 1983), pp. 115–125; C. Hansen, "Punishment and Dignity in China," in *Individualism and Holism: Studies in Confucian and Taoist Values*, ed. D. Munro, pp. 359–383.
3. Cf. *Shang-shu ta-chuan*, IV, 23a8.
4. Po I was a minister in the court of Yao and Shun. See Legge, III, p. 47. He should not be confused with the Po I of the early Chou period.
5. Legge, III, p. 595.
6. All non-*SPTK* editions have *hsien*[a] instead of *hsia*.
7. The *KTT* follows the *Shang-shu ta-chuan*, IV, 23a10, which reads *tien-li*, instead of *tien* as the *Shu-ching* reads.
8. Cf. *Analects*, Legge, I, p. 146.
9. "Wen-tzu—the General Wei" is the title of the sixtieth chapter of the *Ta-tai Li-chi*, VI, 3b7. Sung Hsien, Tsukada Tora, and the commentator of the *Ta-tai Li-chi* state that the name of General Wen-tzu was Mi Mou.
10. *Tsukada Tora*, II, 1b4, states that Mr. Kung-fu was an honorary title given to a judicial officer by the name of Ching[c]. However, I have not yet been able to find any reference in the sources that would support *Tsukada Tora*'s affirmation.
11. Cf. *Shang-shu ta-chuan*, IV, 25a8.
12. Cf. *Analects*, Legge, I, p. 146.
13. Cf. Legge, III, pp. 58–59; *K'ung-tzu chia-yü*, VII, 10a9.
14. For the use of the metaphor of the "reins and the whip" in other discussions of "punishment" see *Yen t'ien lun*, VI, 34, 16a2; *K'ung-tzu chia-yü*, VI, 4a2.
15. This is a direct citation from the *Book of Odes*. See Legge, IV, p. 129.
16. I.e., the border, barbarian, tribes of the south.
17. The *Shang-shu ta-chuan*, IV, 23b6, reads: "According to the customs of Wu and Yüeh males and females go bathing together in the river." The *Han-shu*, vol. 9, p. 2834, reads: "The people of Lo-yüeh go bathing together with their children in the river."

18. Cf. *Mencius*, Legge, II, pp. 239–240.

19. I.e., the promoting of the wise and the transformation of the people for the better.

20. *Shang-tao* may also mean "official robbery," hence the pun.

21. I.e., the Yin (Shang) dynasty, 1751–1112 B.C.

22. Legge, III, p. 390.

23. Cf. *Shang-shu ta-chuan*, IV, 23b1.

24. Cf. *Han-shu*, vol. 4, p. 1109.

25. Legge, III, p. 600.

26. Ibid., p. 608.

27. Cf. *Shang-shu ta-chuan*, IV, 25b2.

28. Cf. *Ta-hsüeh*, Legge, I, p. 364.

29. The pseudo-K'ung An-kuo commentary, *Shang-shu*, 11b8, reads: "Do not follow the (false) arguments; just follow the basic evidence." See also Legge's discussion of this commentary in III, p. 608.

30. Legge, III, p. 388.

31. Cf. *Shang-shu ta-chuan*, IV, 24b2.

32. Legge, III, p. 606.

33. Ibid., p. 608.

34. Cf. *Shang-shu ta-chuan*, IV, 24b8; *Shuo-yüan*, VII, 4b3.

35. Cf. *Shang-shu ta-chuan*, IV, 24a8.

36. Emend *chai* for *chih*[b] in accordance with most editions.

37. Legge, III, p. 605.

38. Ibid., p. 59.

39. Ibid., p. 389.

40. Cf. *Shang-shu ta-chuan*, IV, 24a1.

41. I.e., Meng Wu Po.

42. Cf. *Analects*, Legge, I, p. 161.

Chapter 5

1. Tzu-ssu, whose name was Chi[a], was Confucius's grandson.

2. For the use of the same metaphor cf. Legge, V, p. 613; *KTT*, B, 62b4.

3. The *KTT*, A, 66b3, has *pu-ssu* for *pu-hsiao*, i.e., not befitting the father's image. In that case the term translates: "Unlike a true son."

4. Read Chi[a], Tzu-ssu's personal name, instead of *chi*[c], in accordance with all non-*SPTK* editions.

5. Kuan-tzu, or Kuan Chung (d. 645 B.C.), the famous statesman of the state of Ch'i and the reputed author of the *Kuan Tzu*.

6. Read *wei*[b] instead of *hu* in accordance with the *Shang-shu ta-chuan*, V, 11b2; *Tsukada Tora*, II, 8a2.

7. Cf. *Han Fei-tzu*, XIII, 8a3, Liao, tr., vol. 2, p. 108, reads: "Not to ruin the result of observation with the object of suspicion is difficult."

8. Chao Chien-tzu or Chien-tzu is Chao Yang (ca. 516 B.C.), a noble of Chin. For more data on Chien-tzu see *Mencius*, Legge, II, pp. 262–263.

9. Tou Ming-tu and Shun Hua were wise counsellors of Chin. See *Shih-chi*, vol. 6, p. 1926.

10. Cf. ibid.; *K'ung-tzu chia-yü*, V, 20b3; *San-kuo-chih*, vol. 3, pp. 613–614.

11. Tsou was Confucius's birthplace in the state of Lu.

12. The phoenix was an auspicious omen. Here it is a symbol for the elite scholars. See *Analects*, Legge, I, p. 219.

13. *Hsiao-ch'ih*, an owl, or as Legge points out, "A bird which, when grown, eats its mother." See Legge, IV, p. 561. *Tsukada Tora* suggests that the owl in this case symbolizes corrupt government.

14. I.e., the messenger that was sent to invite Confucius to Chin.

15. I.e., the state of Chin, previously referred to as the T'ang province.

16. I.e., the execution of Tou Ming-tu and Shen Hua.

17. The hill here denotes the Imperial Court.

18. Mt. T'ai was the eastern of the five sacred mountains and was worshipped as a god.

19. Liang-fu is a small mountain located at the foot of Mt. T'ai.

20. The King of Ch'u is probably King Chao of Ch'u. See *KTT*, I, 20b2.

21. Jan Yu was one of Confucius's disciples. For more data on Jan Yu see Lau, *Analects*, pp. 207–209.

22. T'ai Kung is the popular title of Lü Shang, who escaped the tyrannous rule of Chou Hsin, 1122 B.C., and went into exile.

23. King Wen met T'ai Kung during a hunting tour and made him his chief counsellor. At that stage T'ai Kung was eighty years of age.

24. Hsü Yu, one of the four secluded philosophers of Miao-ku-she Mountain. When he was offered the throne by Emperor Yao he regarded the offer as defiling and immediately rushed to wash his ears.

25. In comparing T'ai Kung, who accepted the royal appointment when he was eighty, with Hsü Yu, who rejected official appointment completely, the disciples are trying to find out whether the Master is going to accept the invitation of the King of Ch'u or not.

26. *Tsukada Tora*, II, 9b5, reads wu^a instead of wei^c. In that case the line would read: "Rites have no basis." In his commentary, Chang Chao-hsi points out that the meaning of the line is that rites are strictly kept by the secluded wise.

27. Shu Sun (ca. 482 B.C.) was an officer in Lu. See *Tso-chuan*, Legge, V, pp. 833–834.

28. Cf. ibid.; *Shih-chi*, vol. 6, p. 1942; *K'ung-tzu chia-yü*, IV, 16b3.

29. A side street in Lu, and the burial place of Confucius's mother. According to the *K'ung-tzu chia-yü*, IV, 16b3, the unidentified creature "was thrown outside the suburbs."

30. Kao Ch'ai or Tzu-kao[a] was one of Confucius's disciples.

31. I.e., Jan Yu.

32. Lin^c, the unicorn. For a discussion of the term see Legge, V, p. 834.

33. Yen Yen or Tzu-yu was one of Confucius's disciples.

34. The lin, phoenix, turtle, and dragon are the four spirits, *ssu-ling*, in ancient Chinese mythology. For more about *ssu-lin* see *Li-chi*, Legge, tr., vol. I, p. 384.

35. T'ang and Yü denote the periods when Yao and Shun ruled. They should not be confused with T'ang and Yü, the founders of the Yin (Shang) and Hsia dynasties.

Chapter 6

1. Professor Ch'i-yün Ch'en has suggested to me that *Tsa hsün* should mean "Miscellaneous Teachings." Nevertheless, when one reads the whole of 6.1, one can see that the *hsün* that occurs in the title does not relate to the *tsa* at all, which is followed by *shuo* (doctrines), but rather to the instructions given by the Master as to the foundation of learning.

2. Tzu-shang, whose name was Po, was Tzu-ssu's son.

3. The *tsa* here means the various non-Confucian doctrines and should not be confused with the *Tsa-chia*, the Eclectic school. The *SPTK* edition reads: "Tzu-shang asked Tzu-ssu for a subject to be learned." All other editions, however, read: "Tzu-shang asked about the practice of the various doctrines." At any rate, in the light of the context of 6.1, and especially when one focuses on the final line of 6.1, the preferability of the non-*SPTK* editions becomes clear.

4. I.e., Confucius.

5. I do not think that the *li* and *yüeh* here refer to the three *Classics of the Rites* and to the lost pre-Han *Classic of Music*, but rather to two of the six arts (see Legge, I, p. 196). As was seen in 2.1, p. 79, the main body of classical works, according to the *KTT*, consists of Classics that include neither the *Books of Rites* nor the lost *Book of Music*.

6. Cf. *Analects*, Legge, I, pp. 302–303; *Hsün Tzu*, I, 8a2; *Shuo-yüan*, III, 9b5.

7. According to *Sung Hsien*, II, 7b3, Hsien-tzu was a man of Lu whose name was Suo. I could not find any other reference to this figure in the sources.

8. I.e., Confucius.

9. Tzu-ch'an was a contemporary of Confucius and the chief minster of the state of Cheng. See *Analects*, Legge, I, p. 178.

10. Chi-sun is Chi K'ang-tzu of the *Analects*, Legge, I, p. 152. Tzu-yu is Yen Yen, one of Confucius' disciples.

11. For the use of the same metaphor in regard to the comparison between Tzu-ch'an and Confucius, see *Shuo-yüan*, V, 11b5.

12. I.e., Chi-sun.

13. Cf. *Tao Te Ching*, *Ssu-pu pei-yao* edition, B, 1a4. I assume that the replacement of *yu* by *wu* is a total innovation of the author of the *KTT*. As far as I know, there is no version of chapter 38 of the *Tao Te Ching* that has *wu* instead of *yu* in the opening statement of the chapter. For various textual variations of chapter 38 of the *Tao Te Ching* see Chiang Hsi-ch'ang, *Lao-tzu chiao-ku* (Taipei, 1973), pp. 243–252.

14. I.e., Mencius.

15. Ch'eng-tzu is Ch'eng Pen-tzu of Ch'i, a contemporary of Confucius. The forged text *Tzu Hua-tzu* was ascribed to him from the Sung onward. For other similar descriptions of that meeting see *Han-shih wai-chuan*, 2, 10a5, Hightower, tr., pp. 54–55; *Shuo-yüan*, 8, 20b3; *K'ung-tzu chia-yü*, 2, 8b2, Kramers, tr., p. 237.

16. For the rites concerning the sending off of a guest see *Li-chi*, ch. 34, Legge, tr., vol. 2, pp. 365–368.

17. The rites in the present case refer to the relations of kindred among themselves. See *Li-chi*, 18, ch. 8, 17a9, Legge, tr., vol. 1, p. 356.

18. I.e., Confucius.

Chapter 7 173

19. Cf. *Li-chi*, 10, ch. 16, 8b10, Legge, tr., vol. 2, p. 62.

20. *Li-chi*, 10, ch. 16, 8a8, Legge, tr., vol. 2, p. 61.

21. Cf. *Li-chi*, 10, ch. 16, 9a10, Legge, tr., vol. 2, p. 63.

22. Duke Mu of Lu (409–377 B.C.) was a contemporary of Mencius with whom he held consultations. See *Mencius*, 1B, 12, Legge, II, pp. 172–173.

23. *Analects*, Legge, I, pp. 297–298.

24. Read *cheng*[a] instead of *cheng*[b] in accordance with all non-*SPTK* editions.

25. For a discussion of the way the three first dynasties chose the first month of their calendar see *Analects*, Legge, I, p. 298. For discussions of the Chinese calender see Bodde, *Festivals in Classical China*, pp. 26–41; Needham, *Science and Civilization in China*, vol. 3, pp. 390–408.

26. Cf. *Tso-chuan*, Legge, V, p. 666; tr., p. 668: "Hsia are the more correct deductions from the heavens."

27. Cf. *KTT*, B, 6, 41a8.

28. The Canons of the Duke of Chou are the *liu-tien* of the *Chou-li*, traditionally ascribed to the Duke of Chou. See *Shih-chi*, vol. 5, p. 1522, which attributes to the Duke of Chou the composition of the *Chou-kuan*, i.e., the *Chou-li*. See also Cheng Hsüan's commentary to the *Chou-li*, I, 1a3, where he ascribes the composition of all the *liu-tien* of the *Chou-li* to the Duke of Chou.

29. Po I K'ao was the eldest son of King Wen, but he was set aside in favor of his younger brother, King Wu.

30. For more data on the Viscount of Wei (ca. 1122 B.C.) see Legge, I, p. 331; Legge, III, pp. 273–274.

31. I.e., Mencius.

32. Cf. *Mencius*, Legge, II, pp. 125–126.

33. *Chou-i*, I, 2a7.

34. *Chou-i*, VIII, 4a5.

35. This passage is not what it seems to be—a reversal of the well-known argument in the opening section in *Mencius* (Legge, II, pp. 125–126), where Mencius forced King Hui of Liang silently to admit that only "benevolence and righteousness" and not "profit" should guide human actions. In this instance the *KTT* does not abandon the basic principles of Confucianism, but rather copes with the analytical criticism of Wang Ch'ung (A.D. 27–100), who argued that Mencius's understanding of the concept of "profit" was biased and that his whole argument against King Hui was therefore flawed. See A. Forke, tr., *Lun-heng*, vol. 1 (New York, 1962), p. 418. Apparently the author of the *KTT* assumed that the reader of Wang Ch'ung's criticism of Mencius, on turning to the *KTT*, would realize that Mencius's argument was sound because he had been instructed by Tzu-ssu on this issue and was therefore aware of the distinction between two kinds of profit.

Chapter 7

1. According to *Sung Hsien* the Prince of Wei mentioned in 7.1 is Duke Chao (r. 431–426 B.C.).

2. All commentators refer to Kou Pien as a "Man of Wei." I could not find any other reference to this figure in the sources.

3. According to *Sung Hsien* the Prince of Ch'i mentioned in 7.2 is Duke Ping (r. 480–456 B.C.).

4. Cf. *Analects*, Legge, I, p. 265.

5. For a somewhat similar description of the sages' external appearance see *Po Hu T'ung*, VI, 7a, Tjan, tr., vol. 2, pp. 531–532. See also *Hsün Tzu*, III, 3a3.

6. Emend shao^a to shao^b in accordance with *Tsukada Tora*, III, 2b2.

7. The three sacrificial animals are the pig, sheep, and ox.

8. Cf. *Shen Tzu*, 11a2.

9. Yin Wen, a fourth-century B.C. philosopher. For more data on Yin Wen see Fung Yu-lan, *A History of Chinese Philosophy*, vol. 1 (Princeton, 1952), pp. 148–153.

10. Tan Chu and Shang Chün were the two untalented sons of Yao and Shun. See *Mencius*, Legge, II, pp. 359–360.

11. Shen Hsiang^a, or Shen Hsiang^b, is Tzu-chang's son. See ibid., p. 229.

12. Hsieh was the ruler of Shang, and Shun's minister of instruction. According to tradition he is the figure from whom the emperors of the Shang (Yin) dynasty descended. See Legge, III, pp. 43–44.

13. T'ang is Ch'eng T'ang (1766 B.C.), traditionally the first emperor of the Shang (Yin) dynasty.

14. Ch'i was Hsieh's half-brother, and the ruler of T'ai. He was Shun's minister of agriculture. Traditionally he is the figure from whom the emperors of Chou descended. See Legge, III, p. 44.

15. King Wu (1122 B.C.) was the first emperor of the Chou dynasty.

16. I.e., Hsieh and Ch'i.

17. According to tradition, Emperor K'u was the father of Hsieh and Ch'i, and the great grandson of the Yellow Emperor (2697 B.C.). See *Shih-chi*, vol. 1, p. 13.

18. King T'ai was the grandfather of King Wen, whose son, King Wu, was the first king of the Chou dynasty. See *Chung-yung*, Legge, I, pp. 400–401.

19. King Chi was King T'ai's son and King Wen's father.

20. Kings T'ai, Chi, and Wen were the founders of the Chou dynasty. See *Book of Documents*, Legge, III, p. 311.

21. For a description of the dispute over land between Yü and Jui see the *Book of Odes*, Legge, IV, p. 441.

22. For the background of King Wen's attack on Ch'ung see *Shih-chi*, vol. 1, p. 116.

23. For a reference to the war that King Wen launched against the barbarian tribes of the Western border see *Shih-chi*, vol. 5, p. 1478.

24. I.e., the northern barbarian tribes.

25. Cf. *Mencius*, Legge, II, pp. 175–177.

26. *She Chi*, the gods or altars of earth and grain, the symbol of the nation.

27. *Mencius*, Legge, II, p. 176, says that they built a town at the foot of Mount Ch'i; *Tsukada Tora*, III, 6a1, comments that since King Wen's state was a state of a thousand chariots, the number three thousand of the present text is dubious.

28. King Ch'eng (r. 1115–1079 B.C.) was the son of King Wu.

Chapter 7

29. I have been unable to find a single reference to this figure in the sources.

30. The ancient imperial rulers referred to here are King Wu and his son King Ch'eng.

31. See *Shih-chi*, vol. 1, p. 126; *Shih-chi*, vol. 5, p. 1549; *Li-chi*, IV, ch. 5, 3a8; Legge, tr., vol. 1, p. 213.

32. The two dukes were the Duke of Chou, who was King Wen's son, and Duke Shao, who was said to be the son of King Wen's concubine.

33. Duke Shao, also called the Count of the West, was granted all the states west of the Shan river, while the Duke of Chou, also called the Count of the East, was given all the states east of the Shan. Legge, tr., *Li-chi*, vol. 1, p. 213, interchanges West with East.

34. Hou-chi, Lord Millet, the legendary founding ancestor of the Chou royal line, and traditionally assumed to be Shun's minister of agriculture and the ruler of T'ai. See Legge, III, p. 44.

35. That is, how could King Wen, who lived in the period of the feudal lords, be titled with the rank identical to that of Duke Shao, who lived in a period of central kingship? For more data concerning King Wen's title as the Count of the West see *Shih-chi*, vol. 1, p. 116.

36. Emperor Ti-i of the Yin dynasty, traditionally r. 1191–1155 B.C.

37. The ninth rank, or the ninth symbol, was the highest grade of distinction. See *Li-chi*, IV, ch. 5, 3b10; Legge, tr., vol. 1, pp. 214–215.

38. For a discussion of these two special grants see Tjan, tr., *Po Hu T'ung*, vol. 2, pp. 506, 509.

39. *Tsukada Tora*, III, 6b4, suggests that when Tzu-ssu arrived in Sung he was twenty-six and not sixteen. The *Shih-chi* 47, vol. 6, p. 1946, refers to this anecdote but does not specify Tzu-ssu's age at the time of his arrival in Sung. The *K'ung-tzu chia-yü*'s postscript, Kramers, tr., p. 103, mentions the anecdote, but it also makes no note of Tzu-ssu's age. At any rate, since in 7.10 itself, 45b1, Yüeh Shuo labels Tzu-ssu a "youngster," it is reasonable to assume that the age of sixteen does not need any modification.

40. There are no details available on Yüeh Shuo in the sources.

41. The *Book of Yü* consists of the following four chapters: "The Canon of Shun," "The Counsels of the Great Yü," "The Counsels of Kao Yao," and "I and Chi." See Legge, III, pp. 29, 52, 68, 76.

42. The *Book of Hsia* consists of the following four chapters: "The Tribute of Yü," "The Speech at Kan," "The Songs of the Five Sons," and the "Punitive Expedition to Yin." See Legge, III, pp. 92, 152, 156, 163.

43. Ibid., pp. 621–625.

44. Ibid., pp. 626–630.

45. For the chapters that form the *Book of Chou* see ibid., pp. 281–630.

46. *Tsukada Tora*, III, 7a3, maintains that Yüeh Shuo is referring to the difficult phrases contained in the six chapters of "Announcements" in the *Book of Chou*.

47. The ancestors of the K'ung family came from Sung. See *Shih-chi*, vol. 6, p. 1905.

48. King Wen was held prisoner in Yu-li by King Chou of the Shang dynasty.

49. I.e., Confucius.

50. See *Mencius*, Legge, II, p. 486.

51. Cf. *Shih-chi*, vol. 6, p. 1946; Kramers, tr., *K'ung-tzu chia-yü* postscript, p. 103.

Chapter 8

1. *Sung Hsien* says that Ch'en Chuang-po was a counsellor in Ch'i. *Tsukada Tora* says that he was the grandson of Ch'en Ch'eng-tzu (ca. 481 B.C.). See *Analects*, XIV, 22, Legge, I, p. 284.

2. The Feng and Shan sacrifices were performed by the emperor at Mount T'ai and addressed to Heaven and Earth. More on these two sacrifices is found in *Shih-chi*, vol. 4, p. 1355; Watson, tr., vol. 2, p. 14; *Po Hu T'ung*, V, 1a–4a, Tjan, tr., vol. 1, pp. 239–243.

3. Duke Huan of Ch'i (d. 641 B.C.) and Duke Wen of Chin (d. 626 B.C.) were two feudal lords whose conspicuous role in the Ch'un-ch'iu period denied them the approval of both Confucius and Mencius. See *Analects*, XIV, 16, Legge, I, p. 281. See also *Mencius*, I.a.7, Legge, II, p. 137, whose refusal to discuss the history of these two dukes is replicated and reaffirmed here by the author of the *KTT*.

4. Cf. *Analects*, Legge, I, p. 188.

5. I.e., to be able to live and see the days of the Feng and Shan sacrifices.

6. All non-*SPTK* editions add *ch'ing* before *tao*. In that case the sentence would translate: "After the road had been cleared for the imperial carriage." Nevertheless, since the whole paragraph is modeled on the *Li-chi*, VI, ch. 7, 1b–2a; Legge, tr., vol. 1, pp. 314–315, and since the *Li-chi* does not have *ch'ing* in 2a8, I have decided to follow the *Ssu-pu ts'ung-k'an* edition in my translation.

7. Cf. *Li-chi*, VI, ch. 7, 5a9; Legge, tr., vol. 1, p. 324.

8. Cf. *Shang-shu ta-chuan*, I-B, 7a2.

9. The four rivers are the *Chiang*, *Ho*, *Huai*, and *Chi*^{d}.

10. *Tai-tsung* is either "the venerated Mt. Tai" (a variation of *t'ai*, Mt. T'ai), see Legge, III, p. 35, or else *Tai-tsung*, the name of the mountain peak in the East. See Tjan, tr., *Po Hu T'ung*, p. 502.

11. *Shang Ti*, the Supreme Ancestor or the Sovereign on High. For a discussion of this apotheosized ancestor and the progenitor of the Chou people see E. Werner, *Dictionary of Chinese Mythology* (New York, 1969), pp. 410–411; Bodde, *Festivals in Classical China*, pp. 255–257; and Creel, *The Origins of Statecraft in China*, pp. 493–503.

12. Cf. *Shu-ching*, Legge, III, p. 35. For a description of the "burnt-offering" and the "*wang*^{b} sacrifice," see Tjan, tr., *Po Hu T'ung*, vol. 1, p. 332.

13. Cf. *Li-chi*, XIV, ch. 24, 14b4; Legge, tr., vol. 2, p. 232.

14. The four mountains were the central points in the empire to which different quarters of it were referred. See Legge, III, pp. 24, 531.

15. I.e., throwing light on his achievements. Cf. *Li-chi*, XIV, ch. 25, 21a11–12. Legge, tr., vol. 2, p. 250, reads: "acting according to the idea in the bright and expanding (course)."

16. *Shih*ᶜ (director of markets) is also called *tien-shih* or *ssu-shih*. See Hucker, *Titles*, #5762.

17. I.e., inferring their likes and dislikes from the price list.

18. Cf. *Li-chi*, IV, ch. 5, 4b6; Legge, tr., vol. 1, pp. 216–217.

19. Cf. *Mencius*, 6.b.7; Legge, II, pp. 435–436.

20. I.e., Mt. Hengᵃ.

21. I.e., Mt. Hua.

22. I.e., Mt. Hengᵇ.

23. *Yu-ssu*. See Hucker, *Titles*, #8081.

24. *Li*ᵇ, the Chinese unit for road measurement, varies in different localities. For a discussion of the term and its usages see Legge, tr., *Li-chi*, vol. 1, p. 209.

25. Cf. *Li-chi*, IV, ch. 5, 1a6. Legge, tr., vol. 1, p. 209.

Chapter 9

1. Kung-i Hsiu was a chief minister in Lu at the time of Duke Mu (409–377 B.C.). See *Shih-chi*, vol. 10, p. 3101. Cf. *Kao-shih chuan*, *Ssu-pu pei-yao* ed., 4a.

2. *Sung Hsien* and *Tsukada Tora* state that Lü-ch'iu Wen was a counsellor in Ch'i. I am unable to find any other reference to this figure in the sources.

3. P'ang Lan, as *Tsukada Tora* states, is not mentioned in the sources. P'ang was most probably a name of a village and not a family name as is the case in *Han Fei-tzu*, XVI, 1a4; Liao, tr., vol. 2, p. 172, which reads "The son of the Chinᵃ family in the village of P'ang." The *Lun-heng*, X, 7b1; Forke, tr., vol. 1, p. 442, reads "P'ang Hsien."

4. That is, the book also consists of Confucius's authentic sayings.

5. Some editions read "Hu-mu Pao." Both *Sung Hsien* and *Tsukada Tora* state that he was a man in Lu. I am unable to find any other reference to this figure in the sources.

6. Cf. *K'ung-tzu chia-yü*, V, 12b1–13a3.

7. Po-ch'in, son of the Duke of Chou.

Chapter 10

1. Tseng Shen was Tseng Tzu's son.

2. *K'ang*, "holding firm" or "upholding." Cf. A, 65a8.

3. All commentators and dictionaries agrees that *kuan*ᵇ is a kind of a huge fish.

4. Duke Mu of Lu died in 377 B.C.

5. Add *chi kung* before *yü*ᵃ in accordance with all non-*SPTK* editions. Cf. also *I-li*, XI, 11b3; J. Steele, tr., *The I-li*, vol. 2 (Taipei, 1966), p. 24.

6. Cf. *Analects*, Legge, I, p. 256.

7. Legge, III, p. 317.

8. The logic of Tzu-ssu's *reductio ad absurdum* argument is identical with that of Chuang Tzu's argument in the discussion of the "Happiness of Fish" with Hui Tzu. See B. Watson, tr., *The Complete Works of Chuang Tzu* (New York, 1970), pp. 188–189. Both Tzu-ssu's and Chuang Tzu's problem is how to force the opponent, whether

the Prince of Wei or Hui-tzu, to admit that they themselves do not think that his first argument holds true. In the case of Chuang-tzu, Hui-tzu admits that the way he articulated his first argument rules out any attempt to make a meaningful statement about the inner state of beings other than oneself and that, therefore, Chuang-tzu's statement about the happiness of the fish is sustained. In the present case, Tzu-ssu's pun forces the Prince of Wei to admit that he was insincere, and that he did not really think that his government was flawless.

9. I have been unable to find a reference to this Wen-tzu in the resources.

10. For the title *Ssu-t'u*, minister of education, see Hucker, *Titles*, #5801.

11. Unbleached hempen cloth, worn in the mourning period of three months for distant relatives. See *I-li*, XI, 25b3; and 21a4; Steele, tr., vol. 2, pp. 41, 36.

12. The hemp fillet is worn when one grieves over one's friend. See *I-li*, XI, 24b2; Steele, tr., vol. 2, p. 41.

13. For an elaborate discussion of the degrees and proper dress for mourning see Legge, tr., *Li-chi*, vol. I, pp. 202-208 and the preceding attached tables.

14. For more information on the $yü^b$ sacrifice see ibid., vol. 1, p. 171; vol. 2, p. 48.

15. Both *Sung Hsien* and *Tsukada Tora* state that Kung-shu Mu is Kung-shu (ca. 496 B.C.). See *Tso-chuan*, Legge, V, p. 785.

16. Omit *tse i* and read the following passage in accordance with all non-*SPTK* editions.

17. I was unable to find a reference to Lung Mu in the sources.

18. There is no reference to Ch'iao Tzu-liang in the sources.

19. Read $chin^b$ instead of *ta* according to all non-*SPTK* editions.

20. Shu^d, "political methods" or "administrative techniques." For a discussion of the term see H. Creel, *Shen Pu-Hai* (Chicago, 1974), pp. 125-134. For various usages of the term see A. Rickett, *Guanzi* (Princeton, 1985), p. 475, and R. Ames, *The Art of Rulership* (Honolulu, 1983), p. 275.

21. Cf. *Shen Tzu*, 30b9; *Huai Nan Tzu*, II, 4a11.

22. Cf. *Shen Tzu*, 30b10; *Huai Nan Tzu*, II, 4a12.

23. Cf. *Lü-shih ch'un-ch'iu*, XX, 6a5, 7.

24. Cf. *Huai Nan Tzu*, II, 4a12; *Mencius*, Legge, II, p. 464.

25. Cf. A, 63a7-8.

26. *Tsukada Tora* suggests that Pi might denote Tzu-yang's hometown in Lu.

27. Cf. *Shih Tzu*, quoted in *I-wen lei-chü*, vol. 1, p. 623.

28. Wei Tzu, the Viscount of Wei (ca. 1122 B.C), whose name was $Ch'i^b$, retired from the Shang court before the Chou conquest. See Legge, III, pp. 273-274; *Mencius*, Legge, II, p. 401; *Analects*, Legge, I, p. 331.

29. Around 690 B.C., the state of Ch'i was planning to annex the state of Chi. The third brother of the ruler of Chi foresaw that Chi was doomed. He therefore joined Ch'i, together with his district, as an attached state. See *Tso-chuan*, Legge, V, 75.

30. During the construction of King Wen's sacred pond, the bones of a dead man were discovered. King Wen ordered the immediate reburial of the bones in a proper funeral. See *Lü-shih Ch'un-ch'iu*, X, 10b8.

31. Chou, the symbol of tyranny and the last king of the Shang dynasty.

32. According to the pseudo-K'ung An-kuo commentary to the *Shang-shu*, VI, 5a2; Legge, III, p. 295, Chou was amazed to see on a winter morning a group of people wading across a cold stream. Since he thought that their legs had a unique power to bear such cold he ordered them cut off in order to examine their marrow.

33. K'ang Shu (1115–1079 B.C.), the first Duke of Wei.

34. Emend *ts'ang* to *tsang*, in accordance with all non-*SPTK* editions.

35. Cf. A, 66a2.

36. Cf. A, 63a8.

37. See Legge, tr., *Li-chi*, vol. 1, p. 354 (3); vol. 2, p. 295.

38. I.e., he discussed the case with his father, the ruler, who approved the grant.

39. Cf. *Li-chi*, I, 4a1; Legge, tr, vol. 1, p. 67. In the case of the *Li-chi*, the son declines the third gift of horses and carriage because he does not want to appear superior to his father in social position. Tzu-ssu suggests that the Duke's son should also not try to take precedence over his father and let him confer the favor in person.

40. I.e., Duke Mu.

41. Cf. A, 65b1.

42. Cf. A, 64a8.

43. Cf. *Lü-shih Ch'un-ch'iu*, XVIII, 1b1: "You have surely heard that the superior man is like a bird—when startled it takes off."

44. I^d is both "to frighten" and "to doubt," and hence the pun.

45. There are no details concerning this figure in the sources.

46. I.e., the King of Ch'i.

47. I.e., greediness and excessive indulgence in sex.

48. Lao Lai-tzu is said to be the same as Lao Tzu; see Hsiao Kung-chuan, *A History of Chinese Political Thought* (Princeton, 1979), p. 744. According to the *Shih-chi*, vol. 7, p. 2141, Lao Lai-tzu was a contemporary of Confucius from Ch'u. He was said to have written a book about the applications of Taoist teaching. For an anecdote connected with Lao Lai-tzu's activity see also *Kao-shih chuan*, Han Wei ts'ung-shu edition, vol. 4 (Taipei, 1983), p. 1477 [A, 9b4].

49. Cf. A, 66b3.

50. Cf. J. Crump, *Chan-Kuo Ts'e* (Oxford, 1970), p. 252; *Shuo-yüan*, X, 4b5.

Chapter 12

1. For a translation and discussion of a similar passage which forms the introduction of the *Kung-sun Lung-tzu* see Y. Mei, "The *Kung-sun Lung-Tzu* with a translation into English," *Harvard Journal of Asiatic Studies*, vol. 16 (1953), pp. 404–420. Kung-sun Lung was the reputed leader of the School of Names in the third century B.C. For the dating and authenticity of the *Kung-sun Lung-tzu* see A. Graham, "The Composition of the *Gongsuen Long Tzyy*," *Asia Major*, n.s. 2 (1957), pp. 147–183. For excellent recent discussions of the "White Horse Discourse," see C. Hansen, *Language and Logic in Ancient China* (Ann Arbor, 1983); A. C. Graham, "The Disputation of Kung-sun Lung as Argument about Whole and Part," *Philosophy East and West* (April 1986), pp. 89–106.

2. Ping-yüan chün (d. 250 B.C.) is the title of Chao Sheng, a leading figure in the

state of Chao who was the great patron of thousands of retainers. He played a central role in the events that preceded the establishment of the Ch'in dynasty (221–206 B.C.). For his biography see *Shih-chi*, vol. 7, p. 2365.

3. *Hsing-ming*, in the third century A.D.: "Forms and names." See A. Graham, *Later Mohist Logic*, p. 67. For other usages of the term from the pre-Ch'in period up to the Han see H. Creel, *What is Taoism?* (Chicago, 1970), pp. 79–91.

4. Hu Tao-ching claimed in his *Kung-sun Lung-tzu k'ao*, pp. 23–24, that the *KTT*'s systematic correction of Kung-sun Lung's thesis, "A white horse is not a horse," to "A white horse is not a white horse" was a typical late error of the Han to Chin era. My conviction is that the author of the *KTT* did not fully grasp the subtle philosophical implications of the original "white horse" argument and therefore awkwardly rendered it throughout the *KTT*'s twelfth chapter. Both in the case of "A white horse is not a 'white' horse" and in the following case of "Mr. Tsang's three ears," the author of the *KTT* takes the entire philosophical enterprise of Kung-sun Lung as only a sophisticated diversion which has nothing to do with the real state of things. At any rate, both Liu Chün's commentary to the *Shih-shuo hsin-yü*, tr. Mather, *A New Account of Tales of the World*, p. 105, and the *I-wen lei-chü*, vol. 2, p. 1614, quote the *KTT* as saying "A white horse is not a horse." These references indicate that there was at least one copy of the *KTT* that had a correct rendering of Kung-sun Lung's "white horse" argument. Moreover, a careful reading of the *KTT*, A, 74a6, translated in the last four lines of p. 131, indicates that there is at least one point in the debate where Tzu-kao demonstrates that he understands the distinction between a "white horse" and a "horse."

5. Confucius's descendant of the sixth generation.

6. *Hsiao pien*, "petty distinction" or "trivial discriminations." Cf. *Shuo-yüan*, XVI, 2b1; *Ta-tai Li-chi*, 74, 1a6; *K'ung-tzu chia-yü*, II, 22a4, Kramers, tr. pp. 249, 357 (& 17).

7. Emend $shih^d$ to $hsien^a$ in accordance with almost all non-*SPTK* editions.

8. Read *so* instead of *fei* in accordance with almost all non-*SPTK* editions.

9. Cf. *Lü-shih Ch'un-ch'iu*, XVI, 19b4.

10. I.e., Confucius.

11. Cf. *Shuo-yüan*, XIV, 6b5.

12. *Ju-shu*, the Confucian arts, or the Way of a Confucian. For a discussion of the term of ju^b see Hsiao, *A History of Chinese Political Thought*, p. 87. See also Hucker, *Titles*, #3063.

13. For the author of the *KTT*, li^a, "principle," in philosophical discussion is always the principle by which right, $shih^a$, is distinguished from wrong, *fei*. See *KTT*, B, 54b8.

14. Legge, V, p. 170.

15. *Ch'un-ch'iu Kung-yang chuan*, V, 16a1.

16. Legge, IV, pp. 85–86.

17. *Li-chi*, XII, ch. 20, 1a8.

18. Emend li^c to li^d. I could not find li^c in any source or dictionary. The "Hsiao Erh-ya," however, lists li^d, which usually means 'black horse,' as purely black color. See A, 64a4.

19. Cf. A, 9b5.

20. Cf. *Lü-shih Ch'un-ch'iu*, XVIII, 11b9.

21. The *Lü-shih Ch'un-ch'iu*, XVIII, 11b9, has *pien*^{a} instead of *pien*^{b}. The *KTT*, A, 64b7, has *ch'i-pieh* for *pien*^{b}. It is clear, however, that the author of the *KTT* regards scholars who make distinctions (*pien*^{b}) as eloquent debaters. See also B, 54b8, where he explicitly identifies the *lun pien che* with those who make distinctions between principles of right and wrong.

22. For the various forms of this enigmatic statement and for its analysis see Graham, "The Composition of the *Gongsuen Long Tzyy*," pp. 164-165.

23. There is no reference to this figure in the sources.

24. There is no reference to this figure in the sources either.

25. Cf. *Hsiao-ching*, XIV, 13a7.

Chapter 13

1. Cf. Legge, tr., *Li-chi*, vol. 2, p. 402: "Dress of a scholar," and Kramers, tr., *K'ung-tzu chia-yü*, p. 215: "Robe of a Ju." For a discussion of the term of *ju* see Hsiao, *A History of Chinese Political Thought*, p. 87; Hucker, *Titles*, #3063.

2. Cf. *K'ung-tzu chia-yü*, II, 16b7; Kramers, tr., p. 244: "Official robe and cap." I have decided to omit the "cap" because Wang Su himself refers to *kung-mien* as embroidered clothing and makes no mention of a cap in his commentary to the above paragraph of the *K'ung-tzu chia-yü*.

3. *Liu-i*, the six arts, i.e., rites, music, archery, riding, writing, and arithmetic.

4. Cf. *Mencius*, 7.b.37; Legge, II, p. 498.

5. I have found no references to these two individuals in the relevant sources.

6. Read *chu*^{a} instead of *i* in accordance with almost all non-*SPTK* editions.

7. Cf. *Mencius*, Legge, II, p. 201.

8. *Chung*^{a}, a jar, and *ku*, a beaker, were ancient wine vessels. For the measure of *chung*^{a} see A, 70b5-6.

9. Tzu-lu or Chi-lu, whose name was Chung Yu, was a prominent disciple of Confucius. See Lau, *Analects*, pp. 209-212.

10. I follow *Tsukada Tora*, V, 8a4, who explains *k'o-k'o* as *shao-yin*.

11. Cf. *Lun-heng*, VII, ch. 25, 16b8.

12. I.e., Confucius.

13. Nan Tzu was the notoriously lewd wife of Duke Ling of Wei. See *Analects*, Legge, I, p. 193.

14. For a parallel of this anecdote see *Han-shih wai-chuan*, I, 1b8, Hightower, tr., p. 13.

15. Cf. *Li-chi*, ch. 19, 7a2; Legge, tr., vol. 2, p. 408.

16. Read *i*^{e} instead of *tsai* according to most non-*SPTK* editions.

17. Read *wen pu i* instead of *se pu tsai i* according to several non-*SPTK* editions.

18. See *Analects*, Legge, I, p. 294.

19. For a description of the manner of this meeting see *Shih-chi*, vol. 6, p. 1920.

20. The presence of the wife in these great feasts was disdained. See Legge, tr., *Li-chi*, vol. 2, p. 298.

21. The *KTT*, A, 64b1, defines *huo* with *te*. Chu Hsi, in his *Shih chi chuan* (Taipei,

1981), XVI, 20b4, explains *pu huo* as "losing the Way." *Tsukada Tora*, V, 9a5, explains *fu huo* as loosing grasp of the rites.

22. The troops of Ch'in surrounded Ta-liang, the capital of Wei, at the time of King An Hsi (r. 276–247 B.C.). The anecdote is recorded in the *Shih-chi*, vol. 7, p. 2377.

23. Wu Chi, the youngest son of King Chao of Wei, r. 295–276 B.C. For his biography see ibid.

24. The *wu ti* here do not represent a group of five legendary emperors but rather the five gods or spirits that correspond to the five phases. See *K'ung-tzu chia-yü*, VI, 1a7, and Wang Su's commentary on it.

25. The East correlates with green, the South with red, the Center with yellow, the West with white, and the North with black. See Needham, vol. 2, pp. 262–263, for a table of symbolic correlations of the five phases.

26. Eight correlates with the East, seven with the South, five with the Center, nine with the West, and six with the North.

27. The East correlates with sheep, the South with fowl, the Center with ox, the West with dog, and the North with pig.

28. The five arms were the bow and the arrow, the *shu* lance, the spear, the lance, and the halberd.

29. This paragraph appears in non-*SPTK* editions as a separate piece.

30. The question is probably asked with reference to the *Shu-ching*, Legge, III, p. 155.

31. *Chu^b* is replaced by *tu* in some non-*SPTK* editions. In both cases it represents the execution at the altar of the God of the Earth, as exemplified in the pseudo-K'ung An-kuo commentary to the *Shu-ching*, III, 10b10, which reads: "The guilty was executed before the altar of the God of the Earth."

32. Cf. *Mo-tzu*, VIII, 6b6; Watson, tr., p. 100.

33. I have found no reference to Ch'en Wang in the sources. *Sung Hsien*, IV, 8a1, states that he was a man from Wei, but he gives no further details about him.

34. There is no reference to this figure in the sources.

35. Kuan Shu and Ts'ai Shu were the elder and younger brothers of the Duke of Chou. For their biography see *Shih-chi* 35, vol. 5, pp. 1563–1574. See also *Shu-ching*, Legge, III, pp. 357–359, where their malicious attitude toward their brother, the Duke of Chou, is recorded.

36. The original quotation in the *Shu-ching*, Legge, III, p. 70, is transposed.

37. Ts'ao-tzu is Ts'ao Kuei of Lu (ca. 680 B.C.). He is mentioned in the *Tso-chuan*, Legge, V, p. 85.

38. This is a condensed version of the anecdote that is fully recorded in the *Ch'un-ch'iu kung-yang-chuan*, III, 13a5–13b11; *Tso-chuan*, Legge, V, pp. 90–91.

Chapter 14

1. *Sung Hsien*, IV, 9a5, states that the King of Wei mentioned here is King An Hsi, who reigned in Wei during the years 276–243 B.C.

2. There is no reference in the sources to this particular Chang Shu.

3. There is no reference in the sources to this particular Fan Wei.

4. Po-lo is a nickname of a famous horse trainer in remote antiquity. He is mentioned in various sources. See, for instance, Hightower, tr., *Han-shih wai-chuan*, p. 229; Liao, tr., *Han Fei Tzu*, vol. 1, p. 244; Watson, tr., *The Complete Works of Chuang Tzu*, p. 104.

5. Mr. Pien is Pien Ho from Ch'u, who was afflicted with terrible pains throughout his life because of his persistent claim that the stone he had found in the mountain was genuine jade. For a full exposition of this famous anecdote see B. Watson, tr., *Han Fei Tzu, Basic Writings* (New York, 1964), p. 80.

6. Emend *ch'i*^{c} to *mei*, in accordance with all non-*SPTK* editions.

7. Cf. *Analects*, Legge, I, p. 257.

8. *Sung Hsien*, IV, 10a6, states that this King of Ch'i is King Hsüan (r. 332–314 B.C.).

9. Lord Shang (ca. 359–338 B.C.) was executed in the same way. See Crump, tr., *Chan-Kuo Ts'e*, p. 55.

10. *Wu-ch'ang*, or *wu-lun*, the five norms of human relationships between ruler and subject, father and son, husband and wife, brother and brother, and friend and friend. Sometimes *wu-ch'ang* denotes the five fundamental virtues, namely, benevolence, righteousness, rites, knowledge, and honesty. For the relationships between *wu-ch'ang* and human feelings such as sorrow and joy see Legge, tr., *Li-chi*, vol. 2, pp. 92–93, and p. 107.

11. Cf. *Chung-yung*, Legge, I, p. 384. Most non-*SPTK* editions omit *pu* after *wu*^{a}. In that case the paragraph would translate: "Man is also expressed in the feelings of sorrow, joy, pleasure, and anger. These feelings should never be allowed to run beyond their proper degree. However, when this happens, one's sense of righteousness is undermined." In the light of the preceding sentences, however, which argue that the King's severe law denies his people their natural expression, it seems that the reading is correct and that the *pu* should not be omitted.

12. *Tsukada Tora*, V, 14b2, as many other non-*SPTK* editions, has *chung*^{b} instead of *chu*^{a}. In his punctuation he inserts a full stop after the *chung*^{b}. In that case the two sentences would translate: "The ruler must cooperate with all the officials. If a great state faces difficulties and yet carries out brutal punishments which intimidate people near and far, then. . . ."

13. Lung-p'ang, who is usually referred to by the name Lung-feng, is Kuan Lung-feng, who was executed by Chieh (ca. 1818 B.C.), the last tyrant-king of the Hsia dynasty, because of his critical stands against his king. See *Hsin-yü*, VII, 1b5. See also Watson, tr., *Chuang Tzu*, p. 55.

14. Pi Kan is Prince Pi Kan, who was brutally executed by Chou (ca. 1154 B.C.), the last tyrant-king of the Shang dynasty, because of his firm stand against his king. See *Analects*, Legge, I, p. 331.

15. Emend *t'ao* to *hsien*^{b} according to all non-*SPTK* editions.

16. *Chi-tzu*, the Viscount of Chi, who was, as Pi Kan, the uncle of Chou, the last tyrant of the Shang dynasty. The Viscount of Chi was thrown into jail and then forced to retire from court because of his criticism of the king. See *Analects*, Legge, I, p. 331.

17. *Sung Hsien*, IV, 11a5, states that Kuan Mu was a worthy man in Ch'i. However, I could not find any indication of this figure in the sources.

18. Chao Wen-tzu is the posthumous title of Chao Wu (ca. 545 B.C.), who was a counsellor of Chin. See *Tso-chuan*, Legge, V, p. 528.

19. Read "six feet" and not "three feet" in accordance with the *T'ai-p'ing yü-lan*, 382, 4b9, which consists of some lines of the present paragraph. The ancient Chinese foot, *ch'ih*, is said to be about three-quarters of the present foot. Yen-tzu was indeed short, even by ancient Chinese standards, but certainly not a dwarf. The *T'ai-p'ing yü-lan*'s "six feet" agrees with the *Shih-chi*, vol. 7, p. 2135, which also has "six feet" as Yen-tzu's height.

GLOSSARY

An Hsi 安釐
An-kuo 安國
chai 扱
Chan-kuo ts'e 戰國策
chang-chü 章句
Chang Fan 張璠
Chang Hsin-ch'eng 張心澂
Chang-sun Wu-chi 長孫無忌
Chang-yen 長彥
Chao Ch'i 趙岐
Ch'ao Kung-wu 晁公武
Ch'ao-san lang 朝散郎
Chao Sheng 趙勝
Chao Yang 趙軼
Ch'en 陳
Ch'en Chen-sun 陳振孫
Ch'en Ch'eng-tzu 陳成子
Ch'en K'uei 陳騤
Ch'en She 陳涉
Ch'en Sheng 陳勝
Ch'en shih-i 陳士義
cheng[a] 正
cheng[b] 政
Ch'eng 丞
Cheng Ch'iao 鄭樵
Cheng Hsüan 鄭玄
Ch'eng Jung 程榮
Ch'eng T'ang 成湯
Chi[a] 伋
Chi[b] 冀
chi[c] 亟

Chi[d]	濟
ch'i[a]	七
Ch'i[b]	啓
ch'i[c]	契
Chi-fa	祭法
Chi-i	記義
chi kung	寄公
Chi-lu	季路
Ch'i-lu	七錄
Ch'i lüeh	七略
Ch'i Mo	詰墨
ch'i-pieh	詰別
Chi-tzu	箕子
Chi-wen	記問
Chi-yen	季彥
Chia	甲
Chia I	賈誼
Chia-yen	嘉言
Chia-yü	家語
Chiang	江
Chiang Chao-hsi	姜兆錫
Chiang-yu	江右
Chien-yang	建陽
ch'ien	前
Ch'ien-an-tzu	潛菴子
Ch'ien Hsi-tso	錢熙祚
Ch'ien Mu	錢穆
chih[a]	之
chih[b]	枳
ch'ih	尺
Chih-chai shu-lu chieh-t'i	直齋書錄解題
Chih-chieh	執節
Chih-hai	指海

Glossary

Chin^a 糷
chin^b 進
Chin-shih 進士
Ch'in shih-huang-ti 秦始皇帝
Chin Shou-shen 金受申
ching^a 經
Ching^b 荊
Ching^c 靖
ch'ing 清
Ching-chou 荊州
Ching-i tsa-chi 經義雜記
ch'ing-t'an 清談
Ching-tien shih-wen 經典釋文
Ch'iu 求
Chiu T'ang-shu 舊唐書
Chiu T'ang-shu ching-chi-chih 舊唐書經籍志
Chou Ch'in Han Wei Chu-tzu chih-chien shu-mu 周秦漢魏諸子知見書目
Chou Chung-fu 周中孚
Chou-kuan 周官
Chou-li 周禮
Chou Tzu-i 周子義
chu^a 諸
chu^b 主
Chu-hou 諸候
Chu Hsi 朱熹
Chu Hsi pien wei-shu 朱熹辨偽書
Ch'u-hsüeh chi 初學記
chu-tzu 諸子
Chu-tzu chih-yao 諸子治要
Chu-tzu hui-han 諸子彙函
Chu-tzu pien 諸子辯
Chü Wei 居衛
Ch'uan 穿

chüan 卷
chün 鈞
Chün-chai tu-shu-chih 郡齋讀書志
Ch'un-ch'iu 春秋
Ch'ün-shu chih-yao 群書治要
chün-tzu 君子
Chung 忠
chung[a] 鍾
chung[b] 衆
Chung Hsing 鍾惺
Chung-hsing kuan-ke shu-mu 中興館閣書目
Chung-hua shu-chü 中華書局
Chung-huang 仲驤
Chung-shu 中書
Chung-sun He-chi 仲孫何忌
Ch'ung-wen tsung-mu 崇文總目
Chung Yu 仲由
Chung-yung 中庸
erh 而
Erh-ya 爾雅
fei 非
Fu 鮒
fu[a] 賦
Fu Chia 鮒甲
Fu Hsüan 傅玄
fu huo 弗獲
Fu-tzu 傅子
Han-chi 漢紀
Han Fei Tzu 韓非子
Han-shih wai-chuan 韓詩外傳
Han-shu 漢書
Han-shu I-wen-chih 漢書藝文志
Han-tan shu-mu 邯鄲書目
Han-tan t'u-chih 邯鄲圖志

Glossary

Han-Wei ts'ung shu　漢魏叢書
Heng^a　衡
Heng^b　恆
Ho　河
Ho-nan　河南
Ho Yün-chung　何允中
hou　後
Hou-Han-shu　後漢書
hsia　下
Hsia-kuan　夏官
Hsiang　襄
hsiang-chin yü k'an t'an chi han shu yeh　相近於坎壇祭寒暑也
hsiao　小
Hsiao Erh-ya　小爾雅
hsiao pien　小辨
hsiao-ch'ih　梟鴟
Hsiao-ching　孝經
Hsiao Wu　孝武
hsien^a　先
hsien^b　陷
Hsin-hsing　新興
hsin-hsing chih li　心性之理
Hsin-hsü　新序
Hsin T'ang-shu　新唐書
Hsin shih　心史
Hsing-lun　刑論
hsing-ming　刑名
Hsü　徐
Hsü Chien　徐堅
Hsü Kuang　徐廣
hsüan-hsüeh　玄學
Hsün-shou　巡狩
Hsün Tzu　荀子
hu　乎

Hu Tao-ching　胡道靜
Hu Ying-lin　胡應麟
Hu Yü-chin　胡玉縉
Huai　淮
Huang　黃
Huang Chang-chien　黃彰健
Huang-fu Mi　皇甫謐
Huang Ti　黃帝
Huang Yün-mei　黃雲眉
Hui　惠
Hung Mai　洪邁
huo　獲
I^a　易
i^b　義
i^c　議
I^d　疑
i^e　己
I-ching　易經
I-lin　意林
i-tsu　一足
I-wen lei-chü　藝文類聚
I-yin　伊尹
Jan Yu　冉有
jang chi　禳祈
Jen　仁
Jen Ho　仁和
Jen-jen wen-k'u　人人文庫
ju^a　汝
ju^b　儒
Ju-chia　儒家
Ju-chia-yen　儒家言
Ju-fu　儒服
ju-shu　儒術
Juan Hsiao-hsü　阮孝緒

Glossary

Jung-chai sui-pi 容齋隨筆
k'ang 抗
K'ang-chih 抗志
K'ang Sang-tzu 亢桑子
K'ang Shu 康叔
K'ang Ts'ang-tzu 亢倉子
kao 誥
Kao-shih-chuan 高士傳
Kao Ssu-sun 高似孫
Kao yang 羔羊
Kao Yu 高誘
K'o[a] 榾
K'o[b] 軻
k'o k'o 嗑嗑
ku 觚
Ku Chieh-kang 顧頡剛
Ku-chin wei-shu k'ao 古今偽書考
Ku-shih-pien 古史辨
Ku-wen Shang-shu 古文尚書
kuan[a] 冠
kuan[b] 鯤
Kuan-chih 貫之
Kuan Lung-feng 關龍逢
Kuan Shu 管叔
Kuang Han-Wei ts'ung-shu 廣漢魏叢書
K'uei 夔
Kuei Ku-tzu 鬼谷子
Kuei Yu-kuang 歸有光
K'ung 孔
K'ung An-kuo 孔安國
K'ung Chi 孔伋
K'ung Chia 孔甲
K'ung-chih 孔志
K'ung Ch'uan 孔穿

K'ung Fu 孔鮒
K'ung Hsiang 孔襄
K'ung Hui 孔惠
Kung-i 公儀
K'ung Meng 孔猛
kung-mien 袞冕
K'ung Shang-ta 孔尚達
K'ung-shih tsu-t'ing kuang-chi 孔氏祖庭廣記
Kung-shu Shu 公叔戍
Kung-sun Lung 公孫龍
Kung-sun Lung-tzu 公孫龍子
K'ung Tsang shu 孔臧書
K'ung-ts'ung 孔叢
K'ung-ts'ung[a] 孔藂
K'ung-ts'ung cheng-i 孔叢正義
K'ung-ts'ung-tzu 孔叢子
K'ung-tsung[a]-tzu 孔藂子
K'ung-ts'ung-tzu chiao-cheng 孔叢子斠證
K'ung-ts'ung-tzu shih-wen 孔叢子釋文
K'ung-tzu chia-yü 孔子家語
K'ung Yin-chih 孔胤植
K'ung Ying-ta 孔穎達
K'ung Yü-ch'i 孔毓圻
K'ung Yü-yen 孔毓埏
K'ung Yüan-ts'o 孔元措
Kuo P'o 郭璞
Kuo yü 國語
Lan-yen 讕言
Lao Tan 老聃
Lao Tzu 老子
Li 鯉
li[a] 理
li[b] 里
li[c] 犧

Glossary

li[d] 驪
Li-chi 禮記
Li Lien 李濂
Li Shan 李善
Li Shu 李叔
Li Tao-yüan 酈道元
Liang 梁
Lien-ts'ung-tzu hsia 連叢子下
Lien-ts'ung-tzu shang 連叢子上
Lin[a] 琳
Lin[b] 林
lin[c] 麟
ling-t'ai 靈臺
Liu Chao 劉昭
Liu Chün 劉峻
Liu Hsiang 劉向
Liu Hsin 劉歆
Liu Hsü 劉煦
liu-i 六藝
Liu Pei 劉被
liu-tien 六典
liu-tzung 六宗
lo 樂
Lo Ken-tse 羅根澤
lu 戮
Lü-shih ch'un-ch'iu 呂氏春秋
Lu Te-ming 陸德明
Lun-heng 論衡
lun pien che 論辨者
Lun-shih 論勢
Lun-shu 論書
Lun-yü 論語
Lung-tzu 龍子
Ma Jung 馬融

Ma Kuo-han	馬國翰
Ma Tsung	馬總
mei	美
Mei Ch'eng	枚乘
Meng K'o	孟軻
Meng Tzu-chü[a]	孟子居
Meng Tzu-chü[b]	孟子車
Mi Mou	彌牟
Mi-shu chiu-chung	秘書九種
Mo Tzu	墨子
Mou	茂
Nagasawa Kikuya	長澤規矩也
Nan Tzu	南子
nei-hsüeh	內學
Ou-yang Hsiu	歐陽修
Ou-yang Hsün	歐陽詢
Pan Ku	班固
P'an Yü	盤盂
P'ang Hsien	龐掮
pao	報
Pei-t'ang shu-ch'ao	北堂書鈔
P'ei Yin	裴駰
Pi	費
Pi Kan	比干
Pieh-lu	別錄
pien[a]	辯
pien[b]	辨
p'ien	篇
Pien Ho	卞和
Ping-yüan Chün	平原君
Po	白
Po-ch'in	伯禽
Po Hu T'ung	白虎通
Po I K'ao	伯邑考

Glossary

Po-lo 伯樂
Po-shih 博士
Po Yü 伯魚
pu 不
pu huo 不獲
Pu Shang 卜商
pu-ssu 不似
pu-tiao 不雕
San-kuo-chih i-wen-chih 三國志藝文志
se pu tsai i 色不在己
shan-lin 山林
shang 上
Shang-chia 上甲
Shang-shu 尚書
Shang-shu cheng-i 尚書正義
Shang-shu ta-chuan 尚書大傳
shang-tao 上盜
Shang Ti 上帝
shao[a] 邵
shao[b] 邵
Shao I-ch'en 邵懿辰
Shao-shih shan-fang pi-ts'ung 少室山房筆叢
shao-yin 少飲
She 涉
She Chi 社稷
Shen 慎
Sheng-cheng-lun 聖證論
Shen Chia-pen 沈家本
Shen Hsiang[a] 申祥
Shen Hsiang[b] 申詳
shih[a] 是
Shih[b] 詩
Shih[c] 市
shih[d] 失

Shih-chi 史記
Shih-chi chi-chieh 史記集解
Shih-chi-ch'uan 詩集傳
Shih-ching 詩經
Shih-shuo hsin-yü 世說新語
shu^a 書
Shu^b 蜀
Shu^c 書
shu^d 術
Shu-ching 書經
Shu-sun T'ung 叔孫通
Shui-ching-chu 水經注
shun 順
shuo 說
Shuo-yüan 說苑
so 所
ssu 緦
ssu-ch'en 四臣
Ssu-ch'uan 四川
Ssu-k'u chien-ming mu-lu piao-chu 四庫簡明目錄標注
Ssu-k'u ch'üan-shu 四庫全書
Ssu-k'u ch'üan-shu ts'ung-mu 四庫全書總目
ssu-lin 四鄰
ssu-ling 四靈
Ssu-ma Piao 司馬彪
Ssu-pu pei-yao 四部備要
Ssu-pu ts'ung-k'an 四部叢刊
Ssu-shih 司市
Ssu-t'u 司徒
ssu yü Ch'en hsia 死於陳下
Sui-shu 隋書
Sui-shu ching-chi chih 隋書經籍志
Sun Chih-tsu 孫志祖
Sun Lin-fu 孫林父

Glossary

Sung Ch'i 宋祁
Sung Hsien 宋咸
Sung Lien 宋濂
Sung-shih i-wen-chih 宋史藝文志
Suo 瑣
ta 達
Ta hua 大化
Ta-liang 大梁
ta-lu[a] 大麓
Ta-lu[b] 大錄
Ta-tai li-chi 大戴禮記
Ta wen 答問
t'ai 泰
Tai chen 戴震
T'ai-chia 太甲
T'ai-p'ing yü-lan 太平御覽
T'ai-shih 太師
T'ai Tien[a] 太顛
T'ai Tien[b] 泰顛
Tai-tsung 岱宗
tao 道
t'ao 謟
te 得
Teng 騰
Ti-wang shih-chi 帝王世紀
t'i-yao 提要
t'iao 祧
tien-li 典禮
Tien-shih 典市
T'ien-tzu 天子
Ting Yen 丁晏
tsa 雜
Tsa-chia 雜家
Tsa-hsün 雜訓

tsai	在
Ts'ai Shu	蔡叔
Ts'an-yen	譖言
Tsang	臧
tsang	臧
ts'ang	藏
Tsang Lin	臧琳
Ts'ao Kuei	曹劌
Ts'ao Ming	曹明
tse i	則亦
Tseng t'ing Han-Wei ts'ung-shu	增訂漢魏叢書
ts'o	錯
Tso-chuan	左傳
ts'o hsing	錯刑
tsu	祖
Tsu-chia	祖甲
tsu-ying	祖迎
Tsukada Tamon	冢田多門
Tsukada Tora	冢田虎
ts'un	寸
tsung	宗
ts'ung	叢
ts'ung[a]	縱
tu	土
Tu-chih	獨治
T'u-shu shih-chih	圖書十志
Tui Wei-wang	對魏王
T'un-t'ien	屯田
T'ung	桐
T'ung-chih	通志
Tung Chung-shu	董仲舒
T'ung Tien	通典
tzu	子
Tzu-ang	子卬

Glossary

Tzu-ch'ao　子鈔
Tzu-chia　子家
Tzu-chien　子建
Tzu-chih　子直
Tzu-chü[a]　子居
Tzu-chü[b]　子車
Tzu-feng　子豐
Tzu-fu　子鮒
Tzu-ho　子和
Tzu-hsiang　子襄
Tzu Hua-tzu　子華子
Tzu-hui　子彙
Tzu-kao　子高
Tzu-kao[a]　子羔
Tzu-kuo　子國
Tzu-li　子立
Tzu-lu　子路
Tzu-lüeh　子略
Tzu-lüeh Mu　子略目
Tzu-shang　子上
Tzu-shun　子順
Tzu-ssu　子思
Tzu-ssu Tzu　子思子
Tzu-wen　子文
Tzu-yu　子游
Tzu-yü　子魚
Tzu-yüan　子元
Wa-koku-bon shoshi taisei　和刻本諸子大成
wang[a]　亡
wang[b]　望
Wang Ch'ung　王充
Wang Chuo　王晫
Wang Lang　王朗
Wang Lin　王麟

Wang Mo	王謨
Wang Shih-yüan	王士元
Wang Su	王肅
Wang Yao-ch'en	王堯臣
Wang Yün-wu	王雲五
Wei[a]	微
wei[b]	謂
wei[c]	為
Wei Cheng	魏徵
Wei-Chin	魏晉
Wei-shu	偽書
Wei-shu t'ung-k'ao	偽書通考
Wei Tzu	微子
Wen Chen-meng	文震孟
Wen-chi	文集
Wen chün-li	問軍禮
Wen-hsüan	文選
Wen-hsüan-chu	文選注
wen pu i	問不已
wo	我
Wu	武
wu[a]	無
wu-ch'ang	五常
Wu Chi	無忌
Wu-kao chieh	五誥解
wu-lun	五論
wu ti	五帝
Wu Ting	武丁
Wu yang	無羊
Yang	楊
yang[a]	陽
Yao Chen-tzung	姚振宗
Yao Chi-heng	姚際恆
Yen[a]	彥

Glossary

Yen[b]　兗
Yen Ch'in-nan　閻琴南
Yen Ling-feng　嚴靈峯
Yen Shih-ku　顏師古
Yen-tzu ch'un-ch'iu　晏子春秋
yin　陰
Yin Min　尹敏
ying　迎
yu　有
Yü　豫
yü[a]　寓
yü[b]　虞
Yü Chung-jung　庾仲客
Yü-han shan-fang chi-i-shu　玉函山房輯佚書
Yü-lei　語類
Yü Shih-nan　虞世南
Yu-ssu　有司
Yung　雍
Yung-lo ta-tien　永樂大典

BIBLIOGRAPHY

Throughout the bibliography the *Ssu-pu ts'ung-k'an* edition is abbreviated as SPTK.

Editions and Commentaries of the KTT Consulted

Kō-sō-shi 孔叢子. In *Wa koku bon shoshi taisei* 和刻本諸子大成, vol. 1. Edited by Nagasawa Kikuye 長澤規矩也. Tokyo: Koten Kenkyū Kai, 1975. See figure 5.

K'ung-ts'ung cheng-i 孔叢正義, by Chiang Chao-hsi 姜兆錫. See figure 14.

K'ung-ts'ung-tzu 孔叢子. *Han Wei ts'ung-shu* 漢魏叢書 edition. Taipei: Hsin-hsing Press, 1967. See figure 6.

K'ung-ts'ung-tzu 孔叢子. *Ssu-k'u ch'üan-shu* 四庫全書 edition. Reprinted in the multiple-volume reproduction of the *Ssu-k'u ch'üan-shu*, vol. 695, pp. 307–368. Taipei: Commercial Press, 1985. See figure 11.

K'ung-ts'ung-tzu 孔叢子. *Ssu-pu pei-yao* 四部備要 edition. Taipei: Chung-hua shu-chü, 1970. See figure 16.

K'ung-ts'ung-tzu 孔叢子. SPTK edition. Reproduced in *Ssu-pu-ts'ung-k'an cheng-pien* 四部叢刊正編, vol. 17. Taipei: Commercial Press, 1979. See figure 1.

K'ung-ts'ung-tzu 孔叢子. *Tseng-ting Han Wei ts'ung-shu* 增訂漢魏叢書 edition. Taipei: Ta hua Press, 1983. See figure 8.

K'ung-ts'ung-tzu 孔叢子. *Tzu-hui* 子彙 edition. Reprinted. Taipei: Commercial Press, Jen-jen wen-k'u, 1971. See figure 4.

K'ung-ts'ung-tzu chu 孔叢子注, by Sung Hsien 宋咸. See figure 3.

Tsuka-chū Kō-sō-shi 冢註孔叢子, by Tsukada Tora 冢田虎. See figure 15.

Classical Chinese Works and Traditional Sinology

Chan-Kuo Ts'e 戰國策. SPTK.

Cheng-t'ang tu-shu-chi 鄭堂讀書記, by Chou Chung-fu 周中孚. 3 vols. Peking: Commercial Press, 1959.

Chih-chai shu-lu chieh-t'i 直齋書錄解題, by Ch'en Chen-sun 陳振孫. 3 vols. Taipei: Kuang-wen shu-chü, 1979.

Chin-shu 晉書. 10 vols. Peking: Chung-hua shu-chü, 1974.

Ching-i tsa-chi 經義雜記, by Tsang Lin 臧琳. Taipei: Chung-ting wen-hua, 1967.

Ching-tien shih-wen 經典釋文, by Lu Te-ming 陸德明. SPTK.

Chou-i 周易. SPTK.

Chou-li 周禮. SPTK.

Ch'u-hsüeh-chi 初學記, by Hsü Chien 徐堅. 3 vols. Peking: Chung-hua shu-chü, 1962.

Chu-tzu pien 諸子辨, by Sung Lien 宋濂. Taipei: Commercial Press, Jen-jen wen-k'u, 1978.

Chu-tzu yü-lei 朱子語類, by Chu Hsi 朱熹. 8 vols. Taipei: Cheng-chung shu-chü, 1962.

Chün-chai tu-shu-chih 郡齋讀書志, by Ch'ao Kung-wu 晁公武. 4 vols, Taipei: Kuang-wen shu-chü, 1979.

Ch'un-ch'iu Ku-liang chuan 春秋穀梁傳. SPTK.

Ch'un-ch'iu kung-yang chieh-ku 春秋公羊解詁. SPTK.

Ch'ün-shu chih-yao 群書治要 or *Chu-tzu chih-yao* 諸子治要, by Wei Cheng 魏徵. SPTK.

Chung-hsing kuan-ko shu-mu chi-k'ao 中興館閣書目輯考, by Ch'en K'uei 陳騤. Compiled by Chao Shih-wei. Peking: P'eiping T'u-shu-kuan, 1933.

Chung-kuo li-tai ching-chi-tien 中國歷代經籍典. 8 vols. Taipei: Commercial Press, 1970.

Ch'ung-wen tsung-mu 崇文總目, by Wang Yao-ch'en 王堯臣. In *Hou-chih pu-tsu-chai ts'ung-shu* 後知不足齋叢書, vols. 7–8. Taipei: Hua-wen shu-chü, 1969.

Erh-ya 爾雅. SPTK.

Fa-yen 法言. SPTK.

Han-chi 漢紀. SPTK.

Han Fei-tzu 韓非子. SPTK.

Han-shih wai-chuan 韓詩外傳. SPTK.

Han-shu 漢書. 12 vols. Peking: Chung-hua shu-chü, 1975.

Hou-Han-shu 後漢書. 12 vols. Peking: Chung-hua shu-chü, 1965.

Hsiao-ching 孝經. SPTK.

Hsiao Erh-ya i-cheng 小爾雅義證, by Liu Shih-heng 劉世珩. In *Chü-hsüeh-hsüan ts'ung-shu* 聚學軒叢書, vol. 19. Taipei: I-wen yin-shu, n.d.

Hsiao Erh-ya shu-cheng 小爾雅疏證, by Ko Ch'i-jen 葛其仁. Taipei: Commercial Press, 1965.

Hsin-hsü 新序. SPTK.

Hsin T'ang-shu 新唐書. Peking: Chung-hua shu-chü, 1975.

Hsün Tzu 荀子. SPTK.

Huai Nan Tzu 淮南子. SPTK.

I-li 儀禮. SPTK.

I-lin 意林, by Ma Tsung 馬總. SPTK.

I-wen lei-chü 藝文類聚, by Ou-yang Hsün 歐陽詢. 2 vols. Hong Kong: Chung-hua shu-chü, 1973.

Jen wu chih 人物志, by Liu Shao 劉邵. SPTK.

Jung-chai sui-pi wu-chi 容齋隨筆五集, by Hung Mai 洪邁. 3 vols. Shanghai: Commercial Press, 1937.

Bibliography

Kao-shih chuan 高士傳, by Huang-fu Mi 皇甫謐. In *Tseng-ting Han Wei ts'ung-shu*, 增訂漢魏叢書, vol. 4, pp. 1469–1497. Taipei: Ta-hua shu-chü, 1983.

Ku-chin wei-shu k'ao 古今偽書考, by Yao Chi-heng 姚際恆. In *Ku-chin wei-shu k'ao pu-cheng* 古今偽書考補證, by Huang Yün-mei 黃雲眉. Taipei: Chin-sheng ko ta shu-chü, 1972.

Ku-shu-mu san-chung 古書目三種, by Shen Chia-pen 沈家本. 2 vols. Peking: Chung-hua shu-chü, 1963.

Kung-sun Lung Tzu 公孫龍子. In *Chu-tzu chi-ch'eng* 諸子集成, vol. 6. Taipei: Shih-chieh shu-chü, 1972.

K'ung-tzu chi-yü 孔子集語, by Sun Hsing-yen 孫星衍. Taipei: Shih-chieh shu-chü, 1970.

K'ung-shih tsu-t'ing kuang-chi 孔氏祖庭廣記, by K'ung Yüan-ts'o 孔元措. Taipei: Commercial Press, 1965.

K'ung-tzu chia-yü 孔子家語. SPTK.

Kuo-yü 國語. SPTK.

Li-chi 禮記. SPTK.

Li-chi-chu 禮記注, by Wang Su 王肅. In *Yü-han shan-fang chi-i-shu* 玉函山房輯佚書, by Ma Kuo-han, 馬國翰, vol. 2, pp. 914–927. Taipei: Wen-hai Press, 1968.

Lieh-tzu 列子. SPTK.

Lü-shih ch'un-ch'iu 呂氏春秋. SPTK.

Lun-heng 論衡, by Wang Ch'ung 王充. SPTK.

Mencius 孟子. SPTK.

Mo-tzu 墨子. SPTK.

Pei-t'ang shu ch'ao 北堂書鈔, by Yü Shih-nan 虞世南. Taipei: Shin-hsing shu-chü, 1978.

Po Hu T'ung 白虎通. SPTK.

San-kuo-chih 三國志. 5 vols. Peking: Chung-hua shu-chü, 1973.

San-kuo-chih i-wen-chih 三國志藝文志, by Yao Chen-tzung 姚振宗. In *Erh-shih-wu shih pu-pien* 二十五史補編, by Liu Fu-ch'in 劉甫琴, vol. 3. Taipei: k'ai-ming shu-chü, 1974.

Sang-fu yao-chi 喪服要記, by Wang Su 王肅. In *Yü-han shan-fang chi-i-shu*, vol. 2, pp. 825–826.

Shang-shu cheng-i 尚書正義, by K'ung Ying-ta 孔穎達. In *Ssu-pu ts'ung-k'an kuang-pien*, 四部叢刊廣編, vol. 3. Taipei: Commercial Press, 1981.

Shang-shu-chu 尚書注, by Wang Su 王肅. In *Yü-han shan-fang chi-i-shu*, vol. 1, pp. 401–419.

Shang-shu K'ung-chuan 尚書孔傳. SPTK.

Shang-shu ta-chuan 尚書大傳. SPTK.

Shang-shu yü-lun 尚書餘論, by Ting Yen 丁晏. In *Huang-Ch'ing ching-chieh hsü-pien* 皇清經解讀編, by Wang Hsien-ch'ien 王先謙, vol. 194.

Shao-shih shan-fang pi-ts'ung 少室山房筆叢, by Hu Ying-lin 胡應麟. 2 vols. Shanghai: Chung-hua shu-chü, 1964.

Shen Tzu 慎子. SPTK.

Sheng-cheng-lun 聖證論, by Wang Su 王肅. In *Yü-han shan-fang chi-i-shu*, vol. 4, pp. 1951–1969.

Shih-chi-chuan 詩集傳, by Chu Hsi 朱熹. In *Ssu-pu ts'ung-k'an kuang-pien*, vol. 4. Taipei: Commercial Press, 1981.

Shih-chi 史記. 10 vols. Peking: Chung-hua shu-chü, 1972.

Shih-shuo hsin-yü 世說新語. SPTK.

Shih Tzu 尸子, *Ssu-pu pei-yao* edition.

Shui-ching chu 水經注. SPTK.

Shuo-yüan 說苑. SPTK.

Ssu-k'u chien-ming mu-lu piao-chu 四庫簡明目錄標注, by Shao I-ch'en 邵懿辰. Peking: Chung-hua shu-chü, 1959.

Ssu-k'u ch'üan-shu tsung-mu t'i-yao 四庫全書總目提要, by Chi Yün 紀昀 and others. In *Ho-yin Ssu-k'u ch'üan-shu tsung-mu t'i-yao chi Ssu-k'u wei-shou shu-mu chin-hui shu-mu* 合印四庫全書總目提要及四庫未收書目禁燬書目. 5 vols. Taipei: Commercial Press, 1971.

Sui-shu 隋書. 6 vols. Peking: Chung-hua shu-chü, 1973.

Ta-tai Li-chi 大戴禮記. SPTK.

T'ai-p'ing yü-lan 太平御覽, by Li Fang 李昉, 4 vols. Taipei: Kuo-t'ai, 1980.

T'ang-shu ching-chi I-wen ho-chih 唐書經籍藝文合志. Shanghai: Commercial Press, 1956.

Tao Te Ching 道德經, *Ssu-pu pei-yao* 四部備要 edition. Taipei: Chung-hua shu-chü, 1972.

Tso-chuan 左傳. In *Ch'un-ch'iu-ching-chuan chi-chieh* 春秋經傳集解. SPTK.

T'ung-chih 通志, by Cheng Ch'iao 鄭樵. In *Chung-kuo li-tai ching-chi-tien*, vol. 4.

T'ung-tien 通典, by Tu Yu 杜佑. Taipei: Hsin-hsing Press, 1963.

Tzu-lüeh 子略, by Kao Ssu-sun 高似孫, *Ssu-pu pei-yao* edition. Taipei: Chung-hua shu-chü, 1977.

Tzu-lüeh (mu) 子略目, by Kao Ssu-sun. N.p.: Commercial Press, 1939.

Tzu-ssu Tzu 子思子. Compiled by Huang I-chou 黃以周. Taipei: Kuang-wen shu-chü, 1975.

Wei-shu-k'ao wu-chung 偽書考五種. Taipei: Shih-chieh shu-chü, 1965.

Wen-hsüan 文選. 2 vols. Hong Kong: Commercial Press, 1974.

Yen t'ien lun 鹽鐵論. SPTK.

Yen Tzu Ch'un-ch'iu 晏子春秋. SPTK.

Yin Wen Tzu 尹文子. SPTK.

Yü-han shan-fang chi-i-shu 玉函山房輯佚書, by Ma Kuo-han 馬國翰. 6 vols. Taipei: Wen-hai Press, 1968.

Yung-lo ta-tien 永樂大典. 100 vols. Taipei: Shih-chieh shu-chü, 1962.

Recent Works in Chinese and Japanese

Chang Hsin-ch'eng 張心徵. *Wei-shu t'ung-k'ao* 偽書通考. 2 vols. Taipei: Ting-wen shu-chü, 1973.

Ch'en Shih-k'o 陳士珂. *K'ung-tzu chia-yü shu-cheng* 孔子家語疏證. Taipei: Commercial Press, Jen-jen wen-k'u, 1976.

Chiang Ch'üan 江瑔. *Tu-tzu chih-yen* 讀子巵言. Shanghai: Commercial Press, 1927.

Chiang Hsi-ch'ang 蔣錫昌. *Lao-tzu chiao-ku* 老子校詁. Taipei: Ming-lun, 1973.

Ch'ien Mu 錢穆. *Ch'ien-Ch'in chu-tzu hsi-nien* 先秦諸子繫年. 2 vols. Hong Kong: Hong Kong University Press, 1956.

Chien Po-hsien 簡博賢. "Chin-ts'un san-kuo liang-chin ching-hsüeh i-chi k'ao" 今存三國兩晉經學遺籍考. Ph.D. diss., National Taiwan University, 1980.

Chin Shou-shen 金受申. *Chi-hsia-p'ai chih yen-chiu* 稷下派之研究. Shanghai: Commercial Press, 1930.

———. *Ku-chin wei-shu-k'ao K'ao-shih* 古今偽書考考釋. Peking: N.p., 1924.

Chou Feng-wu 周鳳五. "Wei ku-wen Shang-shu wen-t'i chung-t'an" 偽古文尚書問題重探. Ph.D. diss., National Taiwan University, 1974.

Chou Shao-hsien 周紹賢. *Wei-Chin ch'ing-t'an shu-lun* 魏晉清談述論. Taipei: Commercial Press, 1966.

Ch'u-hsüeh chi so-yin 初學記索引. Peking: Chung-hua shu-chü, 1980.

Chung-kuo jen-ming ta-ts'u-tien 中國人名大辭典. Taipei: Commercial Press, 1974.

Chung-kuo wen-hsüeh-chia ta-ts'u-tien 中國文學家大辭典. 2 vols. Taipei: Shih-chieh shu-chü, 1974.

Fujiwara Tadashi 藤原正. *Kōshi zenshū* 孔子全集. Tokyo, Iwanami, 1931.

———. *Shi-shi-shi* 子思子. Tokyo: Iwanami, 1935.

He Ch'i-min 何啓民. *Kung-sun Lung yü Kung-sun Lung-tzu* 公孫龍與公孫龍子. Taipei: Hsüeh-sheng shu-chü, 1976.

———. *Wei-Chin ssu-hsiang yü t'an-feng* 魏晉思想與談風. Taipei: Hsüeh-sheng shu-chü, 1978.

Hsü Ch'un-hsiung 許春雄. *Wang Su chih Shang-shu hsüeh* 王肅之尚書學. Taipei: Shang-chuan hsüeh-pao, 1975.

Hsü Fu-kuan 徐復觀. *Liang-Han ssu-hsiang shih* 兩漢思想史. 3 vols. Taipei: Hsüeh-sheng shu-chü, 1979.

Hu Tao-ching 胡道靜. *Kung-sun Lung-tzu k'ao* 公孫龍子考. Taipei: Commercial Press, Jen-jen wen-k'u, 1970.

Hu Yü-chin 胡玉縉 and Wang Hsin-fu 王欣夫. *Ssu-k'u ch'üan-shu tsung-mu t'i-yao pu-cheng* 四庫全書總目提要補正. Shanghai: Chung-hua shu-chü, 1964.

Huang Chang-chien 黃彰健. *Ching chin-ku-wen hsüeh wen-t'i hsin-lun* 經今古文學問題新論. Taipei: Commercial Press, 1982.

Huang Yün-mei 黃雲眉. *Ku-chin wei-shu-k'ao pu-cheng* 古今偽書考補證. Taipei: Chin-sheng ko ta shu-chü, 1972.

Ku Chieh-kang 顧頡剛. *Ssu-pu cheng wei* 四部正偽. Taipei: Hua-lien, 1968.

Li Chen-hsing 李振興. "Wang Su chih ching-hsüeh," 王肅之經學. 3 vols. Ph.D. diss., National Cheng-chi University, 1971.

Liu Ta-chieh 劉大杰. *Wei-Chin ssu-hsiang lun* 魏晉思想論. Taipei: Chung-hua shu-chü, 1973.

Lo Ken-tse 羅根澤. *Meng-tzu-chuan lun* 孟子傳論. Taipei: Commercial Press, Jen-jen wen-k'u, 1969.

———. *Wei-Chin liu-ch'ao wen-hsüeh p'i-p'ing shih* 魏晉六朝文學批評史. Taipei: Commercial Press, Jen-jen wen-k'u, 1966.

Lo Ken-tse 羅根澤 and Ku Chieh-kang 顧頡剛, eds. *Ku-shih-pien* 古史辨. 7 vols. Reprint. Taipei: Ming-lun, 1970.

Ma Tzung-huo, 馬宗霍. *Chung-kuo ching-hsüeh shih* 中國經學史. Taipei: Commercial Press, 1976.

Mou Tzung-san 牟宗三. *Ts'ai-hsing yü hsüan-li* 才性與玄理. Taipei: Hsüeh-sheng shu-chü, 1978.

P'i Hsi-jui 皮錫瑞. *Ching-hsüeh li-shih* 經學歷史. Taipei: Commercial Press, Jen-jen wen-k'u, 1972.

Takeuchi Yoshio 武內義雄. "Shi-shi-shi nitsuite" 子思子に就いて, *Shinagaku* (February 1921), pp. 488–494. Kyoto.

T'ang Chün-i 唐君毅. *Chung-kuo che-hsüeh yüan-lun* 中國哲學原論. 6 vols. Hong Kong: Hsin-ya shu-yüan, 1966–1977.

Wang Yün-wu 王雲五, ed. *Ching chin-ku-wen hsüeh* 經今古文學. Taipei: Commercial Press, 1967.

Yao Ming-ta 姚名達. *Chung-kuo mu-lu-hsüeh nien piao* 中國目錄學年表. Taipei: Commercial Press, 1971.

Yen Ch'in-nan 閻琴南. *K'ung-ts'ung-tzu chiao-cheng* 孔叢子斠證. Taipei: Chung-kuo wen-hua hsüeh-yüan, 1975.

Yen Ling-feng 嚴靈峯. *Chou Ch'in Han Wei chu-tzu chih-chien shu-mu* 周秦漢魏諸子知見書目. 6 vols. Taipei: Cheng-chung shu-chü, 1979.

Works in Other Languages

Aland, K. "The Problem of Anonymity and Pseudonymity in Christian Literature of the First Two Centuries." *Journal of Theological Studies*, n.s., vol. 12 (1961), pp. 39–49.

Ames, Roger T. *The Art of Rulership: A Study in Ancient Chinese Political Thought*. Honolulu: University Press of Hawaii, 1983.

Ariel, Yoav. "A World with No Punishment: A Third Century Confucian View." *Bulletin of the Chinese Philosophical Association*, vol. 3 (1985), pp. 737–754.

Balazs, Etienne. *Chinese Civilization and Bureaucracy*. Edited by A. F. Wright; translated by H. M. Wright. New Haven: Yale University Press, 1964.

Bauer, Wolfgang. *China and the Search for Happiness*. New York: Seabury Press, 1976.

Berti, Enrico. "Ancient Greek Dialectic as Expression of Freedom of Thought and Speech." *Journal of the History of Ideas*, vol. 39, no. 3 (1978), pp. 347–370.

Bielenstein, Hans. *The Bureaucracy of Han Times*. Cambridge: Cambridge University Press, 1980.

Bodde, Derk. *China's First Unifier: A Study of the Ch'in Dynasty as Seen in the Life of Li Ssu (280?–208 B.C.)*. Leiden: E. J. Brill, 1938.

———. *Essays on Chinese Civilization*. Princeton: Princeton University Press, 1981.

———. *Festivals in Classical China*. Princeton: Princeton University Press, 1975.

Chan, Wing-tsit. *Neo-Confucianism Etc.: Essays by Wing-Tsit Chan*. New York: Oriental Society, 1969.

———. *Source Book in Chinese Philosophy*. Princeton: Princeton University Press, 1963.

Ch'en, Ch'i-yün. *Hsün Yüeh and the Mind of Late Han China*. Princeton: Princeton University Press, 1980.

———. *Hsün Yüeh: The Life and Reflections of an Early Medieval Confucian*. Cambridge: Cambridge University Press, 1975.

Ch'ü, T'ung-tsu. *Law and Society in Traditional China*. Paris: Mouton, 1961.

Creel, Herrlee Glessner. *The Origins of Statecraft in China*. Vol. 1. *The Western Chou Empire*. Chicago: University of Chicago Press, 1970.

———. *Shen Pu-Hai, a Chinese Political Philosopher of the Fourth Century B.C.* Chicago: University of Chicago Press, 1974.

———. *What is Taoism? and Other Studies in Chinese Cultural History*. Chicago: University of Chicago Press, 1970.

Crump, J. I., Jr. *Chan-Kuo Ts'e*. Oxford: Clarendon Press, 1970.

Cua, A. S. "The Logic of Confucian Dialogues." In *Studies in Philosophy and History of Philosophy*. Edited by J. K. Ryan. Vol. 4 (1969), pp. 18–33.

Cua, A. S. "Reasonable Action and Confucian Argumentation." *Journal of Chinese Philosophy*, vol. 1 (1973), pp. 57–75.

Daor, Dan. "The Yin Wenzi and the Renaissance of Philosophy in Wei-Jin China." Ph.D. dissertation, University of London, 1973.

de Crespigny, Rafe. *The Records of the Three Kingdoms*. Occasional Paper 9. Canberra: The Australian National University, 1970.

DeFrancis, John. *The Chinese Language, Facts and Fantasy*. Honolulu: University Press of Hawaii, 1984.

Dobson, W.A.C.H. *Late Han Chinese*. Toronto: University of Toronto Press, 1964.

Dull, J. L. "The Confucian Origins of Neo-Taoism." Paper delivered at the Second International Conference on Taoist Studies, Harvard University, 1972.

Dutton, Denis, ed. *The Forger's Art*. Berkeley: University of California Press, 1983.

Eber, Irene, ed. *Confucianism: The Dynamics of Tradition*. New York: Macmillan, 1986.

Fang, Thome H. *Chinese Philosophy: Its Spirit and Its Development*. Taipei: Linking, 1981.

Farrer, J. A. *Literary Forgeries*. London: Longmans & Green, 1907.

Fong, Wen. "The Problem of Forgeries in Chinese Painting." *Artibus Asiae*, vol. 25 (1962).

Forke, Alfred. *Geschichte der alten chinesischen Philosophie*. Hamburg: Cram, 1964.

———, tr. *Lun-heng*. 2 vols. Reprint. New York: Paragon Book Gallery, 1962.

Fung Yu-lan. *A History of Chinese Philosophy*. Translated by Derk Bodde. 2 vols. Princeton: Princeton University Press, 1952.

Gale, Easson M. *Discourses on Salt and Iron*. Leiden: E. J. Brill, 1931.

Ganzel, Dewey. *Fortune and Men's Eyes, the Career of John Payne Collier*. Oxford: Oxford University Press, 1982.

Goodman, Howard L. "Exegetes and Exegeses of the Book of Changes in the Third Century A.D.: Historical and Scholastic Context for Wang Pi." Ph.D. diss., Princeton University, 1985.

Graham, A. C. "The Composition of the *Gongsuen Long Tzyy*." *Asia Major*, n.s. 2 (1957), pp. 147–183.

———. "The Date and Composition of Lieh Tzyy." *Asia Major*, n.s. 8 (1961), pp. 139–198.

———. "The Dialogue Between Yang Ju and Chyntzyy." *Bulletin of the School of Oriental and African Studies*, vol. 22 (1959), pp. 291–299.

———. "The Disputation of Kung-sun Lung as Argument about Whole and Part." *Philosophy East and West* (April 1986), pp. 89–106.

———. *Later Mohist Logic, Ethics and Science*. Hong Kong: The Chinese University Press, 1978.

Bibliography

———. *Studies in Chinese Philosophy and Philosophical Literature*. Singapore: Institute of East Asian Philosophies, 1986.

———. "Two Dialogues in the *Kung-sun Lung-tzu*: 'White Horse' and 'Left and Right.'" *Asia Major*, n.s. 11 (1965), pp. 139–140.

———. *Yin-Yang and the Nature of Correlative Thinking*. Occasional Paper and Monograph Series no. 6. Singapore: Institute of East Asian Philosophies, 1986.

Grant, R. M. "The Appeal to the Early Fathers." *Journal of Theological Studies*, n.s. vol. 11 (1960), pp. 13–24.

Harvard-Yenching Sinological Index Series no. 26: *Wen-hsüan-chu yin-shu yin-te*. Reprint. Taipei: Chinese Materials Center, 1966.

Harvard-Yenching Sinological Index Series no. 23: *T'ai-p'ing yü-lan yin-shu yin-te*. Reprint. Taipei: Chinese Materials Center, 1966.

Hamblin, C. L. *Fallacies*. London: Methuen, 1970.

Hansen, Chad. *Language and Logic in Ancient China*. Ann Arbor: University of Michigan Press, 1983.

Henricks, Robert G. *Philosophy and Argumentation in Third-Century China: The Essays of Hsi K'ang*. Princeton: Princeton University Press, 1983.

Hightower, James Robert. *Han-shih wai-chuan: Han Ying's Illustrations of the Dialectic Application of the Classic of Songs*. Cambridge: Harvard University Press, 1952.

Holzman, Donald. "The Conversational Tradition in Chinese Philosophy." *Philosophy East and West*, vol. 6, no. 3 (1956), pp. 223–230.

———. *Poetry and Politics: The Life and Works of Juan Chi, A.D. 210–263*. Cambridge: Cambridge University Press, 1976.

Honderich, Ted. *Punishment: The Supposed Justifications*. Harmondsworth: Penguin, 1971.

Hsiao, Kung-chuan. *A History of Chinese Political Thought*. Translated by F. W. Mote. Vol. 1. Princeton: Princeton University Press, 1979.

Hucker, Charles O. *A Dictionary of Official Titles in Imperial China*. Stanford: Stanford University Press, 1985.

Hulsewe, A.F.P. "The Legalists and the Laws of Ch'in." In *Leyden Studies in Sinology*. Edited by W. L. Idema. Leiden: E. J. Brill, 1981.

———. *Remnants of Han Law*. Vol. 1. Leiden: E. J. Brill, 1955.

Karlgren, Bernhard. *On the Authenticity and Nature of the Tso Chuan*. Göteborg: Elanders Boktryckeri Aktiebolag, 1926.

———. "The Authenticity of Ancient Chinese Texts." *Museum of Far-Eastern Antiquities Bulletin* 1 (1929), pp. 165–183.

———. *The Book of Documents*. Stockholm: Museum of Far-Eastern Antiquities, 1950.

Karlgren, Bernhard. *The Book of Odes*. Stockholm: Museum of Far-Eastern Antiquities, 1950.

Knechtges, David R. *The Han Rhapsody: A Study of the Fu of Yang Hsiung (53 B.C.–A.D. 18)*. Cambridge: Cambridge University Press, 1976.

———. *Wen xuan or Selections of Refined Literature*. Vol. 1, *Rhapsodies on Metropolises and Capitals*. Princeton: Princeton University Press, 1982.

Kramers, R. P. *K'ung-tzu chia-yü: The School Sayings of Confucius*. Leiden: E. J. Brill, 1950.

Lau, D. C. *Confucius: The Analects*. Harmondsworth: Penguin, 1979.

———. *Mencius*. Harmondsworth: Penguin, 1970.

———. *Tao Te Ching*. Harmondsworth: Penguin, 1963.

———. *Tao Te Ching*. Hong Kong: The Chinese University Press, 1982.

Le Blanc, Charles Y. *Huai Nan Tzu, Philosophical Synthesis in Early Han Thought*. Hong Kong: Hong Kong University Press, 1985.

Legge, James. *The Chinese Classics*. 5 vols. Reprint. Hong Kong: Hong Kong University Press, 1961.
- Vol. I: *Lun-yü* (Confucian Analects); *Ta-hsüeh* (Great Learning); *Chung-yung* (Doctrine of the Mean).
- Vol. II: *Meng-tzu* (The Works of Mencius).
- Vol. III: *Shoo-king* (The Book of Historical Documents).
- Vol. IV: *She-king* (Book of Poetry).
- Vol V: *The Ch'un Ts'ew with Tso Chuen* (The Spring and Autumn Annals, with the Tso Commentary).

———. *Li-chi, Book of Rites*. 2 vols. Reprint. New York: University Books, 1967.

———. *The Yi King*. Vol. 16 of *The Sacred Books of the East*. Edited by Muller. Oxford, 1899.

Leslie, Donald. "Argument by Contradiction in Pre-Buddhist Chinese Reasoning." Occasional Paper no. 4. Canberra: The Australian National University, 1964.

———. "Contribution to a New Translation of the *Lun-heng*." *T'oung Pao* 44 (1956), pp. 100–149.

Liu, Shu-hsien. "The Use of Analogy and Symbolism in Traditional Chinese Philosophy." *Journal of Chinese Philosophy* 1 (1974), pp. 313–338.

Liao, W. K., tr. *The Complete Works of Han Fei Tzu*. 2 vols. London: Probsthain, 1959.

Lloyd, G.E.R. *Polarity and Analogy*. Cambridge: Cambirdge University Press, 1966.

Loewe, Micheal. *Chinese Ideas of Life and Death: Faith, Myth and Reason in the Han Period 202 BC–AD 220*. London: Allen & Unwin, 1979.

Luz, Menahem. "The Spurious Platonic Dialogues: A Study of Their Historical and Philosophical Background." 2 vols. Ph.D. diss., The Hebrew University, 1980. (In Hebrew.)

Mather, Richard B. "The Controversy over Conformity and Naturalness During the Six Dynasties." *History of Religions*. Vol. 9, nos. 2–3 (1969–1970), pp. 160–180.

———, trans. *Shih-shuo hsin-yü: A New Account of the Tales of the World*. Minneapolis: University of Minnesota Press, 1976.

Mei, Yi-pao. "The *Kung-sun Lung-Tzu* with a Translation into English." *Harvard Journal of Asiatic Studies* 16 (1953), pp. 404–437.

Moore, Charles A., ed. *The Chinese Mind*. Honolulu: University Press of Hawaii, 1967.

Mote, Frederic W. *Intellectual Foundations of China*. New York: Knopf, 1971.

Mou, Jun-sun. *On the Indulgence in "Discourse and Polemics" by Scholars of the Wei-Chin Time and Its Influence in Subsequent Ages*. Hong Kong: The Chinese University Press, 1966.

Munro, Donald. *The Concept of Man in Early China*. Stanford: Stanford University Press, 1969.

———, ed. *Individualism and Holism: Studies in Confucian and Taoistic Values*. Ann Arbor: Center for Chinese Studies, University of Michigan, 1985.

Needham, Joseph. *Science and Civilization in China*. 9 vols. Cambridge: Cambridge University Press, 1954–.

Nylan, Michael. "Ying Shao's *Feng Su T'ung Yi:* An Exploration of Problems in Han Dynasty Political, Philosophical, and Social Unity." Ph.D. diss., Princeton University, 1982.

Ong, Walter J. *Ramus, Method and the Decay of Dialogue*. New York: Octagon Books, 1974.

Paper, Jordan D. *The Fu-Tzu: A Post-Han Confucian Text*. Leiden: E. J. Brill, 1987.

Passmore, John. *Philosophical Reasoning*. London: Gerald Duckworth, 1970.

Peterson, Willard J. "The Grounds of Mencius' Argument." *Philosophy East and West* 29 (1979), pp. 307–321.

Plaks, Andrew. *Archetype and Allegory in the Dream of the Red Chamber*. Princeton: Princeton University Press, 1976.

Pokora, Timotheus. *Hsin lun (New Treatise) and Other Writings by Huan T'an*. Michigan Papers in Chinese Studies no. 20. Ann Arbor: University of Michigan Press, 1965.

Porkert, Manfred. *The Theoretical Foundations of Chinese Medicine*. Cambridge: MIT Press, 1974.

Rickett, Allyn W. *Guanzi: Political, Economic, and Philosophical Essays from Early China*. Princeton: Princeton University Press, 1985.

Rubin, Vitaly A. *Individual and State in Ancient China*. New York: Columbia University Press, 1976.

———. "The Profound Person and Power in Classical Confucianism." In *Proceedings* of the Academia Sinica. Vol. 8. Taipei, 1981.

Rump, Ariane, and Wing-tsit Chan. *Commentary on the Lao Tzu by Wang Pi.* Honolulu: University Press of Hawaii, 1979.

Saily, Jay. *The Master Who Embraces Simplicity: A Study of the Philosopher Ko Hung, A.D. 283–343.* San Francisco: Chinese Materials Center, 1978.

Scharfstein, Ben-Ami. *Philosophy East Philosophy West.* New York: Oxford University Press, 1978.

Schwartz, Benjamin I. *The World of Thought in Ancient China.* Cambridge: Harvard University Press, 1985.

Shryock, J. K. *The Study of Human Abilities.* Reprint. New York: Kraus, 1966.

Sivin, Nathan. *Chinese Alchemy: Preliminary Studies.* Cambridge: Harvard University Press, 1968.

———. "On the Word 'Taoist' as a Source of Perplexity with Special Reference to the Relations of Science and Religion in Traditional China." *History of Religion* 17 (1978), pp. 303–330.

Soothill, W. E. *The Analects of Confucius.* Reprint. New York: Paragon, 1968.

Speyer, Wolfgang. *Die Literarische Fälschung Im Heidnischen Und Christlichen Altertum, Ein Versuch Ihrer Deutung.* München: C. H. Beck'sche Verlagsbuchhandlung, 1971.

Steele, John. *The I-li or Book of Etiquette and Ceremonial.* 2 vols. Reprint. Taipei: Ch'en-wen, 1966.

T'ang, Chün-i. "The T'ien-ming (Heavenly Ordinance) in Pre-Ch'in China." *Philosophy East and West* 11 (1962), pp. 195–218; 12 (1962), pp. 29–49.

T'ang, Yung-t'ung. "Wang Pi's Interpretation of the *I Ching* and *Lun Yü.*" Translated by Walter Liebenthal. *Harvard Journal of Asiatic Studies* 10 (1947), pp. 124–161.

Tankard, J. "The Literary Detective," *Byte*, vol. 11, no. 2 (February 1986).

Teng, Ssu-yü. *Family Instructions for the Yen Clan.* Leiden: E. J. Brill, 1952.

Teng, Ssu-yü, and Knight Biggerstaff. *An Annotated Bibliography of Selected Chinese Reference Works.* Cambridge: Harvard University Press, 1971.

Thompson, P. M. *The Shen Tzu Fragments.* Oxford: Oxford University Press, 1979.

Tjan Tjoe Som. *Po Hu T'ung: The Comprehensive Discussions in the White Tiger Hall.* 2 vols. Leiden: E. J. Brill, 1949.

Tu, Wei-ming. *Confucian Thought, Selfhood as Creative Transformation.* Albany: State University of New York Press, 1985.

———. *Humanity and Self-Cultivation: Essays in Confucian Thought.* Berkeley: Asian Humanities Press, 1979.

Twitchett, Denis, and Michael Loewe, eds. *The Cambridge History of China.* Vol. 1: *The Ch'in and the Han Empires 221 B.C.–A.D. 220.* Cambridge: Cambridge University Press, 1986.

Waley, Arthur. *The Analects of Confucius.* London: George Allen & Unwin, 1938.

―――. *The Book of Songs*. New York: Grove Press, 1960.

Watson, Burton. *The Complete Works of Chuang Tzu*. New York: Columbia University Press, 1970.

―――. *Han Fei Tzu, Basic Writings*. New York: Columbia University Press, 1964.

―――. *Hsün Tzu, Basic Writings*. New York: Columbia University Press, 1963.

―――. *Mo Tzu, Basic Writings*. New York: Columbia University Press, 1963.

―――. *Records of the Grand Historian of China*. 2 vols. New York: Columbia University Press, 1971.

Welch, Holmes, and Anna Seidel, eds. *Facets of Taoism*. New Haven: Yale University Press, 1979.

Werner, E.T.C. *Dictionary of Chinese Mythology*. New York: Julian Press, 1969.

Winks, Robin W., ed. *The Historian as Detective, Essays on Evidence*. New York: Harper & Row, 1968.

Wylie, A. *Notes on Chinese Literature*. Shanghai: 1867. Reprint. Taipei: Bookcase, 1970.

Zürcher, Erik. *The Buddhist Conquest of China*. 2 vols. Leiden: E. J. Brill, 1959.

INDEX TO THE INTRODUCTION

Administrative techniques, 10
Anachronisms, 58, 59, 67, 68
Ancient Kings, 14, 15, 17
Authenticity. *See* Forgery

Buddhism, 34

Canonical Books, 15
Chang Hsin-ch'eng, 36, 60
Chang-sun Wu-chi, 12, 21, 22
Chan-kuo ts'e, 61, 68
Chao Ch'i, 35, 57
Ch'ao Kung-wu, 24, 29, 38, 153n.81
Ch'en Chen-sun, 24, 30
Ch'en, Ch'i-yün, 151n.55, 152n.70
Cheng Ch'iao, 26
Cheng Hsüan, 32, 33, 63–64, 66, 68
Ch'en She the King, 13, 14, 27, 149n.5
Ch'en Sheng. *See* Ch'en She the King
Ch'i, 28
Chia I, 28
Chiang Chao-hsi, 33–34
Chia-yü, 12
Ch'ien Mu, 36
Chih-chai shu-lu chieh-t'i, 30
Ch'i-lu, 12, 21, 22
"Ch'i Mo," 31
Chin dynasty, 34, 36
Ch'ing dynasty, 32–35
Ching-i tsa-chi, 32–33
Ch'ing-t'an (Pure Conversation), 5, 148n.5
Chin Po-hsien, 62
Ch'in Shih-huang-ti, 15
Chin Shou-shen, 35
Chiu T'ang-shu, 23
Chiu T'ang-shu ching-chi-chih, 38
Chi-yen, 7, 9, 30, 31, 34, 66, 67
Chou Ch'in Han Wei chu-tzu chih-chien shu-mu, 36, 39
Chou Chung-fu, 35
Chou Tzu-i, 31
Chu Hsi, 3, 24, 28–29, 31, 33, 34, 57, 68
Ch'u-hsüeh chi, 23

Chün-chai tu-shu-chih, 29, 38
Ch'un-ch'iu, 59
Ch'ung-wen tsung-mu, 39
Chung-yung, 60
Ch'ün-shu chih-yao, 151n.51
Chu-tzu hui-han, 15
Chu-tzu pien, 30
Confucianism, 4–5, 9, 68
Confucius, 5; death of, 29, 30; image of, 58–59, 63; as subject of *KTT*, 7, 8, 38; and punishment, 61; and Tzu-ssu, 67
Creativity, 60

Dark Learning, 5, 148n.5
Dialecticians, 5
Duke Mu, 29, 30, 59–60
Dynastic history, 22, 23

Education, 9
Eleventh chapter, 10
Erh-ya, 10

Forgery, *KTT* as, 3, 4, 22, 24, 28, 29, 30, 35, 37, 59, 60, 61, 68, 147n.1, 147n.2
Fu Chia. *See* K'ung Fu

Grammatical features, 57, 156n.2

Han dynasty, 10, 34, 36, 64; Former Han, 5, 27, 28, 62; Late Han, 4, 28, 31, 33, 39, 57
Han Fei Tzu, 5, 10
Han-shih wai-chuan, 61, 68
Han-shu, 13, 14, 15, 27, 61, 68
Han-shu I-wen-chih: and *KTT*, 13, 27, 29, 57; and *K'ung-tzu chia-yü*, 28; listing of titles, 37, 38, 39, 69; on Mencius's adult name, 17
Han-tan shu-mu, 23, 29
Heterodox teachings, 10
Hiding the books, 15–16
Historical scope, 4
Hsia dynasty, 13
Hsiao-ching, 15

217

"Hsiao *Erh-ya*," 20, 31, 34, 153n.81
Hsiao Erh-ya, 37, 38, 69
Hsiao Wu, Emperor, 25
Hsin-hsü, 61, 68
Hsin Shih, 35
Hsin T'ang-shu, 23
Hsüan-hsüeh (Dark Learning), 5, 148n.5
Hsü Chien, 23
Hsü Ch'un-hsiung, 62
Hsu Kuang, 13
Hsün Tzu, 61, 68
Hsun Yüeh, 148n.5
Huang Chang-ch'ien, 36, 64, 65
Huang-fu Mi, 16, 17, 19
Huang Yun-mei, 35
Hui, Emperor, 150n.35
Hung Mai, 26–28, 57
Hu Tao-ching, 36
Hu Ying-lin, 24, 30–31
Hu Yü-chin, 35

I-lin, 23, 37
Intellectual setting, 4, 5
Interior applications, 10
I-wen lei-chü, 19–20

Juan Hsiao-hsü, 12, 21
Ju-chia-yen, 38, 39, 69
Jung-chai sui-pi, 26–28

K'ang Sang-tzu, 30, 153n.87
Kao Ssu-sun, 18, 24, 29–30
Kao Yu, 35–36, 57
Kramers, R. P., 15, 37, 65–66, 150n.35
Ku-chin wei-shu k'ao, 32
Kuei Ku-tzu, 25
Kuei Yu-kuang, 15
Kung An-kuo [pseud.]: and Canonical Books, 15; and *KTT*, 28, 32, 33, 35, 36, 63, 64; and Wang Su, 62
K'ung Chi. See Tzu-ssu
K'ung Chia, 13, 14, 29
K'ung-chih, 12, 21
K'ung Ch'uan, 36, 38, 39
K'ung family genealogy, 7, 8
K'ung Fu: and anachronisms, 59; and authorship of *KTT*, 3, 12, 20–23, 29, 30, 56; biographical accounts of, 13–16; critique of Mo Tzu, 60, death of, 151n.55; and eleventh chapter, 38; as Erudite, 14; *KTT* protagonist, 7, 9, 66; Li Lien views of, 31; retirement of, 152n.68
K'ung Hsiang, 15, 150n.35
K'ung Hui, 15
K'ung Meng, 65–66
Kung-sun Lung, 5, 36, 57, 58, 67
Kung-sun Lung-tzu, 10, 34
K'ung Tsang: author of "Lien-ts'ung-tzu," 27, 29, 31, 60; *KTT* protagonist, 7, 9, 38; letters, 10, 25; not author of *KTT*, 56; Tsukada Tora on, 34
K'ung Tsang shu, 37, 38
K'ung-ts'ung cheng-i, 33
K'ung-ts'ung-tzu chiao-cheng, 36
K'ung-tzu chia-yü, 18, 28, 62, 63, 65–67; compared with *KTT*, 15, 32, 33, 35; Postscript, 13, 14–16, 37, 39
K'ung Ying-ta, 15, 150n.35
K'ung Yuan-ts'o, 15, 153n.8
Kuo yü, 61, 68
Ku-shih-pien, 35
Ku-wen Shang-shu, 62, 63, 64

Lan-yen, 37, 38
Lao Tzu, 63
Legalism, 5
Letters in *KTT*, 10, 25, 60
Lexical expositions, 9
Li (truth), 58, 59, 60
Liang dynasty, 12, 28
Liao, Marquis of. See K'ung Tsang
Li Chen-hsing, 62
Li-chi, 32, 61, 68
"Lien-ts'ung-tzu," 27, 29, 31, 34, 60
Li Lien, 24, 31
Li Lien preface, 15, 34
Li Shan, 23, 27
Li Shu, 23
Li Tao-yüan, 17, 19
Liu Chao, 151n.52
Liu Chün, 17, 19
Liu Hsiang, 27
Liu Hsin, 27
Liu Hsü, 23
Liu Pei, 12
Lo Ken-tse, 16, 17, 35, 37
Lun Yü, 12, 15, 23, 61, 68
Lu-shih ch'un-ch'iu, 35–36, 57, 61, 68
Lu Te-ming, 150n.35

Index

Ma Jung, 63
Ma Kuo-han, 38, 39
Ma Tsung, 23
Mei Ch'eng, 27
Mencius: adult name, 16, 17, 35, 57; and Tzu-ssu, 29, 30, 38, 58, 67
Mencius, 57, 61, 68
Meng K'o. *See* Mencius
Meng Tzu-chü, 16, 17
Ming dynasty, 30, 38
Modern Text scholars, 10
Mohism, 5
Morality, 5, 9
Mourning rites, 64
Mo Tzu, 5, 10, 60
Mo Tzu, 59

New Text school, 36, 63

Old Text school, 36, 63
Ou-yang Hsiu, 23
Ou-yang Hsun, 19–20

Pan Ku, 14, 37, 39, 57
P'an Yü, 14, 29
Pei-t'ang shu-ch'ao, 18, 19, 21, 50
P'ei Yin, 13, 14, 17, 19
Philosophical debates, 9, 10
P'ing-yüan, Prince, 58–59
Politics, 9
Punishment, 10, 61, 63
Pure Conversation (*ch'ing t'an*), 5, 148n.5

Rhyme prose, 10, 25, 60
Rites, 9

San-kuo-chih i-wen-chih, 35
Shang-shu, 15, 33, 35, 36, 62, 64
Shang-shu cheng-i, 15
Shang-shu ta-chuan, 61, 68
Shao I-ch'en, 39
Shao-shih shan-fang pi-ts'ung, 30
Sheng-cheng-lun, 16, 17, 64
Shen Chia-pen, 35
Shih (truth), 58
Shih-chi, 13, 14, 15, 29, 68
Shih-chi chi-chieh, 17
Shih-ching, 9
Shih-shuo hsin-yü, 17
Shin Shih, 35

Shu-ching, 9, 15, 32, 57–58, 64
Shui-ching-chu, 17
Shun, 13
Shuo-yüan, 61, 68
Shu-sun T'ung, 14
"Six Honored Ones," 64
Sophism, 36, 57, 58
Ssu-k'u ch'ien-ming mu-lu piao-chu, 39
Ssu-k'u ch'üan-shu tsung-mu, 33
Sui dynasty, 39
Sui-shu ching-chi-chih, 12, 15, 20, 22, 28, 33, 37, 38
Sung Ch'i, 23
Sung dynasty, 3, 16, 30, 31, 38
Sung Hsien, 24, 27, 28
Sung Hsien edition of *I-wen-lei-chü*, 20, 24–26
Sung Hsien preface to *KTT*, 3, 26, 29, 33, 34
Sung Lien, 24, 30, 31
Sung-shih I-wen-chih, 153n.80
Ssu-pu ts'ung-k'an edition, 26

T'ai-p'ing yü-lan, 16, 17, 23
T'ang dynasty, 3, 10, 23, 39, 64
Taoism, 5
Ta-tai li-chi, 61, 68
Textual criticism, 63
Themes of *KTT*, 9–10
Ting Yen, 35, 64
Titles of *KTT*, 19, 37–39
Ti-wang shih-chi, 16, 17
Truth, 58, 59, 60
Tsang Lin, 32–33, 64, 151n.52
Ts'an-yen, 37, 38, 39
Ts'ao Ming, 60
Tso-chuan, 61, 63, 68
Tsukada Tamon. *See* Tsukada Tora
Tsukada Tora, 24, 34
T'ung-chih, 26
Tung Chung-shu, 28, 57
T'ung-tien, 64
Tzu-ch'ao, 18
Tzu-feng, 7, 9, 31, 34
Tzu-fu. *See* K'ung Fu
Tzu-ho, 7, 9
Tzu-hsiang, 15
Tzu-hui, 15, 31
Tzu-kao, 7, 9, 36, 38, 39, 57–59, 66
Tzu-lüeh, 18, 29
Tzu-shun, 7, 9, 13, 14, 59

Tzu-ssu, 7, 8, 29, 37, 58–60, 64, 153n.84
Tzu-ssu, 16, 37–38, 69
Tzu-yü. *See* K'ung Fu

Values, 26, 59, 60

Wang Chuo, 37, 38
Wang Lang, 62
Wang Lin, 24, 26, 39
Wang Shih-yüan, 30
Wang Su, 4, 16, 32, 35–38, 61–69
Wang Yao-ch'en, 23
Warring States period, 9, 13
Way, the, 5, 10
Wei Cheng, 151n.51
Wei-Chin era, 4, 5, 31, 35, 57
Wen Chen-meng, 15

Wen-chi, 28
Wen-hsüan-chu, 23, 27
Wen Tzu, 64
Western sinology, 4, 36–37

Yao Chen-tzung, 35
Yao Chi-heng, 32
Yellow Emperor, 13
Yen Ch'in-nan, 36
Yen Ling-feng, 36, 39
Yen Shih-ku, 14, 17, 28, 39
Yen-tzu ch'un-ch'iu, 61, 68
Yü Chung-jung, 18
Yü-han shan-fang chi-i-shu, 38
Yü-lei, 28
Yung-lo ta-tien, 38
Yü Shih-nan, 18, 19

GPSR Authorized Representative: Easy Access System Europe - Mustamäe tee 50, 10621 Tallinn, Estonia, gpsr.requests@easproject.com